HANDBOOK
OF COST
REDUCTION
TECHNIQUES

HANDBOOK OF COST REDUCTION TECHNIQUES

DAVID HENRY

FRANKLIN WATTS
NEW YORK TORONTO
1986

Library of Congress Cataloging in Publication Data

Henry, David, M.B.A.
Handbook of cost reduction techniques.

Includes index.
1. Cost control. I. Title.
HD47.3.H46   1986   658.1'552   86-7792
ISBN 0-531-15512-9

Copyright © 1986 by Alexander Hamilton Institute, Inc.
All rights reserved
Printed in the United States of America
5 4 3 2 1

CONTENTS

INTRODUCTION — 1

1 ORGANIZING AND DEVELOPING A SUCCESSFUL COST REDUCTION PROGRAM — 3

What management can do about cost reduction — 3
The post of cost reduction coordinator — 4
Identifying the cost reduction specialist — 5
Developing your cost reduction program — 6
Laying the foundation: Waste prevention — 7
Operations analysis: Another key component — 8
Promoting the cost reduction program — 9
Communicating results to all levels — 9

2 A SUCCESSFUL CASE HISTORY IN COST REDUCTION — 11

Initiating the program — 11
Specific results in each area — 13
Plant order handling and production control — 18

3 SUGGESTION SYSTEMS: KEY TO EMPLOYEE INVOLVEMENT IN COST CUTTING — 27

Laying the foundation — 27
The best ways to promote suggestion systems — 28
Using the five-step approach — 29
Suggestion system administration — 32
Deciding on awards — 36

4 FORMS MANAGEMENT IN MODERN BUSINESS — 41

The basis of forms management — 41
Future of forms management — 42
Definition of a form — 43
Creating a forms program — 43
Organizing a forms program — 44
Steps to establish a program — 45
Implementing and maintaining the program — 46
Reports to management — 50
Identifying forms by numbers and titles — 51
Developing a functional file — 53
Classifying by function — 53
Numbering the categories — 56
Using the functional file — 56
Effective forms analysis — 57
Questioning areas — 58
Forms specifications — 64

5 COST CUTTING TECHNIQUES IN FORMS DESIGN — 69

The box principle — 69
Determining space requirements — 70

Typewritten vs. handwritten	71
Utilizing ballot boxes	72
Printing and paper specifications	72
Snapout forms	74

6 TECHNIQUES TO REDUCE THE COST OF PAPERWORK — 87

Some disturbing numbers	87
Analyzing your paperwork costs	88
Checklist procedures	90

7 UTILIZING MRP IN PURCHASING AND INVENTORY — 107

What to look for	108
Making plans complementary	108
Symptoms/problems of MRP	109
Getting started with MRP	110
Other considerations	112
MRP conversion	113
Other MRP variations	113
The purchasing function	114
Value analysis	114

8 IMPLEMENTING INVENTORY CONTROLS TO REDUCE COSTS — 121

Benefits and problems	122
Calculating inventory costs	125
Combining functions	126
Electronic coding	126
Other inventory tips	127

9 PRODUCTIVITY IMPROVEMENT AND COST CONTROL 133

Organizing for productivity improvement 133
Performance measurement and improvement 134
Expected payoff/benefits 135
Introduction to the manual system 136
Automated performance measurement system 142
Applying cost accounting to specific operations 144

10 QUALITY CONTROL AS A COST REDUCTION METHOD 149

What quality control really is 150
Establishing a quality policy 151
Organizing your quality control 151
Analyzing specific processing costs 153
Quality cost components 156
Relationships in quality cost components 156
The relationship between COQ and productivity 157
Employing quality circles productively 161
The role of statistics in quality control 164
Control limits 165
Quality control at work 165

11 PRODUCT ENGINEERING AND PRODUCTION TECHNIQUES 169

PA technologies 169
Computerized techniques 170
The JIT technique 171
More on JIT 172
Product engineering 174
Re-manufacturing 175
The problem of manufacturing counterfeiting 176

12 COST REDUCTION MEASURES IN MAINTENANCE, MACHINES AND EQUIPMENT — 183

Preventive maintenance — 185
More maintenance tips — 186
Energy reduction — 187
More cases of energy conservation — 188
Purchasing machinery — 189
Training and reliability — 191
More machine cost reduction ideas — 192

13 EXPENSE REDUCTION THROUGH AN INTEGRATED MANUFACTURING INFORMATION SYSTEM — 201

Explaining the system — 203
An MIS in action — 205
A final note — 212

14 COST ESTIMATING AND CONTROL TO REDUCE EXPENDITURES — 221

Cost per direct labor hour — 223
Analyzing and charging manufacturing costs — 223
Breakeven point — 226
Impact of parts shortages on labor costs — 227
Cost of processing a sales order — 227
Network analysis — 228
PERT/CPM in action — 230
Calculating time estimates — 231
PERT/COST calculations — 232
Cost reduction ratios — 232

15 COST REDUCTION STRATEGIES IN MARKETING — 237

Computerized marketing research — 238
Segmentation analysis — 238
New product development — 239
Balancing customer satisfaction with cost reduction — 241
The personal touch — 242
Retail customers — 242
Getting down to basics — 243
How to use the 20/80 principle for pruning out losers — 244
More marketing tips — 244

16 ORGANIZING SYSTEMS WITHIN YOUR PROGRAM — 251

Components of a successful system — 252
Systems techniques for cost reduction — 252
Information management — 259
Networks — 259
Effective business communications systems — 260

17 A POTPOURRI OF ACTUAL COST CUTTING TECHNIQUES — 265

Better business planning — 265
Effective corporate cash management — 267
Cash management services — 267
Managing human resources — 268
Improved plant layout and design — 271
Integrated industrial engineering — 272
Improved security — 273
Efficient materials handling — 275

Vehicle economy 277
Office improvement 277
Short interval scheduling 280
Measuring work processes 281
Pay for knowledge 281
Successful electronic data processing (EDP) 282
How to choose a computer systems consultant 284
Reducing costs of air travel 285
Saving money in your mailroom 285
Recycling paper 286
Manufacturing productivity center 287

INDEX   **302**

EXHIBITS

1	A suggested suggestion form	33
2	A dual use form for suggestions	34
3	A decision table for suggestion systems	37
4	A suggestion system award table	38
5	A sample form collection letter	47
6	Sample progress record	49
7	Sample form for creating a case history	51
8	A forms analysis questionnaire	59
9	A worksheet for forms specifications	65
10	Spacing and positioning required for box principle design	70
11	Comparison of box principle enhancements	76
12	Conserving space with the box principle	77
13	Rearranging boxes for space saving	78
14	Setting tabular stops for efficiency	79
15	Rearranging vertical rules for ease of use	80
16	Arrangements for columnal and tabular entries	81
17	Diagonal vs. vertical captions	82
18	Arrangement of captions for maximum effectiveness	83
19	Positive and negative aspects of ballot box design	84

20	Vertical/horizontal ballot box arrangement	85
21	Utilizing space in a forms questionnaire	86
22	A worksheet to estimate paperwork costs	89
23	A worksheet to implement and monitor a paperwork reduction program	91
24	An adaptable document inventory control list	95
25	An actual filled-in document inventory control list	96
26	A ranking report for estimated paper costs	97
27	Sample document value analysis questionnaire	100
28	Actual filled-in cost/benefit analysis	103
29	Form for productivity opportunities and cost/benefit analysis	104
30	Combining the business and production plans	109
31	MRP closed loop system	111
32	Two important inventory control calculations	123
33	A reorder system using EOQ	124
34	An actual workflow performance chart	138
35	A sample QC performance chart	140
36	Actual computer-generated trend analysis	143
37	Planning form for creating a quality control policy	152
38	An actual manufacturing cost analysis	155
39	Calculations for cost of quality components	158
40	Planning process for cost of quality program	159
41	An expert's graphic representation of COQ benefits	160
42	Relationship between accounting and manufacturing information systems	202
43	A classic information flow relationship	203
44	An actual Manufacturing Information System	206
45	Actual sample from MIS	213
46	Creating a job card measurement	224
47	A sample breakeven calculation	226
48	Specific avenues for potential sales order savings	229
49	Questionnaire for new product development activities	240
50	Checklist of attributes for a good systems analyst	253
51	A worksheet to analyze work simplification	255
52	A systematic approach to a systems study	264

ACTION CHECKLISTS

1	Product Simplification and Standardization	21
2	Packaging/Materials Handling	22
3	Materials Handling/Warehouses	23
4	Receiving/Shipping	24
5	Transportation/Construction	25
6	Sales Planning and Distribution	26
7	Manufacturing Resource Planning	116
8	Purchasing	118
9	Value Analysis	120
10	Inventory Control	129
11	Productivity Improvement and Cost Control	146
12	Quality Control	167
13	Production	177
14	Product Engineering	180
15	Maintenance	193
16	Energy	196
17	Machines and Equipment	199
18	Integrated Manufacturing Information Systems	219
19	Cost Estimating and Control	234
20	Marketing	246
21	Tips/Suggestions/Insights	288

INTRODUCTION

Every executive and every manager in today's fiercely competitive marketplace knows that cost reduction efforts are the key to the growth and prosperity of tomorrow's companies. The *Handbook of Cost Reduction Techniques* will work hard for every member of your management team. Tapping its proven insights will generate improvements in dozens of areas, from production and quality control to maintenance and marketing to inventory and forms management.

This unique handbook is practical, full of easy-to-use checklists, forms, and exhibits. It's authoritative—based on actual experiences of over 100 large and small companies in all types of industries. And it's flexible, with just enough information to get you started on your own program, but not so much as to overwhelm you with mountains of irrelevant data.

The end result for you will be an organized, companywide program to:

- reduce wasted time, manpower, and materials
- lower expenses across the board
- increase customer satisfaction, employee morale, and profit potential

- slash operating, paperwork, and clerical costs to a minimum
- identify inefficiencies and streamline procedures
- eliminate costly cash expenditures and unnecessary duplication of effort

The special series of checklists at the end of selected chapters also sets this book apart as an extraordinary management tool. Each checklist contains an action focus item to guide you in your search for cost/expense reducing ideas. These are followed by other columns you and management staffers can use to make judgments and create plans for future actions.

The *Handbook of Cost Reduction Techniques* was created by David Henry in conjunction with the editorial resources of the Alexander Hamilton Institute. Mr. Henry, B.B.A., M.B.A., is an assistant professor of financial management at New York University and Manager of the Productivity Improvement department at Manufacturers Hanover Trust Company. He is a Certified Systems Professional and former vice president of the Association for Systems Management, and has been a lecturer and articles contributor to a number of business organizations and publications.

You'll find just the right amount of critical executive intelligence in the *Handbook of Cost Reduction Techniques* to get your creative juices flowing: modules of information that will spark future exploration on your part; tactics and strategies you can adopt and adapt to your particular circumstances; in sum, the insights, suggestions, and directions you need to create a successful program in this vital area for your company.

1

ORGANIZING AND DEVELOPING A SUCCESSFUL COST REDUCTION PROGRAM

In every company, minimizing waste and inefficiency to keep costs down is *everyone's* job. Employees at all levels should be aware that cost reduction is a companywide goal, and should share in the determination to eliminate waste and inefficiency, and do whatever else is necessary to reduce costs. With such an attitude, a planned cost reduction program will be successful.

Within a company, various specific individuals must shoulder the responsibility for formulating and guiding such a cost reduction program. None are more important than the members of **senior management.** Without the support of management, employees are unlikely to share the team feeling and will be less motivated to behave in the most cost-effective way.

Here are specific actions that management can take to facilitate a successful company cost reduction program.

WHAT MANAGEMENT CAN DO ABOUT COST REDUCTION

Management plays a major role in ensuring that a cost reduction program is successful by taking some or all of these ten steps:

1. Originate the goals of the cost reduction program.
2. Consolidate cost reduction activities into a single organizational function.
3. Assign responsibility for the achievement of the program's goals to a cost reduction specialist.
4. Formulate broad policy guidelines for the implementation of the program.
5. Communicate enthusiasm for the program to all company employees, thereby stimulating morale, awareness, and participation in the cost reduction program.
6. Define the scope of the cost reduction program.
7. Measure the effects of the program on the organization.
8. Budget the amount of money to be spent on the cost reduction effort.
9. Place controls on the program.
10. Determine when the goals have been achieved.

The more important it is for your company to reduce costs, the more active your management should be in all phases of the cost reduction program.

THE POST OF COST REDUCTION COORDINATOR

Although everyone in the company needs to be involved in the cost reduction program, it is most efficient and effective if management appoints one individual to be the **cost reduction (CR) coordinator.** This individual should have above-average abilities with respect to both the technical and administrative aspects of the job.

> *Note:* In small and medium sized companies, such a coordinator will hold other positions and responsibilities besides cost reduction. Your situation will dictate how much time and effort a coordinator will spend on this program.

The primary function of the cost reduction coordinator is to stimulate cost consciousness among other members of the organization.

Most companies are organized to function effectively before a formal cost reduction program is introduced. The manager of each department in the company is responsible for activities in his or her department. And those activities include reducing waste and fully utilizing existing resources—the two keystones of a cost reduction program.

Thus, in every well-run company, cost reduction is built into the daily operational procedure to some extent. Think of a CR coordinator as an individual who works through operating departments to stimulate cost reduction consciousness, not as a person who relieves others of the responsibility of cost reduction activities. In performing this primary function, the cost reduction coordinator should:

1. Feed ideas to heads of individual departments. Motivate them to use their creativity to come up with new ways to reduce costs.
2. Develop forms and procedures useful to the cost reduction program.
3. Gather, organize, file, and distribute cost reduction ideas.
4. Develop a cost reduction staff (if applicable) and supervise it.
5. Submit progress reports to, and discuss problems with, other areas of the company.

A cost reduction coordinator should possess qualities such as enthusiasm, imagination, diplomacy, and communications skills. Whether or not you create a formal position, choose the individual who best exhibits the appropriate combination of skills. In small and medium sized companies, it is not uncommon for the owner or plant manager to assume this role.

IDENTIFYING THE COST REDUCTION SPECIALIST

In contrast to the cost reduction coordinator, you choose a cost reduction specialist to represent a department, such as Purchasing. The CR specialist:

1. Helps to develop, organize, and guide both waste prevention practices and operations analysis.

2. Serves as a communications link—receiving and disseminating ideas and information pertinent to the cost reduction program—among the cost reduction coordinator, department managers, and workers in specific departments.
3. Maintains records and measures results of cost reduction activities and projects.
4. Works with the cost reduction coordinator to develop ideas, make inspections, attend company conferences, and ensure the overall success of the cost reduction program.

The cost reduction specialists representing specific departments will generally contribute the most practical ideas to the cost reduction program. Design your program so that they interact with one another, share ideas and practices, and form a network capable of reducing waste and maximizing use of resources.

DEVELOPING YOUR COST REDUCTION PROGRAM

In addition to suggestions from the coordinator and specialists, ideas for the program may come from:

- written documents, such as magazines, newspapers, journals, and technical reports
- employees within the company
- actions introduced by other companies, even competitors
- seminars and conferences
- independent consultants

As the ideas are collected, organize them for effective use. You can do this manually or with the computer, which allows for easy entry, manipulation, and quick retrieval of information. A simple way to group ideas is by creating the following three broad categories or files:

1. being investigated
2. used
3. rejected

While the third category may be left without further organization, you can further subdivide the other two categories. Start by filing items under such subheadings as Marketing, Industrial Engineering, Purchasing, and so on. Then subdivide further. For example, under the Marketing category, include ideas on advertising, market research, data analysis, sales promotion, etc.

Here are the steps that one company president said proved helpful to his coordinator in developing a cost reduction program:

1. Create an idea source file and a method for evaluating the relative merits of the various ideas.
2. Determine the areas in which volunteers will be needed and obtain the individuals to fill necessary positions.
3. Organize needed committees.
4. Create forms and procedures necessary for the program.
5. Schedule, assign, and supervise cost reduction activities.
6. Initiate operations analysis and waste prevention projects and determine how to evaluate cost savings.
7. Decide how to promote and communicate the program.

LAYING THE FOUNDATION: WASTE PREVENTION

Reducing waste is one of the key elements in any cost reduction program. Recognizing waste before it occurs and preventing waste from recurring are two action steps that all employees can incorporate into their daily routines. With effort directed only to this activity, a cost reduction program will be profitable to your company. Here are seven important points about waste prevention:

1. Reduce pilferage. Many employees consider this a "sport" or an unofficial form of payment due to them. It's a form of waste which

accounts for billions of dollars a year in losses to companies. Make sure pilferage is considered unacceptable behavior at all levels of your organization.
2. Consider all possible ways to salvage, reclaim, recycle, and rework existing materials.
3. Focus the waste reduction program on a high or unusual level or area of loss.
4. Publicize the waste reduction program.
5. Designate a day at some regular interval (say the last work day of each month) as "Waste Prevention Day." This reinforces and heightens consciousness about waste prevention. It also allows all in the company to share ideas about how to recognize, guard against, and prevent waste.
6. Uncover redundant and unnecessary activities.
7. Simplify operations wherever and whenever possible.

OPERATIONS ANALYSIS: ANOTHER KEY COMPONENT

Operations analysis is another crucial aspect of a cost reduction program. Its function is to assess the operations involved in an activity so that they may be simplified, eliminated, or otherwise made more effective, efficient, and less costly. At the heart of operations analysis is the attempt to make improvements in the existing method of operation for the purpose of reducing unit costs.

An excellent tool to help pinpoint areas of operational inefficiency is an operations analysis audit. You can conduct your own audit with the **Action Checklists** you'll find throughout this book.

The various items are assigned importance values by those doing the evaluation. The operations analysis audit, which can include extremely detailed questions about methods of operation, is also useful for identifying the source of such problems as employee turnover and absenteeism. It will pinpoint activities frustrating or otherwise unsatisfying to employees, and indicate where and how improvements can be made.

PROMOTING THE COST REDUCTION PROGRAM

Since holding costs down is everybody's business on a daily basis, you should keep company employees informed of the objectives, plans, and success of the cost reduction program. This instills pride and motivates workers to decrease expenses.

The cost reduction program should also have a "face," and not be perceived by employees as strictly an accounting activity or as an impersonal effort. The task of accentuating the positive and humanizing the program can be accomplished through promotion. The person most responsible for promoting the cost reduction program is the cost reduction coordinator, with the assistance of his or her staff and the cost reduction specialists.

COMMUNICATING RESULTS TO ALL LEVELS

Informing employees at all levels of the company about the people, plans, and progress that distinguish the cost reduction program may be done through newsletters, presentations, and seminars.

In many companies, the workforce receives a monthly *cost reduction newsletter*. In larger companies, a cost reduction committee (headed by the CR coordinator) plays a major role in communicating the results of the cost reduction effort through the newsletter and other communications media.

Of all ways of communicating to the company's employees, reports from top management are the best. This group has the greatest authority and commands the most respect. What senior people say has the most credibility and should powerfully stimulate workers at all levels to greater efforts. Consider having your top management send personal letters congratulating employees for their cooperation and praising them for the success they have helped the company achieve. If the program is not going well, use letters from them to encourage workers to do better.

2

A SUCCESSFUL CASE HISTORY IN COST REDUCTION

You can identify a wide range of cost reduction opportunities by broadly attacking just one topic, namely excess inventory. The case history in this chapter involves a large manufacturing company with multiple plants and distribution centers throughout the United States. While your company may not be similar in size, the process and application of ideas will be similar.

What started out as a concentrated effort to reduce excess inventories expanded to focus in on cost reduction in product simplification, packaging, materials handling, and warehousing. In addition, substantial expense reductions were made as a result of improved sales forecasting, production scheduling, and inventory control. Lastly, operations improvements were made in sales planning and distribution of product.

INITIATING THE PROGRAM

Background: This manufacturing company with multiple plants and distribution centers had a substantial inventory investment scattered over all its facilities.

Problem: Over a period of about six years, the inventory investment rose by 200 percent, but sales increased by only 10 percent. There was also a marked increase in customer complaints.

As a result of these problems, a task force was chosen with representatives from production, marketing, and finance.

Findings:

- Sales forecasts were made on an annual basis with no regard for seasonal changes, no zeroing in of product lines, and no changes as a result of trends in the industry.
- In spite of high inventory, shortages were a problem.
- Thousands of products had very little, if any, sales over the past few years. In fact, over a ten-year period, practically no products had been dropped from the product line, and thousands were added during that same period.
- Production scheduling was done on a **manual** basis. This meant that reaction time was slow.
- A multitude of vendors was used to supply parts and specifications varied from one resource to another.

Conclusion: The task force concluded that ordering from warehouses and plants did not take into consideration economic lot sizes. This resulted in many thousands of small orders with inordinate costs for handling and processing. In addition, quantity discounts and freight allowances were not taken in many cases. There was no control over what a local order clerk could purchase.

There were no standards of how to package items for shipment. Materials handling procedures were sloppy. The lack of inventory control resulted in some products being out of stock in one facility while being overstocked in others.

Often orders were processed even though the items were too small to be economically feasible. Shipping errors were frequent. In many instances, special parts were employed where standard parts could (and should) have been used to save the company money.

Recommendations: The task force identified four major areas of cost reduction:

- product simplification and standardization
- packaging, materials handling, and warehousing

- sales forecasting, production scheduling, and inventory control
- sales planning and distribution

For each of these areas, a separate task force was instituted with a broad representation from the company.

Results: Six months after the start of the program, inventory was pruned by $4 million, bank loans reduced by $5 million. Cost reductions amounted to $1.5 million and profits were up almost a million dollars.

One year after the start of the program, profit was up by $3.5 million compared to a $1 million loss the previous year. Costs were reduced by $3.5 million and, very importantly, inventory investment was down by $10 million. Within two years after the start of the program, profits had almost doubled from the first year's results, and inventories had decreased a total of $12 million. Sales had also increased, by 20 percent.

SPECIFIC RESULTS IN EACH AREA

Product Simplification and Standardization

The task force investigating this area found that about 10 percent of the products produced over 90 percent of sales. Practically no sales were discovered for 20 percent of the items. In several product classes, there were substantial losses or very small profits.

Here is what was done specifically:

- Those lines with downward trends in sales were discontinued.
- Other product lines had engineering improvements and lower production costs as a result of redesign of parts.
- Prices were increased on profitable items.
- Products with unusual rates of breakdown were redesigned.
- Key customers were contacted and asked their opinions about specific product lines and items. Changes were made accordingly.
- Products were studied from the standpoint of design. Many revisions were made to standardize specific parts. This alone resulted in substantial cost reductions.

- In addition to review of the product lines, specific items were analyzed. Many were discontinued because of unprofitable sales.

*Note: Throughout this special report you'll find **Action Checklists** which refer to specific segments of the text. For example, Action Checklist #1 at the end of this chapter deals with product simplification and standardization.*

These Action Checklists should serve as the basis for your own cost reduction efforts. They are not complete. You must add your own insights to tailor them to your specific requirements.

Results: The task force reported a decrease of 40 percent of items, coupled with annual savings of $500,000. Importantly, the loss of customers was minor since all major customers had been contacted on revisions to the products. A new system was designed for product approvals or changes. Distribution centers and factories presented periodic reports of volumes, costs, and so forth.

Packaging, Materials Handling and Warehousing

Problem: Each of the facilities was responsible for its own packaging, materials handling, and warehousing. In addition, positive changes instituted at one facility generally were not communicated or applied to the others.

The task force in this area determined that the cost of these operations accounted for one half of total production costs. The task force set as a goal to reduce costs from 50 percent to 25 percent. The group divided its mission into four parts:

- product packaging and containerization
- materials handling and warehousing
- transportation for construction
- construction

Product Packaging and Containerization: Analysis of this group of functions had as its purpose the determination of whether each package was the best for the product, whether cost reductions were possible, and, in general, how the packaging might be improved. The task force recommended standardizing packaging and coordinating it with the distribution center so that storage was made easier. See Action Checklist #2.

Purchase Materials and Supplies: Many containers were reused rather than simply thrown away, as they had been previously. Other packages were redesigned so that they could be better stocked in the distribution facilities.

Palletizing and Containerizing: A great deal of effort was put into reducing the cost of damaged materials by redesigning the way the materials were handled and wrapped. Whenever possible, padding or other protective materials were placed in the boxes.

Product Preservation: Customer complaints caused basic problems to be spotlighted. Products were cleaned and wrapped properly. As a direct result of this activity, customer complaints were reduced by more than 75 percent.

Materials Handling and Warehousing: Many facilities were outdated and little coordination existed between the distribution facilities and the plant. As a result, the task force made numerous recommendations.

For example, bins and racks were replaced in order to accommodate more items; warehouse layout was standardized; materials handling equipment, such as forklift trucks, hoists, and conveyors was modernized; and changes were made in order picking equipment. Focus areas are listed in Action Checklist #3.

Receiving and Shipping: A significantly greater emphasis on quality control resulted in fewer damaged shipments. Suppliers were asked to show weights on cartons. Better methods were developed in terms of addressing shipments. Action Checklist #4 covers this area.

Safety: Improvements at the facilities reduced accidents by more than 25 percent. In addition, and as a result of this, cost reductions were made because of decreases in insurance claims.

Paperwork: All forms and reports were examined and about 30 percent were eliminated. Other forms were redesigned so that reports could be made more easily. (See chapters on forms design and paperwork reduction.)

Standards: Performance standards were developed for storage and materials handling equipment and for the number of items handled over a specific time. Example: a standard of four hours to receive and store incoming materials resulted in a cost reduction of 50 percent.

Maintenance Improvements: An automated method to get lubricating oil for the machines was substituted for the former manual system where operators did it themselves. In addition to cost reduction, there were savings in storage space and the cost of lubrication oil. (See maintenance chapter.)

Transportation: Less-than-carload lots were made into carloads to be shipped at lower freight rates. Better scheduling in the traffic department and an audit of freight bills also resulted in substantial decreases in expenses. A major effort was undertaken to initiate a preventive maintenance program for vehicles. The importance of traffic management was upgraded so that purchase orders could be released more promptly. Action Checklist #5 pertains to this process and to construction.

Construction Standards: Standards were developed for all facilities—including distribution and materials handling areas, parking lots, maintenance of facilities, security, cleaning, and so on.

Sales Forecasting, Production Scheduling and Inventory Control

Although inventories were increasing, so were customer complaints about shortages and deliveries. The major problems were identified as follows:

- Sales forecasts were made in overall monetary terms, without regard to product lines or individual items. This made them practically useless in terms of production scheduling.
- Each of the plants had its own way of scheduling production.
- Six of the facilities used manual methods for orders, receiving, shipment, and inventory control.

There were no consistent methods of production scheduling. Managers were doing their own estimating. As for orders, clerks were also exercising judgment for order points and quantities.

The distribution centers were using a manual system of perpetual inventory control. In response to shortages, the facilities would sometimes order two times or more the number of products they really needed.

As a result of these serious problems, the task force recommended three ways to attack the inventory program:

- develop better sales forecasting
- improve controls of orders
- improve production scheduling/purchasing

The previous method of *sales forecasting* was to base it on total dollar sales without regard to item-by-item patterns and to look at overall economic indicators for the country. The company did examine its share of market as an overall indicator of performance. But the forecast which was made on a yearly basis was not dynamic enough to take changes into consideration.

The recommendation was a moving quarterly forecast, dropping three months and adding another three months, both by dollars and by product lines. In addition, periodic analyses were made to determine whether the forecasts should be changed as a result of changing marketing conditions, economics, and so on.

The forecasts were sent to the various facilities' inventory personnel, who then converted them to planning forecasts for inventory levels. Everybody in relevant positions in the company participated in producing and altering the forecasts.

In spite of the fact that a marked change was made in the process, it did not completely solve the problem. Field warehouse inventory control was needed. Each warehouse had to look at its particular pattern of sales and make changes. The primary emphasis for the field warehouses was to examine their requirements against their own supplies and ability to stock. Lead times were developed for each supplier from the placement of the order to the receipt of the parts.

In addition, the economic order quantity was agreed upon. The task force also examined inventory carrying costs, which were substantial. Those carrying costs included interest, obsolescence, and storage. The task force agreed on a specific percentage of the inventory costs as a goal. Anything much higher than that would trigger an examination of particular items.

Inventory ordering costs were analyzed and the average amount was determined to be approximately $12.75. Using this as an estimate, product lines and product items were examined and specific actions taken. Scheduling plant deliveries was improved by establishing a particular day of the week for each plant, as well as scheduling full truckload or full carload shipments to substantially reduce freight costs.

The results of these steps were:

- a decrease in inventory of more than 25 percent
- a decrease in customer shortage complaints of 65 percent
- a substantial reduction in materials handling costs

PLANT ORDER HANDLING AND PRODUCTION CONTROL

Previously, plants had used either obsolete computers or manual systems for receiving, shipping orders, invoicing, and payrolls. There was no perpetual inventory system for the slow-selling items. Manual systems were used. The task force decided to concentrate on six focus areas.

One was eliminating existing shortages. Thousands of items were on back-order lists, resulting in many customer complaints. To alleviate this, each facility prepared a list of surplus stocks and items which could be shipped from any one of these facilities. Great concentration was placed on bringing these inventories up to the proper levels. Production bottlenecks were isolated and extra employees were put on to relieve them.

A major effort of cost reduction in this area was to standardize the identification of items. In addition to dollar and unit forecasts, forecasts were now made for *parts* as well, so that all the components would be ready to produce the final item. The computer system was upgraded, and fewer manual steps were taken in terms of production scheduling.

Sales Planning and Distribution

The most alarming aspect of this particular segment was that the company share of market for most of its product lines had gradually decreased over the past decade. This was especially troublesome because sales in the industry had increased by 30 percent, while the company sales remained the same.

Much of the sales decline could be traced to the loss of customers because of product shortages and product design. One of the first things uncovered was that sales costs varied by different customers, whether small or large. This raised a very important question. Was it worthwhile spending valuable sales time on *small* customers, while others were being lost?

In order to determine specifically what the problems were, the financial area was called upon to create a detailed analysis by customer and by salesperson. Besides dropping some of the marginal customers, a distribution change was made so that local distributors could handle some small customers who were worth keeping. National customers continued to be handled by large wholesalers.

Salespersons' time was analyzed by customer, region, and sales territory. Some marginal customers who were still potentially profitable were handled by telephone rather than by a salesperson on location.

Marketing people carefully studied the location of all the distribution centers. As a result, four were closed and four were relocated so that better service could be given at a lower cost.

Results: Cost of handling orders were reduced 25 percent; expenses for salespeople remained the same; sales increased 20 percent over two years; net profits increased by two million dollars per year.

Another area clearly identified was immediate inventory reduction problems. Here is the actual list:

- Inventories up in spite of discontinued items
- Many items with a year's supply or more
- Substantial number of products marginal or slow movers
- Distribution centers accumulating items that were already on hand at other facilities
- Scrap products taking up vital storage space

- Products rejected by quality control still on hand
- High carrying costs and storage costs

And here is a list of the actions taken:

- Scrap all items whose potential sales value is less than $50.
- Begin to discontinue product lines with a potential sales value of less than $50.
- Prepare a list of excess items and circulate it among the various distribution centers. Don't allow facilities to order additional stock until they consult the list.
- Set order quantities on fast, medium, and slow selling items differently, based on sales performance.
- Examine excess tools, category by category. Sell unusable ones wherever possible and convert others so that they are usable.
- Check rejected items for possible conversion in order to reclaim them. Sell the others as scrap. Action Checklist #6 covers a few of the avenues in this area.

ACTION CHECKLIST # 1

Product Simplification and Standardization

ACTION FOCUS	N/A	STRONG	SATIS-FACTORY	NEEDS SOME IMPROVEMENT	WEAK: NEEDS MAJOR IMPROVEMENT	ACTION PLAN, RESPONSIBILITY
Discontinue product lines with downward sales trends						
Review engineering improvements and parts redesign						
Increase prices on profitable items						
Redesign products with unusual breakdown rates						
Contact key customers and ask their opinion						
Standardize specific parts						

ACTION CHECKLIST # 2

Packaging/Materials Handling

ACTION FOCUS	N/A	STRONG	SATIS-FACTORY	NEEDS SOME IMPROVEMENT	WEAK: NEEDS MAJOR IMPROVEMENT	ACTION PLAN, RESPONSIBILITY
Improve product protection: more durable packaging						
Improve product protection: more weather resistant packaging						
Study distribution center layouts and space requirements						
Study distribution center systems for materials handling						
Make packaging more attractive at same or lower cost						
Enhance identification of cartons' contents to save time in picking stock						

ACTION CHECKLIST # 3

Materials Handling/Warehouses

ACTION FOCUS	N/A	STRONG	SATIS-FACTORY	NEEDS SOME IMPROVEMENT	WEAK: NEEDS MAJOR IMPROVEMENT	ACTION PLAN, RESPONSIBILITY
Adjustable shelves to allow for different package sizes						
Adjustable shelves for volume peaks and valleys						
Adaptable loading dock ramps for different heights of vehicles						
Gravity feed instead of manual movement of inventory						
Ball-bearing conveyors						
Kit of commonly used items (tape machines, cutters, package markers)						
Clear assignments for production employees' simple equipment maintenance						
Solicit suggestions from employees						

ACTION CHECKLIST # 4

Receiving/Shipping

ACTION FOCUS	N/A	STRONG	SATIS-FACTORY	NEEDS SOME IMPROVEMENT	WEAK: NEEDS MAJOR IMPROVEMENT	ACTION PLAN, RESPONSIBILITY
Emphasis on quality control to reduce damaged shipments						
Suppliers show weight on cartons to speed stocking						
Legibility of shipping addresses to reduce handling time						
Standards for receiving and storage time of inventory						

ACTION CHECKLIST # 5

Transportation/Construction

ACTION FOCUS	N/A	STRONG	SATIS-FACTORY	NEEDS SOME IMPROVEMENT	WEAK: NEEDS MAJOR IMPROVEMENT	ACTION PLAN, RESPONSIBILITY
Reduced freight rates through conversion to full carloads						
Traffic department scheduling to lower distribution costs						
Audit of freight bills to uncover overcharges						
Preventive maintenance of company vehicles						
Standards for construction of distribution facilities						
Standards for creation of parking lots, building security						

ACTION CHECKLIST # 6

Sales Planning and Distribution

ACTION FOCUS	N/A	STRONG	SATIS-FACTORY	NEEDS SOME IMPROVEMENT	WEAK: NEEDS MAJOR IMPROVEMENT	ACTION PLAN, RESPONSIBILITY
Discontinue or scrap items less than a current monetary limit						
Circulate list of excess items to distribution centers						
Set different order quantities based on sales performance						
Convert usable excess tools						
Sell unusable excess tools						

3

SUGGESTION SYSTEMS: KEY TO EMPLOYEE INVOLVEMENT IN COST CUTTING

"People will flood you with ideas if you let them!" That's what one company president claimed while discussing suggestion systems. Here are the benefits, considerations, and steps you can take to either install a new suggestion system or improve your current one.

Among the tangible benefits deriving from such a system, your organization will be able to: reduce costs while returning, on average, three to eight times your monetary investment in awards and administration; boost revenues; improve productivity and quality; enhance performance as your employees learn more details of their jobs and overall operations; and conserve energy and resources.

Intangible benefits include the ability to: improve the company's image, increase employee satisfaction and loyalty, develop more team spirit, improve safety, and foster better communications.

LAYING THE FOUNDATION

You should focus on several management considerations as you examine the opportunities for a suggestion system.

Eligibility of subject matter: what is eligible for submission and evaluation, what is eligible for an award, and what is not

Eligibility of suggestor: job responsibility relative to idea/subject, what is highest eligibility level (first line supervisor/manager, executives, etc.)

Acceptable suggestions: should the program only be concerned with cost reduction and/or revenue improvement; should it include safety, housekeeping, public relations

Property rights: the suggestion generally belongs to the company

Award policy: kinds/amounts of awards and how given out

Administration: submission procedure, forms, appeal, etc.

A shrewd executive also looks for reasons for failure as well as steps for success. A survey of suggestion systems at work today reveals these potential problem areas:

- lack of top management support
- lack of set policies or ground rules
- poor promotion
- insignificant awards
- poor administration, not enough personal contact with suggestors
- lack of quick action (recommended goal is to process within thirty to sixty days)
- accepted suggestions not implemented
- turning down the suggestion without a clear, concise reason
- bypassing supervisory personnel, rather than having them take active roles

THE BEST WAYS TO PROMOTE SUGGESTION SYSTEMS

Among the most common methods for promoting suggestion systems are:

1. frequent reminders in newsletters
2. posters, pamphlets for new staff, stuffers in pay envelopes
3. coffee or tea mugs with slogans printed on them
4. communicating outstanding ideas to general public, associations, and local media
5. top management receives status reports

6. awards made in the form of money, merchandise, company stock, or other forms of recognition
7. top management participates in giving out awards
8. inspect suggestion boxes to make sure they are prominently displayed, clean, and well stocked with forms.
9. idea coordinators to help develop and write the suggestions

According to the National Association of Suggestion Systems in the United States, the average award is 10 percent of first year net value (benefits minus implementation costs); the average return is 4.4 times the cost of the program (awards and administration); and approximately one full-time administrator is needed for each 4,000 eligible employees.

In considering participation eligibility, it is difficult to apply one set of rules to all companies. However, most experts agree on two general guidelines. All employees are eligible to make suggestions, and not all employees can receive awards.

A large manufacturer states: "You cannot receive an award for suggestions that are part of or related to your own assigned duties and job responsibilities."

USING THE FIVE-STEP APPROACH

The following method can help your employees focus on valuable suggestions.

1. Take a good look around you
A worthwhile suggestion cuts costs and/or increases revenues. The employee suggestion pamphlet of an electronics manufacturer has a section titled "Tips on developing ideas." Here is a checklist of what it covers.

Does the suggestion

- eliminate or reduce scrap or waste?
- reduce the frequency of equipment repairs?
- improve operating procedures to increase production?

- improve quality at no extra cost?
- make our product in less time?
- combine two operations into one without sacrificing quality?
- substitute a less costly material without sacrificing quality?
- improve a method of handling materials?
- make repairs at less cost?
- provide a better raw material delivery system?
- provide a better, less costly packaging procedure?
- rearrange machines, equipment, benches, or tools for more efficient operation?
- reduce or eliminate down-time on equipment?
- reduce administrative time?
- reduce energy consumption?
- reduce, simplify, or eliminate paperwork?
- combine or simplify reports to make them more useful?
- avoid duplication of effort?
- improve job safety or health?
- improve security?

This corporation, which has about 350,000 employees, processed approximately 200,000 suggestions and adopted almost 50,000 of them.

A leading financial services organization recommends its employees look into:

- misuse of materials
- unproductive meetings
- bottlenecks
- excessive overtime
- jobs that require lots of time and/or "chasing around"
- work that no one uses after completion
- delays in servicing customers

All the above points can be incorporated into your **employee guide** to making suggestions.

2. Select an area for improvement
Have your employees think about their own job only as a beginning.

Depending upon your eligibility rules, they can be very specific or look at an entire workflow. Frequently the "area" is completely outside their own, as long as it presents no eligibility problems.

3. Ask yourself some questions
These queries belong either on your suggestion form or in the employee booklet. They are also appropriate for posters.

List the answers to:

- Who does it?
- What is done?
- Where is it done?
- How is it done?
- How much is done?
- How much time does it take?

Then following each answer, ask:

- Why?
- Is it really necessary?
- Can it be improved?

If the employee discovers an inconsistency, he or she may have identified a costly problem. That's half the battle.

4. Come up with a better idea
Some general suggestions are to:

- combine tasks
- change the order or place in which tasks are done
- eliminate unnecessary processes
- simplify the work process
- improve the product or service

Subjects or approaches *not* eligible for awards or consideration include ideas already being considered, new products under development or not announced, and ideas with no specific solution.

You should have a company or plant contact who can clarify these points for any employee with doubts. In addition, many firms have "idea coordinators" who are familiar with company policy and skilled in writing. Many suggestion systems have floundered because employees were unable or reluctant to clearly express their ideas on paper. The role of the idea coordinator is to take the employee's concept and help him or her write it on a suggestion form.

5. Submit your suggestion

Your company should have an abundant supply of suggestion forms, pamphlets, and other literature pertaining to the program. The lack of forms is one way to guarantee failure of your system.

Exhibit 1 is an example of what a good form contains. Notice that the suggestor's job title is listed so that it can be compared with the subject for eligibility consideration.

SUGGESTION SYSTEM ADMINISTRATION

In addition, many companies provide processing steps, such as evaluation, cost/benefit analysis, suggestion disposition, award amount, payroll notification and employee notification on a separate sheet. You can use a form like the one shown in Exhibit 2 in two ways.

By giving it to the employee, you can generate a more accurate account of just what the benefits may be, although it may not be very precise. But it will get the suggestor thinking "bottom line."

Your suggestion evaluator can use Exhibit 2 to make more precise estimates and create a cost/benefit analysis to help you decide whether to use a particular idea or not. Tailor the form to your own requirements and then use it the way that's most valuable for your company.

The system can succeed or fail based upon the quality and timeliness of your evaluation. The following is a list of points for your evaluators to follow to make the process work:

1. Make sure the suggestion has a high company priority.
2. Approach the evaluation as a positive task.

SUGGESTION FORM # _____

Name _____
Your Title _____
Location _____ Tel. No. _____
Dept. Name _____ Dept. No. _____

( ) Check This Box If You Do Not Want Your Name Disclosed
Did you submit suggestion previously? ( ) Yes ( ) No
If yes, indicate suggestion number _____
Did you collaborate with others? ( ) Yes ( ) No
If yes, enter their names _____

The present situation or problem is: _____

I/We suggest that: (attach additional sheets if necessary) _____

BENEFITS OF THIS SUGGESTION _____
( ) Increase Revenue by Approx. _____ ( ) Reduce Expenses _____ ( ) Unable to Quantify at This Time
Remarks: _____

_____ Signature   _____ Date

Exhibit 1.
A suggested suggestion form

COST/BENEFIT ANALYSIS

Annual $ (By Category)	Current Costs (A) Present $	Estimated Costs		Savings	
		(B) 1st Year $	(C) 2nd Year	(D) 1st Year	(E) 2nd Year
1. Processing (labor)					
2. Supplies (paper, etc.)					
3. Equipment					
4. Occupancy					
5. Other Costs					
6. TOTAL					

Additional Cost Savings Information, Remarks [( ) Documentation Attached]

Intangible Benefits

SUGGESTION COMMITTEE DISPOSITION
( ) Adopted   ( ) Not Adopted   Recommended Award $ _____

NOTIFICATION   REMARKS
( ) Corporate Personnel   ( ) Payroll   ( ) Employee

_____
Suggestion System Administrator

Exhibit 2.
A dual-use form for suggestions

3. Be objective; don't be swayed by the name or responsibility of the suggestor.
4. Be prompt, particularly when there are items of safety, health, or security.
5. Review the writeup carefully so that you understand what the idea is all about.
6. Gather required documents and interview people who can provide necessary facts.
7. Prepare a clear recommendation for adoption or rejection.

You should also consider promoting and administering the system through a high-level committee. Such a committee can be charged with the following responsibilities:

- formulate policies and make decisions
- establish and approve procedures
- review plan's operation periodically and make changes
- assess usefulness and practicality of suggestions
- recommend cash rewards
- guard against infringement and duplication
- distribute information on approved suggestions to managers who will implement them
- follow up on implementation
- review adopted suggestions periodically for possible additional award

A practical staffing plan is to have a committee composed of one permanent member, such as a suggestion system administrator, plus four people who serve on a rotating basis, changing each quarter or year. This assures greater objectivity and prevents arbitrary decisions by one individual.

Your timetable should be to completely process a suggestion within thirty to ninety days.

Direct your committee's attention to three questions: eligibility, previous consideration, practicality. In addition, focus on the five major processing steps in Exhibit 2: cost/benefit analysis, award determination, implementation of adopted suggestions, payroll notification for awards, and employee notification.

Exhibit 3 is a decision table used by one company to address those eight points.

DECIDING ON AWARDS

There are several diverse viewpoints on the subject of awards in an employee suggestion system.

It is most common to reward at a level of 10 to 15 percent of the first year's net savings. Some companies pay higher to draw out profitable ideas. One source claims that 60 percent of all adopted suggestions are still showing benefits ten years later.

Another calculation method is to take nonrecurring implementation expense and prorate it over a four-year period. Take that 25 percent and deduct it from first year savings. (This method is based on the theory that the average life of a suggestion's effectiveness is four years.)

Intangible suggestions awards can range from $10 to $100. Some programs offer 10 percent of savings after direct implementation costs are subtracted, but before overhead costs are deducted. Others differentiate between one-time and recurring savings (for example, maximum $2,500 for the former and $5,000 for the latter).

Some awards are doubled depending upon management concern—suggestions bearing on energy costs, for example, being deemed more important than those dealing with public relations. Others use a sliding scale, for example, 25 percent of first $5,000 savings down to 5 percent of savings over $50,000 with limit of $10,000.

Exhibit 4 is an actual award table based upon three levels of suggestions. The higher percentages go to precise cost quantification. Quality circles get a lower percentage than individuals because the QC group is allotted company time and expert help.

Giving goods instead of cash for a worker's bright idea is increasing. A leading American bank's ten-week suggestion program gave away only merchandise and travel. But it yielded about 900 good ideas and $9 million in savings. Noncash awards are more attractive to some.

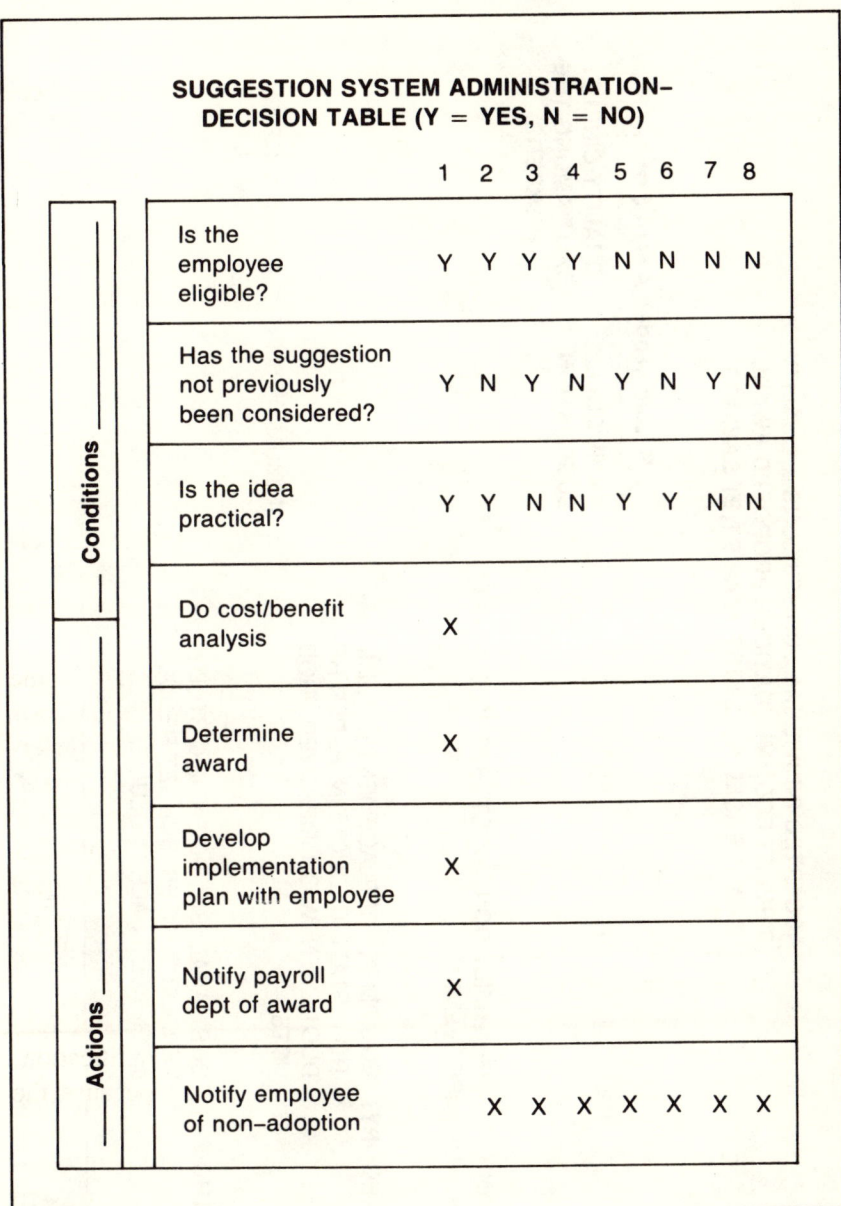

Exhibit 3.
A decision table for suggestion systems

ACCEPTED INDIVIDUAL SUGGESTIONS & QUALITY CIRCLE RECOMMENDATIONS PROPOSED AWARD TABLE BASED UPON 1ST YEAR'S NET SAVINGS

	Recommended Award $ or %	
	INDIVIDUAL SUGGESTION	QUALITY CIRCLE (SPLIT AMONG THE MEMBERS)
LEVEL I		
DEFINITIVE QUANTIFICATION (COST REDUCTION OR REVENUE IMPROVEMENT)	10%	5%
CATEGORY: EQUIPMENT REPLACEMENT OR ELIMINATION, STAFF REDUCTION, PAPER REDUCTION, NEW OR IMPROVED PRODUCTS	(MINIMUM OF $50)	(MINIMUM OF $50 EACH)
METHOD: COST ANALYSIS, SCIENTIFIC STUDY, VENDOR QUOTES, BUDGET REDUCTION, INCREASED SALES VOLUME		

Exhibit 4.
A suggested system award table

SUGGESTION SYSTEMS: KEY TO EMPLOYEE INVOLVEMENT IN COST CUTTING

LEVEL II

SOME QUANTIFICATION (COST AVOIDANCE OR BETTER RESOURCE UTILIZATION)

CATEGORY: BETTER CONTROLS, INCREASED EFFICIENCY, TASK REDUCTION, BETTER UTILIZATION OR EQUIPMENT & RESOURCES	1%–10% (MINIMUM OF $50)
METHOD: STUDY, BUT NO DEFINITE PINPOINTING OF IMMEDIATE $	1%–10% (MINIMUM OF $50 EACH)

LEVEL III

INTANGIBLE BENEFITS

CATEGORY IMPROVED MORALE, COMMUNICATIONS, SAFETY, ETC.	$50
METHOD: ESTIMATE, OPINION, ETC.	$50 EACH

Exhibit 4. *(continued)*

Having something to look at—a TV set, camera, or piano—is a symbol of personal achievement on the job.

Some experts say cash and goods *combined* yield up to triple the level of contributions from workers.

A financial organization awards prizes or shares of stock. Annual savings of more than $5,000 earn a prize worth $1,000. Savings up to $5,000 earn a prize worth from $500 to $1,000. Intangible suggestions earn prizes from $250 to $500. Stock prizes are determined by the suggestion committee (2 to 20 shares).

4

FORMS MANAGEMENT IN MODERN BUSINESS

The progress of modern business greatly depends on obtaining information quickly and accurately. Information is obtained from one or more sources and transmitted to others for further processing or final action. The more efficiently this system is handled, the lower the operating costs.

One of the major tools used for this purpose is the "form." Companies are becoming aware of the need for control of forms and related costs. This chapter provides you with the basic knowledge necessary for the administration of an effective forms program.

THE BASIS OF FORMS MANAGEMENT

For a forms program to be successful, it must provide savings to your organization primarily in two areas.

Savings in physical costs are accomplished through standardizing form design, size, quantity, procurement, printing processes, packaging, warehousing, inventory control, storage, and distribution.

Savings in clerical costs are accomplished by creating forms that require the least clerical effort from employees who use them and which operate efficiently when designed for use with a particular business machine.

The rule of thumb used by most experts is that a forms management program should save your company a minimum of 20 percent of annual printing costs the first year of operation. After that savings can range between 10 percent and 20 percent. This depends on the number of analysts you use, and the amount of time spent questioning and analyzing the forms/system rather than simply maintaining the program. The greater the amount of creativity, the greater the amount of savings.

Experts generally agree that the *other* costs associated with a form equal approximately forty times the cost of printing that form. These other costs are processing (labor), equipment, records management (storage, retrieval, destruction), and so on. To illustrate, if your company's form printing costs are $100,000 a year, the associated annual costs of using the forms would be approximately $4 million. Since you could realize an average 20 percent reduction in costs when an effective forms program is instituted, savings of approximately $20,000 in printing and $800,000 in processing in the first year could result.

A forms program will lose impetus if it cannot justify its existence to management in terms of such savings. In the early stages of a program, the greatest savings will be obtained from reduced printing costs. These initial printing savings can be identified easily and are recurring in nature. They should be counted each year as long as the program continues and the savings remain in effect.

As printing, packaging, storage, distribution, and ordering standards are established and become effective, additional savings from this source will begin to diminish. The emphasis will then shift to the use of the functional file as increased savings from combinations and consolidations of forms are obtained.

FUTURE OF FORMS MANAGEMENT

Forms management is an integral part of all organizational systems. There has been a great deal of talk about the "paperless society." Even though the trend is to move in that direction, the majority of "forms" for the foreseeable future will remain on paper.

As a result of the need for paper reduction, "forms" are being designed and produced in alternative media such as CRT screens, microforms (files and microfiche), optical discs, and the like. These media require creativity and a good deal of technical expertise. But you will still need to know many of the forms analysis and design principles that apply to paper forms management.

DEFINITION OF A FORM

A form is a document which contains printed information with blank spaces provided for inserting data. Entries may be made by hand, typewriter, or other equipment such as computers or word processors.

In addition to the usual types of forms (such as applications, invoices, and letterheads), there are other printed materials which, while not meeting the traditional definition of a form, are included in a forms program. Their design, procurement, and distribution are handled in the same manner. Included are tags, labels, envelopes, and instruction sheets.

Items not classified as forms are booklets, manuals, charts, graphs, advertising, and other graphics work.

CREATING A FORMS PROGRAM

The purposes of a controlled forms program are to analyze, standardize, and design forms which will record and report information quickly, accurately, and economically while keeping printing and other related costs to a minimum. Not only will errors be reduced and workpace expedited in your paperwork operations, but the benefits will extend to any system and procedure in your company which uses the "fill-in" form to obtain data.

Controls are also set up so that only certain individuals within each unit are authorized to approve the initiation of a new form or the revision of an existing one. This reduces the number of unnecessary or inefficient forms in use.

A controlled forms program includes three major activities:

1. *Forms analysis and design.* Every company finds itself bur-

dened with too much paperwork, often using similar or even duplicate forms to record the same information. By applying forms analysis and design principles, you can eliminate unnecessary forms and consolidate similar ones. Forms are standardized and designed in a manner best suited to your needs, taking into consideration related activities such as routing, filing, and final disposition.

2. *Printing and procurement.* Clerical efforts are simplified and processing expedited by selecting the type of construction and production best suited to each particular case. Determining correct ordering quantities and preparing proper printing specifications also contribute to economical printing costs.

A complete forms program also includes methods for procuring forms economically by establishing group ordering and other purchasing techniques. Printing savings are immediate and you can determine them by comparing annual printing costs after the program has been in effect.

3. *Storage and distribution.* Storage and distribution involve taking full advantage of the local facilities available. For example, some companies with limited storage capabilities may order forms in smaller quantities to conserve space. Such companies could set up systems to allow for the production of large quantities of forms at reduced prices, have them stored elsewhere, and shipped in manageable quantities at designated times.

ORGANIZING A FORMS PROGRAM

Before a forms program can be instituted, management must be convinced that it will result in savings to the company.

Once approval is granted, it is essential that high-level management circulate a letter to all departments (or equivalent organizational units) announcing the program, its purpose, and the name of the manager who will be in charge. The directive should request full cooperation with the program so all the managers not only provide information and material when requested, but also adhere to standards and ordering procedures that the forms group subsequently establishes.

The forms administrator should meet with all department managers (or other individuals designated by them) to further delineate the purpose and objectives of the program. Especially during the initial stages of the program, the managers or their representatives will be called on for information and/or material. Their willingness to cooperate fully will depend on whether they consider the effort worthwhile. The best tactic is to use graphic examples to show how, aside from saving the company money, their own departmental operations will benefit.

Request each department or division to designate certain individuals to:

1. Act as contact representatives between the forms administrator or group and the department. These individuals collect samples of all forms used within their units and obtain and provide any information requested by forms management.
2. Approve requisitions for new and revised forms and for reordering existing forms. This prevents unauthorized printing and eliminates unnecessary forms.

Note: Many companies designate a specific executive with other responsibilities (for example, V.P.–Personnel or V.P.–Administration) to handle the forms program. That individual's staff becomes the "forms group." Whether you have a separate person or group or a working executive to handle your program doesn't matter. The text will refer to whomever is in charge as the forms group or forms management for the sake of convenience.

STEPS TO ESTABLISH A PROGRAM

Use the following eight steps to establish a new forms program in your company.

1. Obtain personnel. Forms analysts and designers should have analytical ability and the manual dexterity necessary for drawing and ruling forms. A knowledge of the company's operations is also helpful. The number of people required will depend upon the size and scope of your operations and your programs. One company president said it took two people about one month for each thousand forms in his large firm.

2. *Send collection letters.* Send a collection letter to all department managers or their designated contact representatives requesting samples of all printed forms. Exhibit 5 is a sample collection letter used by an actual manufacturing firm.

3. *Establish liaison with purchasing.* Agree on objectives with the Purchasing Department. Determine operating requirements and procedures.

4. *Obtain tools and supplies.* These are discussed later in this chapter.

5. *Establish standards.* Adopt design standards as described later.

6. *Establish ordering procedures.* Finalize with Purchasing and any stationery or supplies groups a satisfactory system for ordering. Establish stocking and distribution arrangements as well.

7. *Provide for copy preparation.* Composition for original drawings in most cases will be prepared within the company. Obtain any necessary equipment and train operating personnel. If possible, make arrangements with outside suppliers for composition services when work cannot be handled internally.

8. *Prepare internal operating forms.* Provide forms that are used to control and administer the program including:

- forms questionnaire
- printing specification sheet
- form order progress record

IMPLEMENTING AND MAINTAINING THE PROGRAM

The following are some general guidelines for implementing and maintaining a program. Before accepting orders for new or revised forms, you must insure that the forms group is capable of handling the work and meeting delivery schedules. Send a memo to all department managers, contact representatives, and other key personnel

COLLECTING FORMS

To: _____ (Heads of Departments)
From: Forms Management
Subject: Collection of Forms Samples

    As you know, a comprehensive Forms Management Program has been instituted in our company. As the first step a detailed review is being made of all the forms and related documents currently in use. To assist us, please arrange to have five (5) copies of all "forms" used in your organization collected for analysis.

    Include any document which contains printed information with blank spaces for inserting data. Entries may be made by hand, typewriter, or other business machines. This covers, but is not limited to, letterheads, snapouts, continuous forms, envelopes, labels, tags, tabulating cards, etc. Certain other items such as form letters or instruction sheets, are also included since they are designed, printed, and handled in the same manner as forms. If in doubt as to whether a particular document comes under the definition of a form, include it.

    Include samples of forms which are:
—printed internally, purchased from outside suppliers, or otherwise obtained from outside agencies
—produced by *any* method of production (offset, letterpress, copier, etc.)
—permanent or temporary
—used in the office or in the field, warehouse, plant, etc.

Instructions:
1. When collecting the forms:
   A. Obtain samples directly from each unit within your department (not from supply rooms).
   B. Do not compile a list of the samples.
   C. Do not obtain information on the use of the forms.
2. On each collected sample, write:
   A. Name of the using department, division, or section.
   B. Estimated annual usage of the form. (If a form is for tem-

Exhibit 5.
A sample forms collection letter

porary use, indicate this on the sample, show the date it was initiated and the quantity used to date.)
3. Where forms are in sheets, pads, or books obtain only *five* sheets of each different form. (Do not collect the complete book but indicate on the samples that they are bound in a book.) If forms are in sets, provide five complete sets of each form. Do not staple individual forms or otherwise fasten to other forms.
4. Submit samples in the following manner:
   A. Wrap all forms in a package clearly labeled with the name of the department, division, or section and with the name of the person who submitted the collection.
   B. Send package to *(Name and location)* by *(date)*.

For further information, please contact *(Name)* at *(phone number)* who is in charge of the Forms Management Program.

Thank you for your cooperation!
(Signature)

Exhibit 5. *(continued)*

informing them of the ordering procedures for new and revised forms that will be processed through the forms administration. Specify guidelines as to the length of time it normally takes to design and print the various types of forms (for example, flat vs. specialty).

Concurrently with receiving orders for and standardizing new and revised forms, groups of forms within the functional file (see page 52) should be reviewed, standardized, and consolidated. First review the functional file folders containing the largest number of forms, high-usage forms, or expensive forms since they will provide the greatest immediate savings. If certain groups of forms within a system are creating operational difficulties, consider them for early review.

Standardizing these forms involves contacting the originating units. Redesign and consolidation should take place as soon thereafter as possible. As the forms are developed, a Progress Record like the one shown in Exhibit 6 should be created.

A redesigned form is prepared only as a pencil sketch at this juncture. Have the sketch approved by the originating department and

FORMS MANAGEMENT IN MODERN BUSINESS 49

Exhibit 6.
Sample Progress Record

place in a numerical forms folder to await further orders. Make an appropriate note on the progress records to alert the forms designer that the approved sketch will apply at the next printing. At the same time you should send a "hold printing" notice to the purchasing or stationery/supplies office to prevent the automatic reordering of the form. When an internal order is received, an original drawing can be prepared and sent to the originating unit for approval, after which the form is released for production.

REPORTS TO MANAGEMENT

Submit periodic reports to management showing the accomplishments and savings to support the program.

Assure that detailed records are kept by the forms designer showing the savings that result from each redesign, consolidation, standardization, and new procedure. Some savings, such as printing, are tangible and easy to measure monetarily. Other savings, such as clerical, may require more effort to identify and therefore require a different method of analysis.

Detailed record keeping, although time consuming, is especially important during the early stages of the program since some of the greatest savings resulting from redesigning, consolidation, and standardization are *recurring* and will continue for as long as the program is maintained.

To figure printing savings use similar quantities and compare the printing costs of each redesigned form against the cost of the last previous printing before redesign.

With some forms the printing costs will actually increase due to a change in the construction of the form that was made to yield a clerical savings (such as when you change from a flat form to a continuous form). This type of printing cost should be reported separately so as not to affect the statistics on printing savings.

Correctly redesigned forms result in savings by requiring less time to prepare the form and/or by minimizing errors.

In some cases, one or two people, by using a redesigned form, are able to collectively save a few hours a week. Where large numbers of employees are involved, their work output may appreciably

```
┌─────────────────────────────────────────────────────────────┐
│                FORMS MANAGEMENT CASE HISTORY                │
│                                                             │
│  Operation _____    Annual $ Savings _____  │
│  Results gained by:                                         │
│       __ standardization of procedures   __ system conversion│
│       __ consolidation of functions      __ other _____ │
│  Cost reduction due to:                                     │
│       __ less forms expense (design changes)                │
│       __ reduced inventory   __ decreased distribution/handling│
│       __ other_____                               │
│  Details _____│
│  _____│
│  _____│
│  _____│
│  _____│
│  _____│
│  _____│
│                                                             │
│  Prepared by: _____   Approved by: _____  │
│  Date:  / /                     Date:  / /                  │
└─────────────────────────────────────────────────────────────┘
```

Exhibit 7.
Sample form for creating a case history

increase, or fewer people may be required to perform the same operation.

Savings can be reported most effectively by briefly describing the operation before and after, referred to as a "case history." You can use Exhibit 7 to document your case histories.

IDENTIFYING FORMS BY NUMBERS AND TITLES

In a controlled forms program, every form must carry an identifying number and title. The form number is the basic means of identification and control. It is used by the forms management group for record keeping, procurement, storage, and distribution. The form title is no less important. It often is the most significant means of identification for users of the form.

The main function of a form number is to identify and set apart a particular form from all other forms in the company. The numbers also lend themselves to easy filing, retrieval, ordering, and storage.

Most experts recommend you have a two-digit form number prefix to identify the originating department, from 02 through 99 (example, 02 = Accounting; 05 = Controller's). The prefix 01 is reserved for "general" forms—those used by several departments and originated by no specific group. As long as an originating department retains control of the text of a form, the numbering continues to carry that department's prefix even though other departments use the form.

A three-digit form number can be applied to each form within an originating or controlling department. These are usually assigned serially, starting with 001.

Each time a form is revised, a new revision letter is added to the form number to distinguish the revision from previous issues of the form. The initial issue of the form may carry the revision letter A; subsequent revisions may be assigned B, C, D, and so on.

Maintain a register of assigned form numbers to assure that numbers are not duplicated. Start a separate page for each departmental prefix code. Enter each form number and its associated title on the appropriate page as they are issued.

When a form is superseded or obsolete, cross the number off the register with an explanatory note and date. These numbers may be reassigned to new forms after a lapse of time. Normally, a minimum of two to three years is recommended before reusing a number.

Assign a title to every form in the program, including those of a temporary nature or limited usage. A properly assigned title adds an additional identification to the form that acts as a check against the form number. This can be particularly helpful when forms are requisitioned with an incorrect number. Titles also eliminate confusion to the user, especially when several similar-appearing forms are being completed at one time, and they assist new personnel in learning the functions of the various forms they must handle.

The best title is one that is descriptive and specific in the fewest possible words. In the following pages covering **functional file,** the assignment of functions and subjects to each form is described in detail. You can use the same function and subject approach successfully to assign titles. Very often the title becomes obvious from the functional file classification of the form.

DEVELOPING A FUNCTIONAL FILE

An effective forms program must include a means by which functionally related forms can be identified to allow consolidations and combinations of forms. In most cases, you can consolidate forms serving the same or similar purpose into a single form which will serve all users. A series of forms which follow a procedural sequence can be combined so that entries common to all the forms can be made at one writing. Even if a combination of related forms is not possible, there may be areas on each form which should be revised to lessen transferral of information from one form to another.

You can accomplish these results most easily by establishing a functional file. The forms folder maintained for each active form in the program is filed in *numerical* sequence by form number. That makes it possible to determine which forms are functionally similar without an elaborate cross-referencing system. The functional file provides this capability by grouping all forms in the program by function to supplement the numerical file for forms folders.

The simplest and most useful functional file is a collection of one copy or one set of each form used in the organization, classified and filed by functional category. When the categories are chosen properly, you can:

- review for possible consolidations or combinations, thereby reducing the number of active forms in the program
- easily locate forms used in the same procedure
- make a meaningful assignment of form titles

CLASSIFYING BY FUNCTION

In most businesses there are at least twenty-five easily defined and generally accepted functions performed by forms. These may vary slightly from organization to organization and may be affected by local operating conditions. However, most executives start with these functions. You can then add others specific to your particular company.

ACKNOWLEDGE	To recognize as genuine or valid; to recognize the rights, authority, or status of
ADJUST	To bring to a more satisfactory state—for example, to correct errors or omissions; to change, amend, alter, modify, or cancel data, quantities, amounts, and so on
APPLY FOR	To request something that may not be necessarily provided or granted
AUTHORIZE	To empower or sanction; to invest with authority to take action
CERTIFY	To attest authoritatively as being true or as represented; to guarantee
CLAIM	To ask for or demand as a right
CONTRACT	To make a binding agreement in writing
ESTIMATE	To determine approximately or tentatively—for example, to bid, quote, propose, assess, or appraise
FOLLOW UP	To pursue by further action; to remind that supplementary action is required
IDENTIFY	To establish the identity of
INSTRUCT	To teach or give knowledge to
INVOICE	To submit a bill for goods shipped, services, or other charges
LOG	To enter details about an operation in a record

NOTIFY	To give notice of or report the occurrence or status of; to advise
ORDER	To give or place a requirement for materials, work, services, etc.; to direct the payment of money to someone
PASS	To allow or permit to go to or from (usually involving physical movement of someone or something)
PERMIT	To authorize, license, or allow a specific action (usually of limited duration)
RECEIPT	To acknowledge delivery or payment
RECORD	To register facts or data in a permanent manner (usually in writing)
REPORT	To make, issue, or submit an account or statement of action or status (usually in detail required or requested by the recipient)
REQUEST	To ask for something
REQUISITION	To formally require something to be furnished (usually by authority)
ROUTE	To send to a series of persons or places in a specified order
SCHEDULE	To appoint, assign, or designate events to a future timetable; to program
TRANSMIT	To send or transfer from one person or place to another

For the initial classification of the samples, file the forms into the twenty-five functional groups. If the form bears a title, it may not accurately describe the function of the form. Analyze each form to determine its *function* (expressing data) and its *subject* (expressing area of application).

Some typical breakdowns are:

Function	*Subject*
Receipt	Cash
Permit	Parking
Apply for	Employment
Authorize	Overtime

NUMBERING THE CATEGORIES

To simplify the assignment and recording of functional file categories, you need a numbering system. A decimal system is the most effective. Assign a prime number to each of the twenty-five functional groups and use decimals to identify sub-categories. Gaps are usually left in these assignments so that additional categories can be conveniently added later if the need arises.

For example, the initial functional category numbering could be:

5	Acknowledge
10	Adjust
15	Apply for
20	Authorize

Then if the "Apply for" category were broken down further by subject, the numbers could be:

15.1	Apply for - Employment
15.2	Apply for - All other

In the event the category "Apply for - Employment" were found to require a further breakdown, the system reflects its flexibility:

15.1.1	Apply for - Employment (Domestic)
15.1.2	Apply for - Employment (Overseas)

USING THE FUNCTIONAL FILE

As each package of forms samples is received from a user, log in by recording the names of the organizational unit and the individual contact who may have to be consulted later to resolve questions.

Initially, analyze each file folder in the functional file to determine which forms may be consolidated. Usually the folders with the largest number of forms or with expensive or heavily used forms are studied first. They are apt to yield the best opportunities for reducing printing costs and the number of forms in the program.

To identify areas where forms may be combined to produce clerical savings, examine all functional file folders having the same subclassifications by subject. Place these folders in procedural sequence by function. Roughly outline a procedure related to the particular subject. Determine if two or more forms can be combined so that the entries can be made at one writing. The clerical savings resulting from this type of analysis could easily justify a forms program, even if no standardization savings were available.

Once you complete the initial analysis and establish the program, check the functional file each time a new form or one with major revisions is designed. If a form is new, decide on a function classification and search the appropriate files to see if any existing forms can be either used "as is" or consolidated or combined with the new form.

EFFECTIVE FORMS ANALYSIS

Forms analysis is the planning and information-gathering step which precedes forms design. During this stage, the purpose of the form is established, its use justified, and the necessary information obtained to facilitate its design.

An individual using an old form or requesting a new or revised form is often concerned only with immediate needs. On the other hand, the person analyzing the form (forms analyst in a formal program) is interested in the total paperwork system in which the form will be used. He or she questions what happens before, during, and after the form's use in order to achieve maximum efficiency in the design and control of the form. The maximum benefits and savings of a forms management program occur when *all* aspects of a form's use are considered.

Forms analysis begins when either a sketch or description of a required form is provided by the user, or when the analyst is called on to study a complete paperwork system to determine if new forms or revisions to existing ones are required. During the investigation, the analyst should use a questionnaire like the one shown in Exhibit 8.

Depending upon the complexity of the required form, the analyst may obtain this information from the person requesting the form. But the best option is to interview each individual who handles the form as it progresses through the system.

QUESTIONING AREAS

Is the Form Necessary?
One method to reduce forms costs is to prevent unnecessary forms from being initiated. This can be done in various ways.

1. By questioning the originator or by searching the functional file, determine if the same information is recorded elsewhere.
2. Determine if there is a similar form being used in the company that could be modified and consolidated with the proposed form to satisfy the combined requirements.
3. Determine if the cost of the form is justified by its use.

Is Each Item Necessary?
Find out if each field on the form is necessary. This inquiry will also show whether the captions accurately describe the information required for each item. The elimination of unnecessary items results in clerical savings and a less cluttered form. It may also allow use of a more economical form size.

Are All Copies Necessary?
Determine how many copies are made and what happens to each copy.

FORMS QUESTIONNAIRE

Document #	Document Title	Originating Department		Receiving Department		Manual (M) or Computer (C)
		#	Name	#	Name	

How is this item used?
___ No purpose   ___ Information only   ___ Decision support   ___ Control   ___ Other _____

Why eliminate this item?
___ Information obtained elsewhere   ___ Changed conditions   ___ Combined with another _____

What improvements can be made?
___ Get same information from _____   ___ Eliminate selected information   ___ Micrographics
___ On-line inquiry/reporting   ___ Duplex printing   ___ Increase printlines per inch
___ Exception/summary reporting   ___ Electronic mail   ___ Reduce distribution list
___ Change forms design   ___ Reduce frequency (day, week, etc.)   ___ Other _____

What provisions must be made for purchase, storage, and distribution? _____
_____

Exhibit 8.
A forms analysis questionnaire

Additional copies add to the cost of the form and require extra handling and filing. The analyst should consider alternate methods of providing the required information which will reduce to a minimum the number of copies required.

Spacing

Hand filled: Office workers using forms at their desks work under favorable conditions and require minimum fill-in space for entering data. On the other hand, manual or outside workers require more fill-in space due to the nature of their work. They may not be accustomed to paperwork or may have to write while resting the form on any available surface. Take this into consideration when designing spaces.

Machine filled: If a form is prepared by typewriter, computer, or other business machine, the type of machine determines the form, which must be designed to accommodate the machine's spacing and other special features. Various machines print different numbers of characters to the inch and have different vertical line spacing and paper feeding methods.

To determine how much space to allow for entering data, the analyst should obtain an accurate example of what is entered in each space.

Construction

The type of forms construction is based on how the form will be used. For example, forms carried by a person traveling from office to office should be held together during travel and be convenient to use; a multipart form or sales book may fulfill these requirements.

In an office where repetitive forms such as invoices are typed in large quantities each day, considerable handling time can be saved by using *continuous* forms which eliminate the need for manually inserting separate sets into the typewriter.

Identifying Critical Areas of Use

Usually, forms are designed for maximum clerical efficiency for all users. But the analysis might discover that certain phases of processing are more critical than others. The form should be designed to best accommodate these critical requirements.

For example, a form may be filled out by one group, forwarded elsewhere for further entries, and finally sent to data entry. Since errors are most likely to occur in the last stage, it follows that the form design should conform to input requirements.

A form should also be designed for maximum clerical efficiency at the stage where the most clerical savings can result. An employment application is filled out by an applicant only once, but the employment office processes many applications every day. Over and above the obvious requirement that the form be designed to obtain complete and accurate information from the applicant, the first consideration would be to reduce the employment group's clerical processing time.

Sequential Arrangement

After the analysis determines that all items on the form are necessary, entries should be arranged in a logical sequence that corresponds with the flow of work so that entries can be made quickly without wasted motion. (Skipping from one section of the form to another also increases the possibility of error.)

Use writing sequences of left to right and top to bottom whenever possible to suit normal writing habits and reduce clerical time.

Suppose a personnel form contains name, address, telephone number, marital status, and so on. Place these items adjacent to each other on the form for continuity of thought and writing. In some cases the analyst may determine that the correct sequential arrangement on the form is dictated by the *final* user of the information rather than the individual who *first* enters the data.

Information Obtained from Another Form

Determine if the information is obtained or copied from another form. If so, the sequential order of the information on the proposed form should correspond with the form from which it is taken. As an example, if name, account number, and shipping address appear in that sequence on the existing form, they ought to be in the same sequence on the proposed form to facilitate entries and minimize errors.

When some identical information is recorded on two separate forms, consider combining these forms or using a multi-part form (snapout) to serve two or more users having common interests.

Other Forms Affected in the System
The initiation of a new form or the revision of an existing one may affect other forms in the system. Review these related forms to determine whether changes also apply to them and take appropriate measures to see that any necessary changes are made. Resolve all conflicts before the revised or new form is instituted.

Eliminating Restrictive Data
Forms which are general in nature can often be used by more than one department providing the form does not contain restrictive data, such as specific names of people, departments, locations, and so on. If department names or locations must appear on a form, you can still provide one form by printing the items in a list at the top so that the user can check off the appropriate department/name/location.

Avoid data which becomes obsolete when changes occur. For example, "Send copy to John J. Smith, Traffic Manager," can be changed to read "Send copy to Traffic Manager." This prevents the form from becoming obsolete each time a personnel change occurs. As another example, printing the year on a form restricts its use to the current year only. To overcome this, leave a space for the year to be filled in by the user or equipment.

Preprinting Data
The less time it takes to fill in a form, the lower the clerical costs. An effective means of obtaining these savings is to preprint certain constant data, thus eliminating the need for the user to enter this. On a requisition, preprint the company account number. Preprinting a list of code numbers of items from a parts catalog enables the user to check-off items needed instead of writing out each one.

Reviewing Existing Forms
An analyst can obtain valuable clues to the proper presentation of data on a new or revised form by studying filled-in copies of the existing forms in the file. In the case of a form revision, he or she might identify areas on the old form where inaccurate or insufficient information was being provided. For a new form, the same problems can be avoided

FORMS MANAGEMENT IN MODERN BUSINESS   63

by studying the companion forms with which the new one will be used. Here are some items to watch for in reviewing filled-in forms:

1. Notes which are frequently written in the margin or on the face of the form, indicate that the form should be redesigned to accommodate these items in the body of the form.
2. Spaces or boxes repeatedly left unanswered, raise the question of whether they are needed or whether the users clearly understand what is required.
3. Entries which are not confined to the space alloted to them on the form, indicate that more space is required for the entry.
4. Forms which are punched through the text, suggest that margins should be wider or the forms prepunched.

Instructions
Instructions which are vague or complicated tend to confuse the user, resulting in the entry of inaccurate data. Review the instructions to make sure they are complete and can be easily understood by the users of the form.

Often instructions must be given on how many copies to prepare, how to fill in certain items, and where to send each copy. Have these instructions printed on the form where they are most useful to the user.

Routing
Determine where the forms are routed so that full consideration is given to distribution requirements. Give thought to preprinting routing instructions or using different symbols on the form to distinguish the routing, thereby eliminating the need for separate routing slips or addressing envelopes.

If the form is mailed, choose which type of envelope can be used (regular, window, self-mailer, etc.). If automatic inserting machines are used for large mailings, make sure you have the proper form size and envelope in accordance with the machine's requirements.

Filing/Stocking
Find out where and how material is to be filed in order to make pro-

visions in the design of the form for proper placement of the filing data. Filing time is kept to a minimum when the file clerk quickly recognizes the category by which a particular document is filed. Another benefit is the ability of the clerk to retrieve the document easily.

Filing requirements also affect other characteristics of the form such as quality, weight, and size of paper.

Consider the advantages of storing a form in a central stock area where records are maintained and methods for reordering are established.

Individuals who keep an entire supply of forms in their desk or office cabinet often wait until their supply is almost depleted and then submit a requisition for rush printing. This increases printing and clerical costs. Moreover, the supply of forms could be depleted before the new shipment arrives.

When the inventory of forms is controlled by personnel in a stock room, schedules can be developed that allow sufficient time for reordering. Establish procedures for ordering similarly constructed forms at the same time for economy in printing.

FORMS SPECIFICATIONS

A forms specifications worksheet like the one shown in Exhibit 9 contains the data necessary for preparation, construction, and reproduction of a new or revised form. It further acts as a permanent record for contacting the company, department, and responsible individual when revising, superseding, or discontinuing the form.

Prepare a forms specification worksheet for each new form. On a revised form, it is prepared only when the revisions involve changes in the use of the form or its specifications.

The analyst should fill this form out at the first interview with the user. By following the format of the questionnaire, the analyst effectively interviews the user in a minimum of time while assuring that all pertinent information is obtained.

You can tailor Exhibit 9 to the specific requirements of your forms analysis. Remember the following points.

FORMS SPECIFICATIONS

1. Form number _____ ___ New ___ Revised
   Replaces _____ Variation of _____
   Form title _____

2. Purpose _____
   Related forms _____
   Use with envelope # _____

3. Preparation: When, where and how is this form used? _____
   _____

4. Storage: Retention period _____
   Filing equipment used _____

5. Type of form: ___ Flat ___ Snapout ___ Continuous ___
   ___ Other

6. Production specifications: _____

7. Paper and routing: Carbon size: _____
   Routine: _____

8. Stock control: Existing stock _____
   Location of stock _____
   Estimated annual use _____
   Minimum/maximum stock _____ / _____
   Ordering basis ___ as needed ___ low stock
   ___ group order

9. Special notes: _____

10. Contact data: _____ Analyst _____

Exhibit 9.
A worksheet for forms specifications

1. General Information

Form number: Provides a means for identifying the document. If the form is new, assign a number during its design.

New or revised: A new form would indicate that the functional file should be searched before the form is initiated. A revised form indicates that a record of the form exists with the possibility that its original drawing may be usable for making the revision.

Replaces: Often one form replaces several others. This information is necessary so that obsolete forms and their records can be removed from the active files.

Variation of: A form which is very similar in usage and is closely allied to another form always bears the same basic form number as the form it resembles. A numerical suffix is assigned to identify the particular variation.

Title: Reflects (ideally) the purpose and function of the form.

Purpose: Explains the function and use of the form.

2. Relationship to Forms

Related forms: Design the proposed form to correspond in sequence, arrangement, and alignment to related forms with which it will be used. Items in the proposed form may also affect these related forms, which might require change.

Use with envelope #: If an envelope is used, the form design has to fit the envelope into which it is inserted. If the form is used in a window envelope, the address section must coordinate with the window.

3. Preparation

When, where and how the form is used affects spacing, paper, carbon requirements, and construction. If a great number of forms are used, or if peak periods are involved, a special functional construction, such as snapout, may be necessary.

4. Storage

Retention period: Consult official retention schedules and/or legal experts.

Filing equipment used: Size of form should be compatible with size of storage files used.

5. Routing
Number of copies: This aids in determining the type of paper and whether carbon or carbonless material is required.

Reproduction: When a completed form is to be reproduced, the paper on which the form is printed must be compatible with the method of reproduction.

Distribution: A review of where copies are sent may result in a reduction of the number of copies and/or more efficient handling. This also identifies routing instructions that could be included on the form itself.

6. Production Specifications
Type of form: Determines the type of construction that will best fill the user's requirements.

Paper: Conform paper specifications to the standards established under the forms program.

Carbon size: For some types of forms, the carbon is the full width of the form. For others, such as snapouts, the carbon is shorter than the form.

Other specifications: Notes other special physical characteristics necessary to prepare proper printing specifications.

7. Stock Control
Existing stock: Whenever a form is revised and a supply of forms remains in stock, notify the stationery stockroom whether to use or destroy the old stock.

Location of stock: This item is necessary only when there are multiple stockrooms.

Estimated annual use: Determines initial ordering quantity, stocking arrangements, reordering quantity and frequency.

Minimum/maximum stock: Establishes the high and low quantity for ordering based on annual usage.

Ordering basis: Forms may be reordered on an "as needed" basis or by several controlled methods (low stock, group order, etc.).

8. Additional Information

Special notes: The analyst uses this space to record information provided by the user which does not otherwise appear on the questionnaire.

Contact Data: Person(s) to contact for further information and approvals.

Analyst: The location of the analyst is necessary only when the forms program includes analysts who are in more than one area.

5

COST CUTTING TECHNIQUES IN FORMS DESIGN

Forms design begins after you have completed your analysis, collected the necessary data, and resolved all related problems. Information on how the form is used, by whom, how it is processed, produced, stored, and distributed is noted on the forms questionnaires. The sequential arrangements and the spacing required for each entry are entered on a sketch of the proposed form.

Forms design is based upon a set of principles and a group of measures which, when properly applied, result in what is referred to as a "standardized" form. The person designing the form uses the information collected in the analysis and then applies these principles and standards in the most efficient manner to arrive at the finished form. Such a design person must also be knowledgeable in the standards that apply to production elements, such as paper, size, printing, procurement, and storage.

THE BOX PRINCIPLE

The box principle is one of the most useful design techniques available to the forms designer. It conserves space while making it easier

Exhibit 10.
Spacing and positioning required for box principle design—*Use graph paper ruled 12 squares to the inch. Boxes are drawn 4/12" in height. Caption prints in small type flush with left margin or 1/12" from preceding vertical rule, positioned within upper 1/12" of the box. This leaves 3/12" for fill-in.*

to read and enter data on the form. The form is designed as a series of boxes with the captions and entry explanations in the upper left-hand corner of each box. The box caption applies to the data that will be written below it. The entire line is available for fill-in and is suitable for handwritten or machine-filled entries. Exhibit 10 is an example.

This design technique enables entries to be made in a continuous flow from left to right to conform with writing habits as well as typewriter and other business machine requirements. The vertical rules that separate the boxes clearly define the area in which the entry is to be made. By properly aligning the vertical ruling on forms which are machine-filled, you greatly facilitate entries by minimizing the number of required tabular stops. The captions and their explanations are always visible to the typist since they appear at the top of the box. This is illustrated in Exhibit 11.

> *Note:* Exhibits 11 through 21 at the end of this chapter are actual examples created by a noted forms designer. They have been typeset, with comments and notes in the margins and underneath the graphics. It will be easy to make your points with colleagues and subordinates if you make copies of those that are pertinent to your situation.

DETERMINING SPACE REQUIREMENTS

The layout of a form is controlled by the number of items, their sequential arrangement, and the space available on the form. The two factors that control space requirements for each item are a) the length of the caption and b) the space to be allotted for each entry, based mainly on the method of entry (hand, typewriter, etc.). In the case of the hand-filled forms (pen or pencil), the conditions under which the data is entered also determines spacing, as when plant engineers must record numbers as they walk past machines.

Sometimes space must be conserved on a form in order to fit particular items on the same line or in the same block. In such cases, savings of as little as one-quarter of an inch may mean the difference between items fitting or not fitting. In other cases the items must be rearranged to achieve the desired results. There are various alternatives available to the forms designer to suit particular needs, as you can see in Exhibits 12 and 13.

The basic unit of measurement for horizontal spacing is "characters" per inch. A character may be an alphabetic letter, a numeral, any punctuation mark, or even a space between words or numbers. In the vertical direction, the spacing is measured by lines per inch. The spacing between lines may vary based on the method to be used for recording data.

TYPEWRITTEN VS. HANDWRITTEN

Various typewriters print different numbers of characters to the inch horizontally and also may produce different numbers of vertical lines to the inch. The forms questionnaire prepared during the analysis stage should indicate the method of entry and the kind of typewriter used to prepare the form.

Typwriters most commonly print ten or twelve horizontal characters to the inch and six vertical lines to the inch. The minimum space requirements are described below:

Horizontal spacing: Allow $1/12$ or $1/10$ inch for each character, depending on the type pitch of machine to be used. In addition to providing enough space to accommodate the maximum number of characters that could be entered on the line, always allow at least two additional spaces, one for each side of the entry.

Vertical spacing: Specify vertical spacing in multiples of $2/12$ inch to conform to the space of most typewriters. Unless line-to-line spacing is in these exact multiples, the typist must hand roll the typewriter carriage to adjust to the position of each line.

Other business machines: If bookkeeping, data processing, or other business machines are to be used in filling in the form, consider the spacing and mechanical requirements of such equipment.

Exhibits 14 through 17 contain a variety of tips on taking advantage of forms design with typewriters. They cover tabular stops, vertical rules, and diagonal captions.

Unlike machine-filled forms which impose exact spacing demands, the spacing on hand-filled forms is more flexible. For horizontal spacing, it's best to allow $\frac{1}{8}$ inch per character when forms will be used in an office by clerical people. Allow $\frac{2}{12}$ inch per character when forms will be used by manual or outside workers. For vertical spacing, allow $\frac{3}{12}$ inch between horizontal lines for forms used in an office and $\frac{4}{12}$ inch when used by manual or outside workers.

UTILIZING BALLOT BOXES

A technique used to reduce the amount of writing required to enter data on a form is the use of ballot boxes. Most often these are used when entries require a "yes" or "no" answer, or when there is a choice among several predetermined answers. A ballot box is placed directly in *front* of each printed answer. The user marks the desired answer by placing an "X" or a checkmark in the appropriate box.

Ballot boxes eliminate the need for writing out answers, save clerical time, and prevent errors resulting from poor handwriting. The accuracy and alignment of the answers (especially when the form is filled in by machine) make it easier to enter and extract information.

Ballot boxes are used in a variety of ways: horizontally, vertically, and in conjunction with the box principle. You can see positive and negative aspects of this forms design in Exhibits 17 through 21.

PRINTING AND PAPER SPECIFICATIONS

The forms designer should prepare written printing specifications for each form. Verbal specifications given to the printer are subject to

COST CUTTING TECHNIQUES IN FORMS DESIGN 73

misunderstandings and should be avoided. Printing specifications tell the printer what the form's requirements are—the paper to use, punching, registration, special features, and other elements not evident from the form itself.

Written specifications also serve to:

- reduce printing costs by minimizing printing errors caused by inadequate instructions
- establish responsibility in the event the form is printed incorrectly
- eliminate the need for the forms designer to develop specifications each time the form is reordered
- insure consistency in specifications from printing to printing
- enable several printers to bid on identical specifications when forms are sent out for quotations

Consider the following questions when choosing the paper and size best suited to a particular form:

1. How will the form be filled out (by hand or machine)?
2. Will the form be subjected to normal or excessive handling or erasures?
3. Will carbon copies be made? If so, how many?
4. How long will the form be filed?
5. Will the paper be printed on one or both sides of the paper?
6. By what process will the form be printed?

Economy is achieved by utilizing standard paper sizes. In practice, only a few standard sizes are necessary to accommodate the majority of business forms. Nonstandard sizes sometimes may be necessary for forms used with special business machines or filing equipment, or for unusual applications. Under a forms standardization program, you'd want to adopt a limited number of sizes. In addition to savings in paper costs, standard sizes provide these advantages:

- Printing presses are designed to accommodate standard sizes. Use of these sizes enables the printer to utilize the full capacity of the press.

- Binders, folders, filing equipment, and so on, are designed by manufacturers to accommodate the popular standard sizes.
- Combination printing runs can be made more frequently when standard sizes are used.

Forms may be printed on one or both sides of the paper. When printing is required on both sides, you should use opaque paper to prevent the printing and entries from showing through to the other side. Usually 20 lb. or heavier paper is suitable. Also tell the printer how to position the copy on each side (that is, "head to head," "head to foot," or "head to side").

Important: It may sound obvious, but remember that printing on two sides reduces paper consumption by 50 percent.

SNAPOUT FORMS

Snapout forms consist of two or more sheets of paper usually interleaved with carbon paper and bound together into a set by a glued "stub." Sometimes a special chemically treated paper is used (called carbonless paper). The application is the same. Each paper or part of the form may contain variations in text and also may vary in color, size, weight, or grade of paper.

Snapouts offer several advantages when a number of copies of a form are required:

1. Clerical time is saved by eliminating the need for the user to manually gather the individual sheets and insert carbon paper.
2. Sets are kept in alignment while hand or machine entries are made. Collated loose sheets are apt to shift position, causing entries on carbon copies to be out of alignment.
3. If entries on the form must be made at different times or different locations, the parts are kept together during the intervening period, and alignment and registration of all entries are assured.
4. Several related documents which contain certain common information may be filled in with *one* writing by combining them in a set. For example, an incoming order, the invoice, packing list,

bill of lading, and shipping label can all be originated in *one* typing with a snapout.

Snapout forms are costly to produce, so consideration should first be given to using less expensive flat forms, padded if necessary. However, when large numbers of a multi-copy form must be filled in, clerical savings in time (especially during peak periods) can more than offset the additional cost of a snapout.

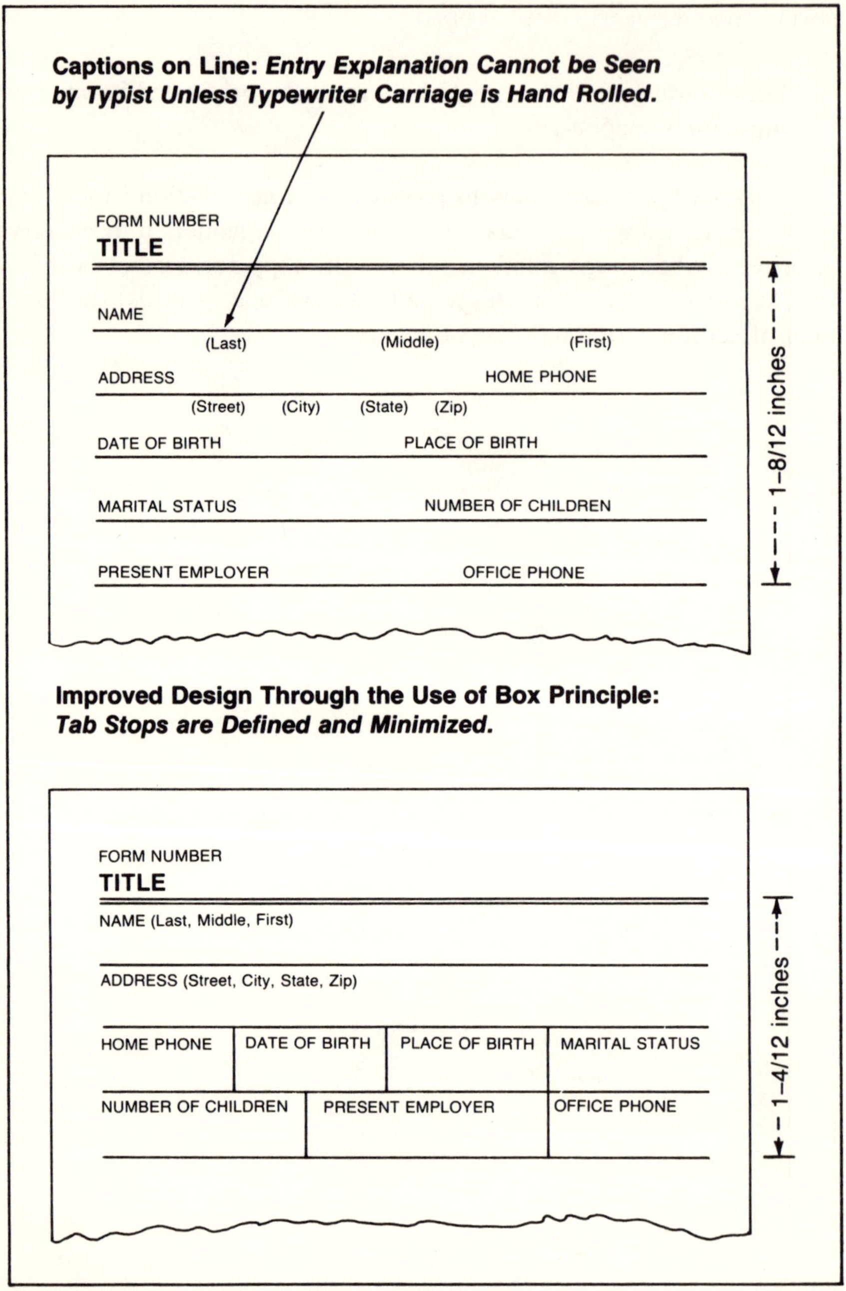

Captions on Line: *Entry Explanation Cannot be Seen by Typist Unless Typewriter Carriage is Hand Rolled.*

```
FORM NUMBER
TITLE
═══════════════════════════════════════

NAME
      (Last)          (Middle)        (First)
ADDRESS                        HOME PHONE
      (Street)  (City)  (State)  (Zip)
DATE OF BIRTH            PLACE OF BIRTH

MARITAL STATUS           NUMBER OF CHILDREN

PRESENT EMPLOYER         OFFICE PHONE
```

↕ 1–8/12 inches

Improved Design Through the Use of Box Principle: *Tab Stops are Defined and Minimized.*

```
FORM NUMBER
TITLE
═══════════════════════════════════════
NAME (Last, Middle, First)

ADDRESS (Street, City, State, Zip)

HOME PHONE | DATE OF BIRTH | PLACE OF BIRTH | MARITAL STATUS
NUMBER OF CHILDREN | PRESENT EMPLOYER | OFFICE PHONE
```

↕ 1–4/12 inches

Exhibit 11.
Comparision of box principle enhancements—
two methods for captioning lines

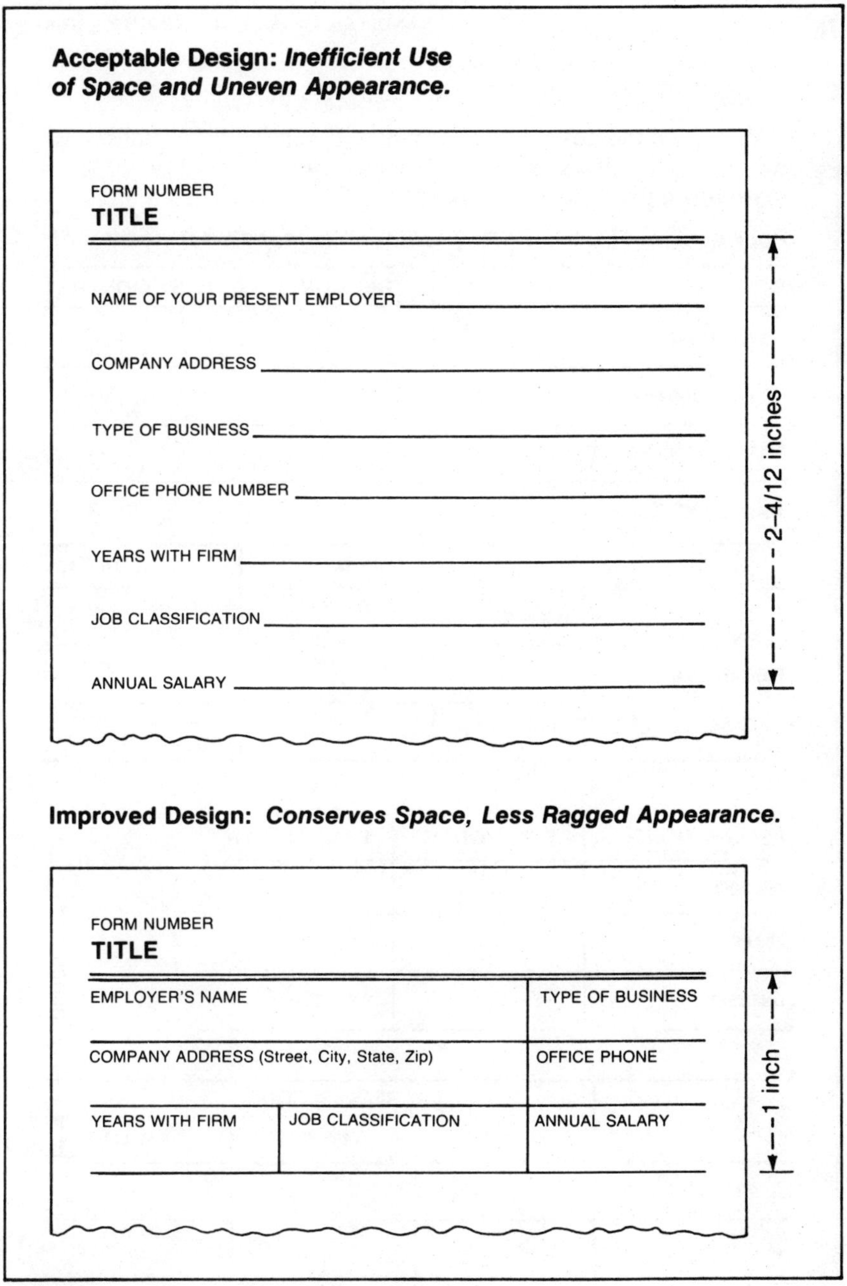

Acceptable Design: *Inefficient Use of Space and Uneven Appearance.*

```
FORM NUMBER
TITLE
========================================

NAME OF YOUR PRESENT EMPLOYER _____

COMPANY ADDRESS _____

TYPE OF BUSINESS _____

OFFICE PHONE NUMBER _____

YEARS WITH FIRM _____

JOB CLASSIFICATION _____

ANNUAL SALARY _____
```

↕ 2–4/12 inches

Improved Design: *Conserves Space, Less Ragged Appearance.*

FORM NUMBER **TITLE**		
EMPLOYER'S NAME		TYPE OF BUSINESS
COMPANY ADDRESS (Street, City, State, Zip)		OFFICE PHONE
YEARS WITH FIRM	JOB CLASSIFICATION	ANNUAL SALARY

↕ 1 inch

Exhibit 12.
Conserving space with the box principle—
designing improvements for space and appearance.

Very often the designer can eliminate excessive or repetitive words or otherwise simplify the headings over columns by rearranging the layout of the boxes.

Poor design: *The word "Requisitions" is repeated unnecessarily.*

	THIS MONTH	LAST MONTH
REQUISITIONS RECEIVED		
REQUISITIONS FILLED		
REQUISITIONS UNFILLED		

Improved designs

		THIS MONTH	LAST MONTH
	RECEIVED		
REQUISITIONS	FILLED		
	UNFILLED		

REQUISITIONS	THIS MONTH	LAST MONTH
RECEIVED		
FILLED		
UNFILLED		

	REQUISITIONS		
	RECEIVED	FILLED	UNFILLED
THIS MONTH			
LAST MONTH			

Exhibit 13.
Rearranging boxes for space saving—eliminating repetition and excessive words.

Eight tabular stops, *indicated by* "▲."

REPORT NO. ▲			
DATE ▲			
DEPT. OR DIVISION ▲			
MANAGER ▲			
CODE	QUANTITY	DESCRIPTION	FOR USE BY
▲	▲	▲	▲

First four items lined up at right, *now only five tabular stops.*

REPORT NO. ▲			
DATE			
DEPT. OR DIVISION			
MANAGER			
CODE	QUANTITY	DESCRIPTION	FOR USE BY
▲	▲	▲	▲

Application of box principle, *reduces tabular stops to four.*

REPORT NO.			
DATE			
DEPT. OR DIVISION			
MANAGER			
CODE	QUANTITY	DESCRIPTION	FOR USE BY
▲	▲	▲	▲

Exhibit 14.
Setting tabular stops for efficiency—box principle applications with tabs.

Vertical rules on forms should be aligned as much as possible to provide a minimum number of tabular stops. On machine-filled forms this permits better use of the machine's tabular stop feature. However, even on forms which are to be hand-filled, this alignment avoids a cluttered appearance.

Twelve tabular stops, *indicated by "▲."*

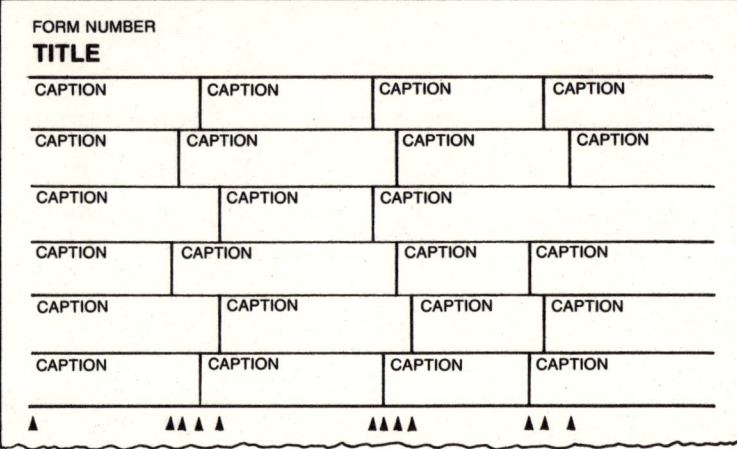

Five tabular stops: *better appearance, easier to fill in and read.*

Exhibit 15.
Rearranging vertical rules for ease of use—tabular stop alignment for vertical lines

COST CUTTING TECHNIQUES IN FORMS DESIGN   **81**

Columnar or tabular arrangements are used when several similar entries can be listed in a column with each heading describing the type of data to be entered in the particular column. By means of this design technique, space can be conserved and repetitive headings eliminated.

FORM NUMBER **TITLE**			
DATE	**REQUISITION NO.**	**FORM NUMBER**	**TITLE**

Horizontal rules may be eliminated if form is machine-filled. Headings centered in box, horizontally and vertically.

When necessary, each major heading may be sub-divided into intermediate and minor headings:

FORM NUMBER **TITLE**					
MAJOR	**MAJOR**				**MAJOR**
	INTERMEDIATE		**INTERMEDIATE**		
	MINOR	**MINOR**	**MINOR**	**MINOR**	

Exhibit 16.
Arrangements for columnar and tabular entries

Diagonal or angle captions: *Used when width of columns prevents horizontal placement of captions.*

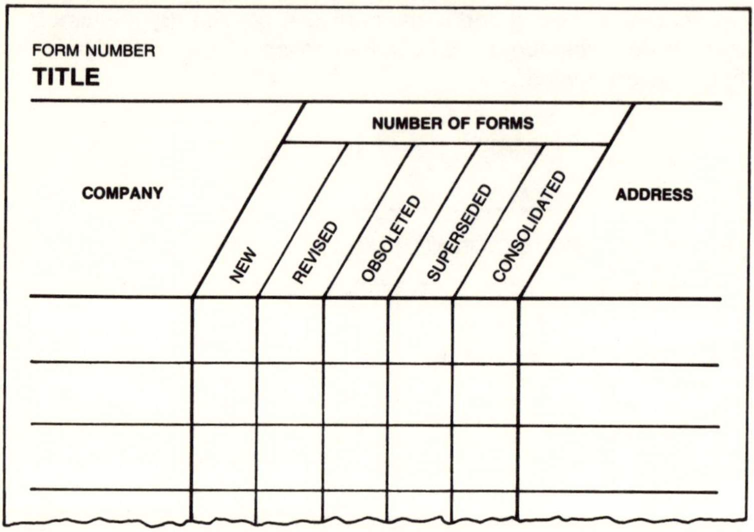

Vertical captions: *Require more vertical space than diagonal captions and are more difficult to read.*

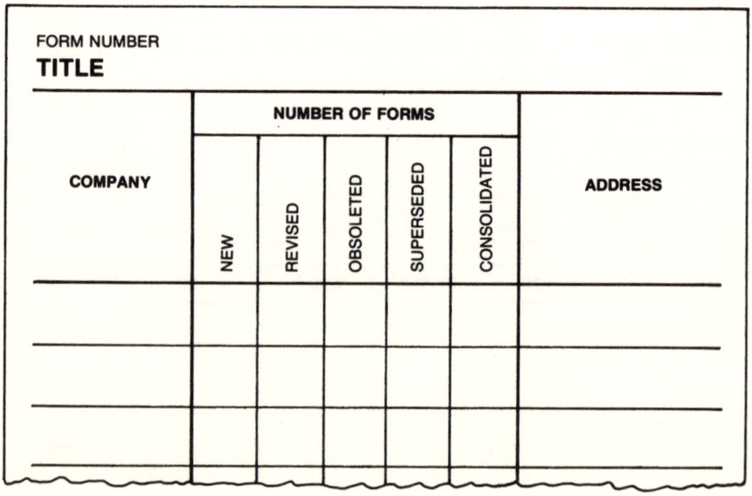

Exhibit 17.
Diagonal vs. vertical captions—utilizing width in caption size designs

COST CUTTING TECHNIQUES IN FORMS DESIGN 83

When there is limited space available on the form, the headings can be arranged in many different ways to utilize the available space.

Captions on side—*These arrangements are also used to save horizontal and/or vertical space.*

	ITEMS	THIS YEAR
NEW YORK	REQUISITIONS	
	RECEIVED	
	FILLED	
	UNFILLED	
	ON BACK ORDER	
	REQUISITIONS	
	FORMS	

Writing line wasted

Acceptable design—Two wasted lines used only for secondary headings where no entries will be made. See better design at right.

	ITEMS	THIS YEAR
NEW YORK		
REQUISI-TIONS	RECEIVED	
	FILLED	
	UNFILLED	
ON BACK ORDER	REQUISITIONS	
	FORMS	

Better design than illustration at left—requires less vertical but more horizontal space, still one wasted line used for "New York."

		ITEMS	THIS YEAR
NEW YORK	REQUISI-TIONS	RECEIVED	
		FILLED	
		UNFILLED	
	ON BACK ORDER	REQUISITIONS	
		FORMS	

Recommended design—all lines are used for entries, easy to read and use.

		ITEMS	THIS YEAR
NEW YORK	REQUISITIONS	RECEIVED	
		FILLED	
		UNFILLED	
	ON BACK ORDER	REQUISITIONS	
		FORMS	

If horizontal space must be further conserved, this design is recommended.

Exhibit 18.
Arrangement of captions for maximum effectiveness

Poor design:
***Boxes not aligned,
cluttered appearance,
difficult to read.***

Function of Responsibility

☐ Makes talks before groups ☐ Maintains proper records

☐ Dresses appropriately to the occasion ☐ Delegates authority

☐ Maintains discipline ☐ Maintains morale and good employee relations

Recommended design:
***Boxes are aligned,
easy to read and use.***

Function of Responsibility

☐ Makes talks before groups ☐ Maintains proper records

☐ Dresses appropriately to the occasion ☐ Delegates authority

☐ Maintains discipline ☐ Maintains morale and good employee relations

Exhibit 19.
Positive and negative aspects of ballot box design

COST CUTTING TECHNIQUES IN FORMS DESIGN

As noted previously, horizontal arrangements of ballot boxes are always preferable. However, each of the following arrangements may be used when available space on the form will not accept horizontal positioning:

Overall Rating.

In comparison with other employees of the same job level, rate this employee's performance using the scale below to qualify your judgment:

☐ **1. Outstanding** — Performs present duties in a manner which is seldom equalled by others in similar positions.

☐ **2. Above Average** — One of the best employees performing the assigned task. Nearly always exceeds the requirements of the position.

☐ **3. Satisfactory** — One of the better employees performing the assigned task. Frequently exceeds the requirements of the position.

☐ **4. Acceptable** — Performance is generally satisfactory but is less than normally expected.

☐ **5. Unsatisfactory** — Performs present duties in a fashion which is not acceptable and which

2/12" between bottom of heading and top of box.

Minimum of 2/12" between boxes.

Overall Rating

☐ Outstanding
☐ Above average
☐ Satisfactory
☐ Acceptable
☐ Unsatisfactory

Color of Paper

☐ White   ☐ Green
☐ Buff   ☐ Canary
☐ Blue   ☐ Gray
☐

1/12" between box and caption.

At least 3/12" (preferably 1/2") between end of caption and start of next box.

Exhibit 20.
Vertical/horizontal ballot box arrangement

Either of the following two arrangements is also appropriate for questions which may be answered with an "X" or "√". They are used because of space limitations or to conform with the design arrangement of the rest of the form. In some instances they are used as variations of ballot boxes when the form would appear too cluttered or confusing if too many ballot boxes were used.

TYPE OF FORM	FLAT	SNAPOUT	CONTINUOUS	LABEL

TYPE OF FORM			
FLAT	SNAPOUT	CONTINUOUS	LABEL

Another variation of the standard ballot box design, for use when space is limited, is placing captions above the box rather than to the right. Several different horizontal design techniques also can be effectively used on the same form:

Caption over the box.

Caption upper left corner.   *Caption to the right of box.*

Exhibit 21.
Utilizing space in a forms questionnaire—variations of spatial arrangement

6

TECHNIQUES TO REDUCE THE COST OF PAPERWORK

What will a paperwork analysis and reduction program do for you? It will:

- increase productivity in your organization
- reduce extraordinary expenses associated with paperwork
- improve the accuracy and timeliness of information

Uncontrolled paper growth and resultant waste have been identified as areas where significant expense reduction can be accomplished. The cost of paper and the expenses associated with preparing, distributing, using, and storing paper have a major impact on the ability to conduct business in a timely and profitable manner. Even with the advent of high-speed data and word processing, information handling is still hindered by various input forms and paper output necessary to develop, monitor, control, and distribute the desired information internally and externally. Automation has not necessarily reduced paperwork.

SOME DISTURBING NUMBERS

The United States Commission on Federal Paperwork reported that the cost of paperwork generated by federal government requirements exceeds $100 *billion* a year. That includes a hefty $25 to 32 billion for private business.

The report also commented on economic burdens that go beyond the direct monetary costs of filling out federal reports. Those costs include maintaining recordkeeping systems and opportunities lost due to the allocation of resources to paperwork instead of to more productive pursuits. This situation exists in many companies and many countries.

Added to the cost of generating paperwork is the cost of storing and monitoring it. It is currently estimated that 20,000 documents exist in storage for each white collar worker in the United States.

One large financial institution reports that it has 13,000 forms, just about one form for every two employees. That same corporation spends over $10 million per year on paper, uses over 170 million pages of computer paper, 72 million sheets of 8½" x 11" white bond paper and over 212,000 8½" by 11" yellow pads per year. The computer paper placed end to end would more than stretch around the world.

A major United States bank conservatively estimates that its average employee generates $1,000 worth of paperwork every year.

Superfluous paperwork robs productive time from individuals at all levels of organizations. Extraneous forms and their processing add enormously to the cost of business. Naturally, companies must maintain certain records and reports to remain competitive, satisfy government regulations, and provide vital information. However, in many cases the growth of paperwork far outpaces the growth of business. Executives know that drains profits and must be controlled.

ANALYZING YOUR PAPERWORK COSTS

Numerous studies have shown that printing costs represent only a small portion of total paperwork expenses. You can see a typical cost distribution in Exhibit 22. It's not unusual for processing, equipment, records management, and other associated costs to be considerably more than actual printing expenditures. This dramatically magnifies the total cost savings associated with eliminating a form or report.

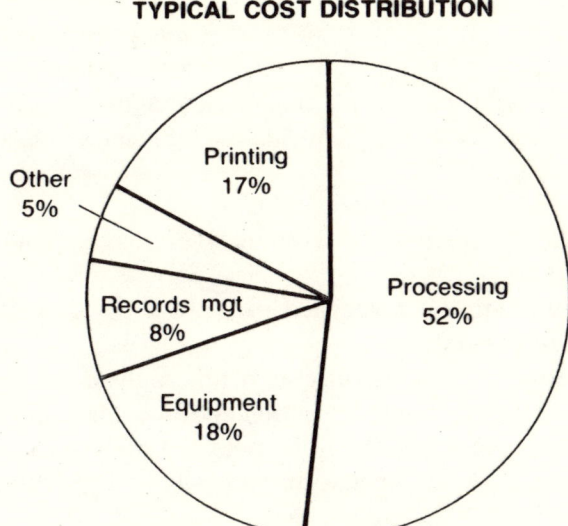

How Does YOUR Operation Compare?

ESTIMATE your annual paperwork cost distribution.

Factor	Dollars	Percent
Printing		
Processing		
Equipment		
Records Management		
Other		
Total		

Exhibit 22.
A worksheet to estimate paperwork costs

Take a minute to make some rough estimates yourself on Exhibit 22. It's a form created by a U.S. firm, which distributes it to many of its managers to keep paperwork cost reduction awareness high.

The program you'll create by applying the techniques in this chapter serves the following functions:

1. provides proven, practical tools to analyze, manage, and control paperwork flow
2. aids in determining all associated paperwork costs—that is, the **actual** cost of paperwork
3. analyzes items selectively since in-depth analysis of all paperwork within an area would be extremely time-consuming; therefore, analysis is performed only on potential high payback items
4. helps determine which paperwork items can be eliminated, combined, or revised
5. provides a means to maintain an open dialogue between users and producers of paper
6. enables the use of alternate media (such as microfilm, graphics, etc.) to distribute information
7. encourages the use of exception reporting and executive summaries to reduce costs of information

Using the following eleven-step checklist, various institutions have saved considerable sums. One financial services corporation reduced expenses by $6 million in just eighteen months. The management estimates that eventual implementation in all parts of the company will decrease paperwork costs by $50 million annually. While your results may not be quite so large, they will be just as important on a percentage basis.

Exhibit 23 is a checklist worksheet to initiate and monitor your efforts. You can reproduce it and use it to encourage the program companywide.

CHECKLIST PROCEDURES

1. Select a Coordinator

The paperwork reduction program should feature a structured ap-

TECHNIQUES TO REDUCE THE COST OF PAPERWORK

PAPERWORK ANALYSIS AND REDUCTION CHECKLIST

Area		Coordinator		
Step No.	Action	Responsibility	Due Date	Done ✓
1	Select coordinator			
2	Get management commitment and support			
3	Define scope			
4	Establish goals			
5	Address the obvious now			
6	Conduct document inventory			
7	Use selective analysis			
8	Conduct detailed analysis			
9	Identify improvement opportunities			
10	Utilize practical paperwork reduction techniques			
11	Implement plan and monitor results			

Exhibit 23.
A worksheet to implement and monitor a paperwork reduction program

proach. The one outlined here is designed to enable an individual in any area to implement the steps using proven techniques and analytical tools with minimal consulting assistance. However, the assigned person should possess basic analytical, organizational, and interviewing skills.

> Note: *You can have a companywide paperwork cost reduction program, concentrate on one department, or even focus only on your individual operations. The text here will refer to a departmental program, but can be adapted for any options you require.*

It is essential that the executive in charge view the paperwork program from an overall vantage point, not from within the confines of a particular department. That individual should have a working knowledge of the entire operation and the ability to communicate effectively with all members of the staff and company likely to be involved. Whether there is a separate coordinator who concentrates solely on this program or not, he or she can achieve success by following these guidelines.

2. Get Management Commitment and Support

User acceptance is an important prerequisite for a successful program. All those concerned should view the effort as an opportunity to enhance rather than deter productivity in their department. In order for the program to be effective, user management must also provide the support and commitment to see it through.

In order to pave the way, send a short memorandum addressed to departmental staff members. Accentuate the benefits of the program, introduce the coordinator, and express your support.

3. Define Scope

After sending the memorandum, arrange to meet with the selected coordinator. In this initial meeting, define the purpose and scope of the project. The agenda for this initial meeting should focus on:

- identifying areas to be included in the study
- assigning contacts for each function (authority/responsibility)

- deciding what types of paperwork will be included (forms, reports, correspondence, etc.)
- including incoming, outgoing, or both form types
- determining milestones for various phases of the program

4. Establish Goals

Determine what the department is spending on paperwork. To accomplish this, look at the budget. Remember that paper and printing expenses represent only a small portion of overall paperwork costs. They do not reflect processing, equipment, records management, occupancy, and so on. Try to establish the total cost of paperwork.

Establish a reasonable, attainable goal for annual reduction (5 to 20 percent is a good start). Setting these goals quantifies expectations and makes staff aware that you are serious about the paperwork reduction effort. More important, it says that you expect results. Start thinking about the mechanics of measuring planned versus actual reduction.

5. Address the Obvious First

Begin reducing/stabilizing paperwork expenses in a department by utilizing practical paperwork reduction alternatives, such as two-sided copying, routing, and the like. These techniques do not require exhaustive studies and can quickly produce measurable results. Among these techniques are:

- decreasing or modifying distribution (example: 10 copies instead of 20)
- reducing frequency (example: weekly rather than daily)
- exception/summary reporting
- form design enhancements
- alternative media, such as micrographics, computer graphics, electronic mail

6. Conduct Document Inventory

Purpose: to identify and estimate costs for all items within the defined scope of the department. This inventory listing can serve as the input document for an automated ranking system. You can use it to highlight those items with the greatest potential payback.

Instructions: Create a document inventory control list like the one shown in Exhibit 24. Plug in the information for each item in the scope of the study.

The first two columns are the document's name and number. The next five boxes involve use/source. Use the legend at the top of the illustration as a guide.

The annual costs/percent of budget area is next. This is the hardest part. You don't have to be exact; just make your best estimates. Look at Exhibit 25 to see how one executive actually filled in such a document and what he included in his cost components by category.

7. Use Selective Analysis

Studies in many companies indicate about 20 percent of the paperwork contributes 80 percent of the costs. Using the selective analysis approach, you can concentrate on those forms and reports which represent the bulk of time and monetary expenditures. You will be left with high impact items requiring further analysis and/or "essential" items with improvement potential, thereby achieving maximum return on investment (ROI). Even those forms/reports which are considered "essential" present opportunities for cost reduction.

One executive found the type of report pictured in Exhibit 26 to be extremely beneficial in this regard. Note that his ranking is by type of cost (printing, processing, equipment, records management, other). A tie score is broken by the budget weight previously assigned (e.g., equipment costs = 64%). For any specific report/form, you can find out which cost element is high, medium, or low and list an appropriate action.

For example:

Item #	High Costs	Possible Action
1	Processing	Analyze processing (labor)
2	Printing	Check form specifications
3, 4	Equipment	Look at computer costs, etc.
5	Other Costs	Examine further (what are they?)
6	None	Postpone analysis until later
7	Records Management	Look at microfiche as alternative
8	None	Disregard (payback not worth it)

TECHNIQUES TO REDUCE THE COST OF PAPERWORK 95

Exhibit 24.
An adaptable document inventory control list

DOCUMENT INVENTORY CONTROL LIST

FORM NUMBER DOCUMENT NUMBER	ITEM NAME	USE (1)	FREQ (2)	SOURCE (3)	ORIG DEPT	REC DEPT(s)

USE (1)
P – Producer
U – User

FREQUENCY (2)
D – Daily
W – Weekly
M – Monthly
Q – Quarterly
R – On Request

SOURCE (3)
M – Manual
C – Computer-Word Processor

COST COMPONENTS BY CATEGORY
(All costs are annual)

1. **PRINTING**
   A. Paper
   B. Reproduction
   C. Padding Collating, Binding, etc.
2. **PROCESSING** (Labor Costs)
   A. Input Preparation
      1. Data Collection
      2. Recording
   B. Machine Operation
      1. Input
      2. Output
   C. Quality Assurance Costs
   D. Distribution to User(s)
3. **EQUIPMENT**
   A. Data Processing
      1. CPU Charges
      2. Connect Time
      3. Input Devices (CRT, Keypunch, Reader/Sorter, Etc.)
      4. Storage (on-line, tape, Etc.)
      5. Printer or other output devices
   B. Auxiliary Equipment
      1. Collator, Decollator, Copier, Shredder, etc including cost of:
         a. purchase
         b. rental
         c. lease
         d. usage expenses charged back to department
         e. maintenance
   C. Other (Specify)
4. **RECORDS MANAGEMENT**
   A. Retention (Storage)
   B. Retrieval (Labor)
   C. Destruction (Labor)

% OF TOTAL BUDGET				
	ANNUAL COSTS			
	1. Printing	2. Processing	3. Equipment	4. Records Mgmt.	Other

ANNUAL COSTS (4)
0 – N/A
1 – Low
2 – Medium
3 – High

Exhibit 25.
An actual filled-in document inventory control list

*** PAPERWORK REDUCTION PROGRAM ***
RANKED REPORT: ESTIMATED TOTAL COST (WEIGHTED)

DEPT: DEPARTMENT 1

Forms/Documents (Item Name/Title)	****** *Rank* ******	Print Costs	Processing Costs	Equipment Costs	Records Mgt Costs	Other Costs	Action/ Comments
12345	1	LOW	HIGH	LOW	LOW	LOW	
12346	2	HIGH	LOW	LOW	LOW	LOW	
12347	3	LOW	LOW	HIGH	LOW	LOW	
12348	4	LOW	LOW	HIGH	LOW	LOW	
12349	5	LOW	LOW	LOW	LOW	HIGH	
12350	6	MEDIUM	MEDIUM	LOW	MEDIUM	N/A	
12351	7	LOW	LOW	LOW	HIGH	LOW	
12352	8	LOW	N/A	LOW	N/A	LOW	

Exhibit 26.
A ranking report for estimated paperwork costs

You can use a computer for this project, or do it manually by circling or otherwise coding the cost codes and then ranking, as this executive has done.

Once you have prepared the document inventory control list and reviewed this type of ranked report, select the items with the highest total cost and best payback potential. During the selection process you may also identify items you know are no longer needed. Although they may or may not represent high impact items, they should be targeted for immediate elimination and thus quick cost savings.

8. Conduct Detailed Analysis

For those items chosen during the Selective Analysis, jointly fill out a paperwork reduction "Document Value Analysis" with the users to determine whether there is a need or alternative for the item.

Exhibit 27 is a key form for any company's paperwork reduction efforts. It is a comprehensive review of every aspect of a form's usefulness. You should make it mandatory to complete this document for all your company's forms and reports.

9. Identify Improvement Opportunities

To make final determination of which items will be analyzed, discussed in depth with producer and user, and ultimately acted upon, review the questionnaires completed by the users and producers. Based on estimated costs and necessity, select those items which can be:

- eliminated outright
- modified with respect to content (the design of form or report), methodology (how it is processed), or procedure (instructions)

10. Utilize Practical Paperwork Reduction Techniques

The successful reduction of expenditures relating to paperwork is limited only by your initiative, creativity, and persistence. In many cases, reducing paper and its associated costs can be accomplished by initiating obvious measures.

Some of the following techniques are easy to institute, others require more planning and coordination. However, they are all proven techniques to decrease paperwork costs, increase productivity, and improve the accuracy and/or timeliness of information.

Print Consolidation: Use each piece of paper to its maximum potential through:

- two-sided copying and two-sided printing
- single vs. double spacing
- increased print density (smaller pitch typeface)
- using second side for redrafts
- central copy centers (costs less than convenience copiers)

Office Practices:

- use lighter bond paper
- route instead of sending multiple copies
- use bulletin boards instead of personal copies
- limit distribution to people who need to know
- update distribution lists periodically by attaching usage questionnaires
- institute inventory control techniques to curb consumption
- cut old paper for work pads instead of using personalized notes
- combine publications
- initiate summary and/or exception reporting
- create central library for magazines and other publications

Office Automation: Various communications media, data and word processing equipment are available to help reduce the need to use paper and incur paper handling costs.

a) *Micrographics:* Reduce the amount of paper being used through micrographics—that is, placing images on film. You get the following advantages over paper:

- expense reduction up to 75 percent
- space savings up to 90 percent
- lower duplicating costs
- file integrity (reduction in lost files)

REPORT/DOCUMENT TITLE		FORM/JOB/DOCUMENT NUMBER
PROCESSING DEPT(S)	USER DEPT(S)	

In the interest of reducing processing, printing, and distribution costs, we are trying to determine if there is still a need for this document. Please complete the following and return promptly to: _____
The estimated cost of ☐ using ☐ producing the document was determined to be:

PRINTING	PROCESSING	EQUIPMENT	RECORDS MANAGEMENT	OTHER COSTS
☐ HIGH ☐ LOW ☐ MEDIUM ☐ N/A	☐ HIGH ☐ LOW ☐ MEDIUM ☐ N/A	☐ HIGH ☐ LOW ☐ MEDIUM ☐ N/A	☐ HIGH ☐ LOW ☐ MEDIUM ☐ N/A	☐ HIGH ☐ LOW ☐ MEDIUM ☐ N/A

USER EVALUATION:

Is the document absolutely necessary? ☐ No ☐ Yes, explain _____

Is the document essential to the performance of a major function? ☐ No ☐ Yes
How is the document used?

☐ Complete a task or activity ☐ Decision support
☐ Control ☐ Information only
☐ Other (Specify) _____

What areas are impacted by this document: _____

Is the information on this document ☐ Critical ☐ Helpful ☐ Not necessary

TECHNIQUES TO REDUCE THE COST OF PAPERWORK 101

To your knowledge, is the information contained on this document available in another form, location, format, etc.?
☐ No ☐ Yes, check one ☐ On-line ☐ Microfiche/Microfilm ☐ Other report (Specify) _____

Could the document be:
☐ Combined with another   ☐ Distributed electronically   ☐ Comments
☐ Reduced to executive summary ☐ Expressed graphically
☐ Produced as an exception report ☐ Filmed (roll, fiche, etc.)

Could the frequency be reduced? ☐ No ☐ Yes, reduce frequency to:
☐ Weekly ☐ Monthly ☐ Quarterly ☐ Yearly ☐ On request

The distribution list should be modified as follows:
☐ Remove the following names/copies: _____
☐ Add the following names/copies: _____

Is the document filed? ☐ No ☐ Yes, complete the following section
RETENTION ☐ Days   ☐ Weeks   ☐ Months   ☐ Years
LOCATION ☐ Local/Personal Files ☐ Departmental ☐ Central Files (and Archives) ☐ Other
MEDIUM   ☐ Paper   ☐ Tape/Disk   ☐ Microform   ☐ Other
REASON   ☐ Legal Requirements ☐ Audit   ☐ Informational   ☐ Other

Based on your answers, document action should be:
☐ Eliminate   ☐ Alternative media used   EXPLANATION
☐ Distribution changed   ☐ Frequency changed
☐ Contents modified   ☐ NO ACTION TAKEN, explain

PREPARED BY	DEPARTMENT NAME	DEPARTMENT NO.	LOCATION	TELEPHONE NO.

Exhibit 27.
Document value analysis

- rapid retrieval of information, particularly with computer assisted retrieval

b) *Computer Graphics:* A graphic representation can convey much more information than rows and columns of figures. Most graphic systems create line, bar, and pie charts with integrated text. Four-color presentations are available. In comparison to paper output, computer graphics:

- significantly reduce time of preparation
- attractively present trends, relationships, and patterns
- clearly illustrate complex data

c) *Electronic Mail:* This can replace conventional types of communications previously sent on paper and enable you to:

- speed up information distribution
- notify many people at the same time
- verify attempts to contact co-workers
- eliminate paper and playing "telephone tag"

d) *Word Processing:* Word processing equipment provides many benefits to people producing a high volume of typed reports, memoranda, and other forms of correspondence, the greatest of which is to multiply an operator's productivity.

Free Forms Analysis: Another practical technique, which is free, involves using vendor-supplied report forms. Some large business forms companies will help you analyze inventory records, usage reports, "slow sellers," and so on.

As part of this step, experts in the field recommend that you complete a Cost/Benefit Analysis like the actual one shown in Exhibit 28. Use Exhibit 29 for your calculations.

The reason for first year and second year estimated costs and savings is to make allowances for nonrecurring versus recurring costs. Example: to change the present method may require nonrecurring (first year) costs such as computer programming, or system analysis.

Annual $ (By Category)	Current Costs (A) Present $	Estimated Costs		Savings	
		(B) 1st Year $	(C) 2nd Year $	(D) 1st Year $	(E) 2nd Year $
1. Processing (labor)					
2. Supplies (printing, paper, etc.)					
3. Equipment					
4. Occupancy					
5. Other costs					
6. Total					

Exhibit 28.
Actual filled-in cost/benefit analysis

PRODUCTIVITY OPPORTUNITY PROPOSAL			REFERENCE ☐ H ☐ S
☐ PRODUCTIVITY IMPROVEMENT ☐ PAPERWORK REDUCTION			
AREA NAME	GROUP NAME		DEPARTMENT NAME

OPPORTUNITY CATEGORY
- ☐ REVENUE IMPROVEMENT ☐ STAFF PLANNING
- ☐ EXPENSE CONTROL ☐ TECHNOLOGY INTEGRATION

ESTIMATED NET ANNUAL SAVINGS AFTER IMPLEMENTATION		REVENUE IMPROVEMENT	
(6D) 1st YEAR	(6E) 2nd YEAR	1st YEAR	2nd YEAR
$	$	$	$

OPPORTUNITY DESCRIPTION

INTANGIBLE BENEFITS

PRIORITY/RECOMMENDED SCHEDULING

☐ VITAL/IMMEDIATELY ☐ OF GREAT BENEFIT/AS SOON AS POSSIBLE
☐ AN IMPROVEMENT/BASED UPON AVAILABILITY OF LABOR, FUNDS, EQUIPMENT, ETC.

DIFFICULTY TO ACCOMPLISH	RISK (EXPOSURE)
☐ HIGH ☐ MEDIUM ☐ LOW	☐ HIGH ☐ MEDIUM ☐ LOW

Exhibit 29.
Form for productivity opportunities and cost/benefit analysis

COST/BENEFIT ANALYSIS

TRANSFER NET SAVINGS (ITEMS 6D and 6E) TO OTHER SIDE IN "ESTIMATED NET SAVINGS AFTER IMPLEMENTATION"

ANNUAL $ (BY CATEGORY)	CURRENT COSTS (A) PRESENT $	ESTIMATED COSTS		SAVINGS	
		(B) 1st YEAR $	(C) 2nd YEAR $	(D) 1st YEAR $	(E) 2nd YEAR $
1. PROCESSING * (LABOR)					
2. SUPPLIES (PRINTING, PAPER, ETC.)					
3. EQUIPMENT					
4. OCCUPANCY					
5. OTHER COSTS					
6. TOTAL					

* FOR AVERAGING LABOR COSTS, USE LOWER SALARY IN MIDDLE THIRD OF APPROPRIATE GRADE. ADD % FOR FRINGE BENEFITS TO ALL SALARIES PER DIVISION CONTROLLER GUIDELINES.

ADDITIONAL COST/SAVINGS INFORMATION, REMARKS.

☐ DOCUMENTATION ATTACHED   HOW ARE COST/SAVINGS DERIVED AND MONITORED? (PROFIT PLAN, I/E ETC)

BENEFITS SCHEDULE BY QUARTER (DIVISION CONTROLLER USE ONLY)

PLAN	1	2	3	4	5	6		8	TOTAL
ACTUAL	1	2	3	4	5	6		8	TOTAL

CHANGE IN VOLUME HANDLING CAPACITY	CURRENT		CHANGE IN UNIT COST	CURRENT
	ESTIMATED			ESTIMATED

APPROVALS

ANALYST	DATE	GROUP CONTROLLER	DATE
DEPARTMENT HEAD	DATE	GROUP HEAD	DATE
		PRODUCTIVITY COMMITTEE REPRESENTATIVE	DATE

Exhibit 29.
Continued

Therefore, savings for the first and second years may be substantially different. Columns D and E (Savings) are used to record the *payback* for the program.

11. Implement Plan and Monitor Results

Develop an action plan to implement changes. The plan should contain:

- a synopsis and/or summary flow charts of current processing
- a list of activities and resources necessary to implement changes
- a time schedule from initiation to completion

Among the first steps to take are:

1. Finalize arrangements with representatives of technical areas. Obtain equipment/programming commitments necessary to adhere to schedules.
2. Summarize proposed costs/savings, current processing, recommended changes, and major implementation dates.
3. Conduct regularly scheduled reviews of existing documents or newly created ones insuring that paperwork costs are maintained at manageable levels.
4. Subject newly created documents to rigorous scrutiny using techniques employed in analysis of existing documents.
5. Periodically evaluate the usefulness and importance of all existing paperwork items.

7

UTILIZING MRP IN PURCHASING AND INVENTORY

Manufacturing Resources Planning (MRP) can reduce inventory while maintaining customer service levels. MRP also involves managing production, coordinating purchasing, and improving cash flow and return on investment. It works closely with the marketing research and financial aspects of your business, providing an overall company plan which improves productivity, provides for better teamwork, and insures a high quality product.

Another important benefit is the simulation capability which will enable you to ask such questions as:

- What will a revision in product mix do to inventory?
- How would this change affect cash flow?
- What will be the increases or decreases in expenses for labor and material?

Note: *Most MRP systems are accomplished with the aid of computers. But even if your process is still manual, you can apply many of the techniques and steps to increase its efficiency and effectiveness. This chapter will give you a taste of what MRP in-*

volves. To institute a complete system, you'll need to get a more extensive review of the subject.

WHAT TO LOOK FOR

Companies have reported measurable benefits such as the following:

- Productivity increases ranging from 5 to 40 percent through reductions in material shortages and production line interruptions
- Reduced indirect labor costs resulting from less paperwork and less need for overtime
- Improved quality control resulting from reduction of time pressures on production people to meet schedules
- Decrease in purchasing costs because of reduced paperwork and increased employment of techniques such as value analysis
- Better customer service due to having the right service level and improved customer information
- Better productivity in the engineering area resulting from reduced time for creating bills of material
- Improved management productivity resulting from team efforts keeping one overall company goal in mind
- From an owner's/shareholder's standpoint, increase in profits due to better utilization of the factors of production, capital, labor, and material

MAKING PLANS COMPLEMENTARY

A specific by-product of MRP is that the production plan and the business plan become mirror images of each other. The production plan, which is in units, concerns itself with sales, production, and inventory. The business plan converts these units into monetary figures and again reports on sales production and inventory. See Exhibit 30 for an example of a production/business plan.

Another important by-product of this planned integration is the ability to use it in simulation to answer "What if?" questions. This capability alone could save you substantial amounts of money and time.

MRP: UNIT PRODUCTION AND $ BUSINESS
(Assuming unit cost of $5.00 per item)
January 19___

		Sales	Production	Inventory
Unit production	Plan	100,000	80,000	120,000
	Actual	100,000	78,000	122,000
$ Business	Plan	500,000	400,000	600,000
	Actual	550,000	390,000	610,000
Variance %		+10.0	−2.5	+1.7

Recommended Action: _____

Responsibility: _____

Exhibit 30.
Combining the business and production plans

SYMPTOMS/PROBLEMS OF MRP

Here are some of the symptoms and some of the comments that MRP seeks to address.

"I don't have the parts."

"We have a schedule but nobody pays attention to it."

"Materials are brought in when somebody gets excited rather than on a planned basis."

A specialist in installing MRP developed the following laundry list of common problems:

1. low inventory turn, resulting from the wrong mix of inventory, excessively high inventories, and inordinate changes by engineering department
2. severe parts shortages because of inventory mix, incorrect priorities, and poor delivery by resources
3. poor customer service (typical are misquoted delivery dates and poor quality control)
4. low labor productivity due to shortages of parts or materials, closing out of production lines, producing the wrong products, and inadequate communication between engineering and production
5. unprofitable sales, which can be caused by poor accounting records, failing to show actual costs/budgets/variances
6. reduction of share of market resulting from poor customer service, uncompetitive prices, and reduction in quality

GETTING STARTED WITH MRP

The first step for you should be to establish a production plan policy. This takes a number of important actions:

1. State the objectives—for example, to control inventory and meet customer demands.
2. Assign accountability for the production plan and its coordination with marketing, manufacturing, finance, and product engineering.
3. Determine the timetables. Your plans should be for at least twelve months to two years. It is ideal that you add a month and drop a month as the plan proceeds.
4. Determine the frequency of review of plan to actual sales.
5. Zero in on the product groups that will be covered.
6. Determine the accuracy of the sales forecast, improving where needed.

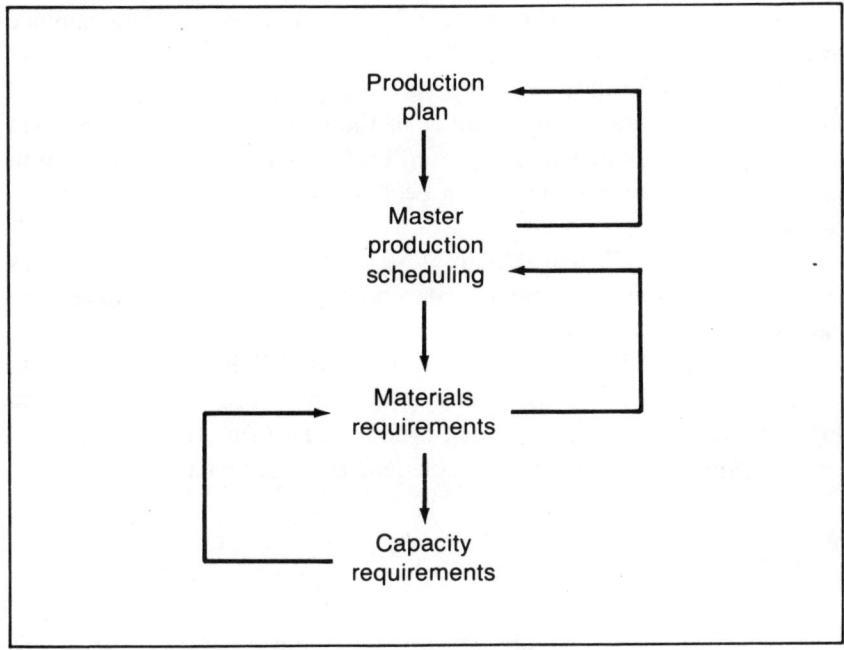

Exhibit 31.
MRP: Closed loop system

7. Provide guidelines for inventory control systems in terms of lead times, safety stock, and so on.

Zeroing in on the various components of MRP, you review the following aspects.

Forecasting—projecting sales, is the key to MRP. This must be done in units and monetary figures. Make sure they correspond to each other.

The master schedule concerns itself with breaking down the overall production plan into units by product.

The closed loop diagram—note that this seems to be a never-ending process but it holds the key to tying together all the operating costs of the manufacturing resource plan. See Exhibit 31.

The capacity requirements plan has as its objective the sequence of operations in producing a product. Moreover, it indicates the number of hours required for each operation as well as the location where the product is made. A by-product of the capacity requirements plan is facilities planning, which is based on looking closely at the equipment and determining how it can best be run under different production plan situations.

The dispatch list—to schedule the production run, by detail work center. This shows the individual schedules for each operation and each priority as it occurs.

Integration with other company systems: MRP interacts with accounts payable to reimburse vendors and employees. It tracks inventory, provides stock status, back-orders and so on. In addition, cost systems are updated to provide standard costs for each operation.

OTHER CONSIDERATIONS

One necessity is a well thought out parts numbering method. Like any other system where something must be identified, this has to be *unique*. It should be simple, short, and instantly recognizable by all functions in the company.

The expenses connected with a computer-generated MRP are:

- the technical costs of systems and computer hardware and software
- the expenses of input into the system
- the labor costs

It is important to distinguish between recurring and nonrecurring costs. Recurring costs are expenses that will be incurred on a day-to-day basis. They are the so-called operating costs. Nonrecurring expenses are generally those that happen once. Typical of these are start-up expenses for new systems, for computer hardware, software, and the like. In performing the cost benefit analysis to evaluate an MRP system, you should carefully distinguish between recurring and nonrecurring costs in terms of your return on investment.

MRP CONVERSION

Typically there are three ways you can convert to MRP.

1. Turn off the old system and turn on the new one simultaneously. This method generally produces the most problems.
2. Run the old and new systems simultaneously and compare the results. This parallel system is a more conservative approach than the first.
3. A pilot system, which is the most conservative, involves a great degree of simulation before the old system is scrapped and the new one is implemented.

There are some more subtle points to consider in converting to MRP.

1. Management should understand the objectives as well as the pros and cons.
2. Supervisors should have a clear idea of the benefits and be made to understand MRP is not a threat.
3. All affected departments should use the same terminology as well as the same data.
4. Timetables should be published and adhered to when possible.

Action Checklist #7 gives a number of areas to review concerning an overall MRP program.

OTHER MRP VARIATIONS

Recently, great emphasis has been placed on isolating bottlenecks and curing them as a way of speeding up the overall process of manufacturing. By definition, a bottleneck is a point in the production process that holds back the amount you can produce. Some causes are narrowing of raw materials flow because of capacity limits on machines, absenteeism of workers with highly specialized skills, or a lack of critical tools.

One of the newer techniques that addresses bottlenecks is called Optimized Production Technology or OPT. It is a product of Creative Output Incorporated. What this system does, basically, is identify people, equipment, and tools that represent bottlenecks in the plant.

It reschedules them to work at the fullest capacity possible and sometimes it rearranges the sequence. The computer programs schedule work to the bottleneck points, thereby keeping production up and lowering the inventory investment.

You should be on the lookout for similar systems in your marketplace which may produce the same positive results for you.

THE PURCHASING FUNCTION

You can improve your purchasing function and lower expenses by coordinating MRP with this department.

To aid in determining whether your purchasing function is operating at low cost and high quality, use Action Checklist #8.

VALUE ANALYSIS

This is a technique which purchasing executives are using to question every detail of a product design. To begin with, four different kinds of value are questioned:

1. Use value: How suitable is the item for the job for which it's intended?
2. Cost value: What is the expense of producing the item, and is it worth it?
3. Esteem value: What about certain features? If the customers have marginal or negative feelings, why should you pay for installing those features in the product?
4. Exchange value: What is the product really worth to the customer?

The technique itself involves a four-step process:

Comparison: Look at the item critically to see if it can be produced for less money. Specifically, can cheaper raw materials be used without affecting the customer's perception of performance? More importantly, can a specific part be eliminated and not affect the product's performance?

Function analysis: Ask five crucial questions, and thoroughly evaluate the results:

- What is the product?
- What does it do?
- How much does it cost?
- What substitute could do the job?
- How much will the substitute cost?

Identify functional areas: Using this method, the product is looked at as a group of parts which performs a specific function, such as play music, transport materials, etc.

Scientific evaluation. In this step, detailed specifications are examined, such as horse power, breaking strength, and so on. Your purchasing and engineering people can then ask about the effect of reducing certain specifications without affecting the safety or performance of the product.

The bottom line of these comparisons is to look at alternatives from the standpoint of customer satisfaction, performance, and cost. You can simply set up a matrix with these factors listing the component or product, the old features, new features, present and proposed cost, and the cost savings. By doing this systematically and objectively, you use value analysis to improve your product safety and quality, increase customer satisfaction, and reduce costs.

Several key areas you should cover in value analysis are contained in Action Checklist #9.

ACTION CHECKLIST # 7

Manufacturing Resource Planning

ACTION FOCUS	N/A	STRONG	SATIS-FACTORY	NEEDS SOME IMPROVEMENT	WEAK: NEEDS MAJOR IMPROVEMENT	ACTION PLAN, RESPONSIBILITY
Measure current system effect on expense reduction						
Check present system effect on cash flow improvement						
Evaluate MRP Re: productivity						
Feasibility of MRP for better systems and data processing						
Practical use of simulation ("what if")						
Reduce excess paperwork						
Tighten controls on inordinate overtime						
Decrease routine Purchasing expenses						
Interact with Product Engineering on better bills of material						
Coordinate production plan (units) with business plan ($)						
Measure goals, actuals, variances of production						
Take action on significant variances						
Order materials on planned (not crisis) basis						
Track number of inventory turns versus comparable periods						
Compare inventory mix to customer demand						

UTILIZING MRP IN PURCHASING AND INVENTORY 117

Check if customer delivery dates are met															
Make provision for standard versus actual costs															
Assign accountability for production plan															
Prepare production timetables for 12–24 months															
Review frequency of production plan relative to sales forecast															
Check practicality of inventory lead times, safety stock															
Evaluate master schedule for proper units by product															
Verify performance of facilities planning															
Employ dispatch list for production work centers															
Set production priorities wherever appropriate															
Integrate MRP with accounts payable to properly reimburse vendors															
Provide for reports of stock status and back-orders															
Interact with payroll system to pay employees accurately															
Set up easily understood parts numbering system															
Examine input/output costs this year versus last year															
Consider pilot versus parallel system for conversion															
Brief supervisors/managers on benefits, operation of MRP															
Identify and rectify production bottlenecks															

ACTION CHECKLIST # 8

Purchasing

ACTION FOCUS	N/A	STRONG	SATIS-FACTORY	NEEDS SOME IMPROVEMENT	WEAK: NEEDS MAJOR IMPROVEMENT	ACTION PLAN, RESPONSIBILITY
Pay attention to rising inventory levels						
Increase awareness of importance of balance between cost and quality						
Use competitive bids by vendors						
Evaluate make versus buy for required parts						
Participate strongly in MRP function						
Research alternative materials and distribution channels						
Rate vendors' performances periodically						
Check resources' financial condition to assure delivery continuity						
Analyze long-term commitments versus short-range contracts						
Verify legal conditions on contracts with counsel						
Coordinate with Product Engineering on matters of common concern						

UTILIZING MRP IN PURCHASING AND INVENTORY

Clear up guidelines on procurement of capital equipment									
Intensify program for getting maximum cash discounts and purchases									
Notify all concerned of approved vendors									
Instruct all resources on routing orders									
Investigate vendors as possible customers									
Prepare contingency plans for natural disasters, strikes, etc.									
Limit signature authorizations based on monetary value of purchase order									
Use economic order quantity where feasible									
Train purchasing agents in basics of procurement									

ACTION CHECKLIST # 9

Value Analysis

ACTION FOCUS	N/A	STRONG	SATIS-FACTORY	NEEDS SOME IMPROVEMENT	WEAK: NEEDS MAJOR IMPROVEMENT	ACTION PLAN, RESPONSIBILITY
Evaluate suitability of product for its intended use						
Compare production cost to product worth						
Examine features from a customer's perspective (esteem value)						
Determine product's true market worth (exchange value)						
Use cheaper materials while maintaining performance						
Explore alternatives which produce identical or comparable functions						
Check detailed specifications (horsepower, tensile strength) for possible revisions						
Concentrate on weight reduction to decrease distribution costs						
Reclassify freight listing to get lower transportation rate						
Encourage vendor recommendations for expense reduction						
Intensify interchangeable/standardized parts, sub-assemblies						

8

IMPLEMENTING INVENTORY CONTROLS TO REDUCE COSTS

Inventories are a current asset of the business and in many manufacturing companies are of significant size. Therefore, they constitute a large investment on the part of the firm.

Most experts divide inventory into three categories:

1. raw materials which are purchased
2. work in process, which is the next stage of converting raw materials—includes a portion of direct labor as well as other manufacturing costs directly identified with the product
3. finished goods which are the end product of the process

Initially, expense reduction can be produced in two major areas. One involves precise sales forecasting and breakdowns of raw materials. This is done in conjunction with estimates of customer demand. The other broad area involves the movement, processing, and storing of parts and materials.

Moreover, a successful inventory control system has to take into consideration the following:

- enough time for ordering materials

- sufficient inventory to fill customer orders
- that the inventory control function coordinates with manufacturing

Specifically, this involves assurance that the required inventory is there when production needs it. These points will further be exemplified in the Action Checklist which accompanies this chapter.

BENEFITS AND PROBLEMS

The specific benefits of a solid inventory control system are:

- smoother production flow
- lower inventories and thus less capital tied up
- greater customer satisfaction through higher service levels
- reduced carrying costs and other expenses

The most difficult aspect of inventory control is the balance between a high inventory which will satisfy customer demand, and a low inventory which minimizes investment. Part of this is timing, which the experts claim "is everything in business." If inventory is too late, customer orders may not be filled on time. However, manufacturing inventory too early can result in more inventory than is needed, along with its high carrying cost.

To address this balancing act, savvy executives use the Economic Order Quantity, or EOQ. Exhibit 32 shows an actual example of how to balance inventory carrying costs with demand to arrive at two important figures:

1. the economic order quantity or that amount which appears on a purchase order
2. the number of annual orders

In the example, the economic order quantity is 163 units and the number of annual orders is six (or one order, each two months). An

IMPLEMENTING INVENTORY CONTROLS TO REDUCE COSTS

(a) *Calculation of Economic Order Quantity and Number of Annual Orders*

$$EOQ = \sqrt{\frac{2 \text{ (Annual demand) (Purchase order cost)}}{\text{(Unit cost) (Inventory carrying cost)}}}$$

$$= \sqrt{\frac{2 (1000) (20.00)}{(0.75) (2.00)}}$$

$$= \underline{\underline{163}}$$

$$\frac{\text{\# of Annual Orders}}{} = \frac{\text{Annual demand}}{\text{EOQ}}$$

$$= \frac{1000}{163}$$

$$= \underline{\underline{6}} \text{ (1 order each 2 months)}$$

(b) $\dfrac{\text{Inventory}}{\text{Turnover}} = \dfrac{\text{Sales}}{\text{Average Inventory}}$

$$= \frac{300{,}000}{60{,}000}$$

$$= 5$$

Exhibit 32.
Two important inventory control calculations

added measure of reducing inventory costs is the ratio of sales to average inventory (turnover). Exhibit 32 shows this calculation. You can reduce inventory costs by increasing sales or decreasing inventory investment.

Using the EOQ, you can employ a system known as "Reorder Point—Order Up To Level." You'll see that calculation illustrated in Exhibit 33, employing three sets of figures:

1. the available inventory
2. economic order quantity
3. reorder point

REORDER POINT—ORDER UP TO LEVEL SYSTEM

Elements: Review time = 2 weeks
Lead time = 3 weeks
Sales forecast = 100 units per week
Safety stock = 50 units

Formulas:

Reorder point = (Lead time + 1/2 Review time) (Sales forecast) + Safety stock

= (3 + 1) (100) + 50

= 350

Reorder quantity = (Weeks supply) (Sales forecast)

= (2) (100)

= 200

Order up to level = Reorder point + reorder quantity

= 350 + 200

= 550

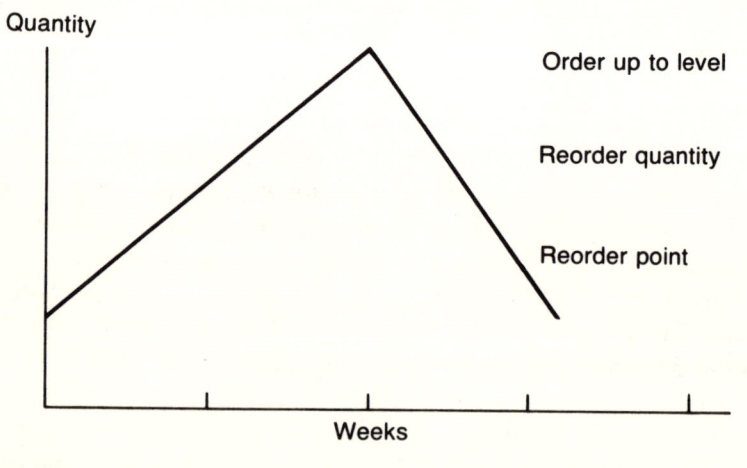

Exhibit 33.
A reorder system using EOQ

CALCULATING INVENTORY COSTS

In order to recognize prime areas for cost reduction in inventory control, you should know how to calculate inventory costs. They are divided into five groups:

1. Capital Costs.
This involves the cost of money. As an example, instead of tying up your assets in inventory, you could invest in money investments at, say, 10 to 15 percent interest. So reduction of inventory has a direct impact on your profit and loss statement.

2. Inventory Service Costs.
These are divided into two subcategories:
   Taxes: If your local or other governmental authority applies taxes on inventory, that is an extra added expense you can avoid.
   Insurance: If your policy is based on the amount in inventory, you can save money by inventory reduction.

3. Storage Space Costs.
This is the expense of storing inventory in various facilities. They would be warehouses or distribution centers you own, rent, or lease.

4. Inventory Risk Costs.
Obsolescence is an expense that results from an item not retaining its original value.
   Damage can result from inventories being shifted around repeatedly.
   Pilferage (theft of an asset) can be a more serious problem. In fact, in order to avoid pilferage, you might have to incur extra costs for security. Therefore, you are getting hit twice.

5. Relocation Costs.
These are connected with shifting inventories from one location to another, in order to maximize use of the inventory itself.
   As you can see, carrying costs can be a major extra burden in an

inventory system. Avoiding these by keeping inventory down to the lowest possible level will be a major cost reduction factor.

COMBINING FUNCTIONS

Another crucial way to reduce the expense connected with inventory control is, wherever possible, to combine this function with order entry, analysis of sales, cost accounting, and so on. To the degree that these are integrated, you will save money by avoiding redundant databases, and the costs of adding, deleting, and changing appropriate records. A number of powerful yet inexpensive computer systems are on the market that integrate these functions. In addition to regular inventory reports, you can have ad hoc capabilities to produce exception reports, back-order items, on-order inventory turnover, and even automatic generation of purchase orders.

Another refinement of using computers for inventory control and related functions is the employment of microcomputers or personal computers with software known as electronic spreadsheets. One of the most powerful options with a microcomputer spreadsheet is the ability to conduct "what if" exercises. You can simulate the effect on customer service levels of varying inventory amounts. Moreover, the goal-seeking option allows you to set a specific service standard—for example, 97 percent in stock—and ask the system to supply the optimum inventory to satisfy this criteria.

ELECTRONIC CODING

You can identify raw materials, work in process, finished goods, and spare parts, as well as conduct physical inventory in an extremely cost effective way through electronic coding, and/or scanning.

Basically, you use optical character recognition (OCR) to scan product codes and so on, on cartons or on shelving. Moreover, the use of bar codes or universal product codes (UPC) permits you to utilize electronic or laser scanners to read and transmit quantity directly to your computer system. Even more money can be saved by conducting your inventory on a cycle basis. This could involve taking 5 percent of your inventory each day rather than altogether once a month—a process which might involve diverting production people, or even incurring overtime.

What are some of the benefits of electronic coding?

- lower costs of periodic or required inventories
- more accuracy, through elimination of transcribing errors that result from calling quantities and then writing them on some official form

This data can be either alphabetic or numeric. Drawing on the experience of some other corporations, one large company which is involved in distribution uses an eleven-digit bar code on its packages. It estimates an accuracy of 99.99 percent in terms of information.

With the advent of less expensive equipment, these scanners may cost as little as $1,000. Some companies are using the scanners to materially reduce the cost not only of inventory but of shipping as well. In one example, as the products leave the factory, a scanner picks up the bar code, automatically prepares the bill of lading, and notifies the various accounting records automatically.

OTHER INVENTORY TIPS

Occupancy expense can be costly. Your present facility may have to be enlarged as production expands. This will result in an increase of fixed costs. There are several ways to avoid this.

One is to have a contract with an outside vendor to store your supplies. The vendor's occupancy cost (expense per square foot) might be cheaper than yours. Labor might be less expensive too.

Another method is to transmit replenishment requests automatically through your computer or manually by terminal, on-line to your outside resource. This also can be done by telephone or mail. Using this method will reduce your labor costs as well as occupancy expense.

Surplus and scrap on your premises don't generate income. They occupy space and require periodic handling. Your local classified telephone directory or manufacturers' association probably has a list of dealers in this area. The components you sell might be able to be recycled or melted down for reuse, thereby conserving natural resources. You should also look into the tax aspects of contributing surplus and scrap to charitable institutions. Local schools might have a need for nonworking models of machines for demonstration purposes. Such donations make for good public relations as well as possible tax write-offs.

Action Checklist #10 details specific things you can do to reduce your inventory investment while maintaining top-notch customer service.

ACTION CHECKLIST # 10

Inventory Control

ACTION FOCUS	N/A	STRONG	SATIS-FACTORY	NEEDS SOME IMPROVEMENT	WEAK: NEEDS MAJOR IMPROVEMENT	ACTION PLAN, RESPONSIBILITY
Calculate degree of investment of inventory versus earning assets						
Use proper mix of raw materials, work-in-process, finished goods						
Improve accuracy of sales forecasts for proper service levels						
Tighten controls over movement, processing, storing of parts and materials						
Set lead time for systematic replenishment						
Calculate sufficient inventory for satisfactory customer service						
Coordinate inventory control with manufacturing process						
Pinpoint cost of capital relative to excess inventories						
Improve timing of raw material deliveries to plant						
Use Economic Order Quantity (EOQ)						
Use optimum # of annual purchase orders calculation						

Employ reorder point-order up to level system											
Compute carrying costs: capital											
Compute carrying costs: inventory service (taxes, insurance)											
Compute carrying costs: storage space (warehouses, etc.)											
Compute carrying costs: inventory risk (obsolescence, damage, pilferage, etc.)											
Compute carrying costs: inventory risk (security, relocation costs)											
Integrate with order entry, sales analysis, cost accounting											
Improve data base management: adding, deleting, changing records											
Use exception reporting back-order reports, automatic order generation											
Explore personal computer with electronic spreadsheets for "what if" simulations											
Try computer simulations of "goal-seeking" for optimum stock levels											
Employ electronic coding for identification and/or physical inventories											
Use optical scanning for inventories, distribution, document preparation											
Conduct cycle inventories rather than all at once											

IMPLEMENTING INVENTORY CONTROLS TO REDUCE COSTS 131

Store supplies, raw materials off site (occupancy, labor costs)	Generate automatic or on-line requests for materials replenishment	Profitably dispose of scrap/surplus to dealers	Contribute scrap/surplus to charitable institutions	Contribute scrap/surplus to educational institutions	Periodically review inventory budget versus actual	Take action on production workers' waiting time for raw materials	Provide special care for delicate components	Place fast-moving parts near production area	Use inventory locator file to easily find desired item	Emphasize increasing rate of inventory turns	Correlate physical inventory to accounting records	Report slow-moving items, obsolete products and overstock	Clear up written instructions for inventory taking and maintenance

9

PRODUCTIVITY IMPROVEMENT AND COST CONTROL

The most widely used definition of productivity is physical units of output divided by number of employee hours needed to produce them. Well-known management consultant Peter Drucker says it is the yield from resources. That is fairly close to this all-encompassing definition: Productivity is the result of the utilization of *all* corporate resources—people, funds, facilities, and materials. Productivity growth results from proper utilization of resources. Gains and/or losses are monitored by use of productivity indicators, ratios, or measures.

ORGANIZING FOR PRODUCTIVITY IMPROVEMENT

Productivity is an integral part of the management process. Most companies place particular emphasis on the productivity issue and formally integrate it into the strategic planning process. Specifically, they measure and quantify operations in terms of people, funds, facilities, and materials.

You can take these concrete steps to create a productivity awareness "culture" at all levels of your organization:

1. Publish productivity goals in company newsletters and other media.
2. Establish a solid system for performance measurement and reporting.
3. Use feedback from the system to determine progress.
4. Set up a research/exchange network in order to find out about other success stories inside your company and outside.

Here's a practical example of team cooperation to increase productivity. At Motorola (an electronics company), more than 95 percent of its employees are involved in the Participative Management Program (PMP). According to Motorola's communications, teams are formed to set the goals, standards, and procedures under which the members do their jobs. Regular meetings of the teams are held. Communication is opened, vertically and horizontally. Performance is rated by standards set by the participants themselves. Excellence is reflected by many forms of compensation, not the least of which is financial. Targeted goals are charted, posted, and—most important of all—then surpassed. The magic ingredient is: "Quality and productivity through employee participation in management."

As you review the rest of this chapter, keep in mind these two fundamental principles for reducing manufacturing expenses:

- Define each worker's production goals and measure actual performance versus the standards.
- Plan/schedule the workflow for maximum efficiency.

PERFORMANCE MEASUREMENT AND IMPROVEMENT

Today's manufacturing executive must manage a process that provides a higher quality product at a lower unit cost, enabling that product to remain competitive in a very demanding marketplace. At the same time, the "mix" of his products has become more complex, requiring tighter controls. Despite advances in automation, which have allowed managers to cope with the surge in volume, there is still a considerable price tag on measuring performance and improving it.

Performance measurement and improvement techniques can generate positive results such as measurable cost savings and operating improvements.

An effective performance measurement system need not be mysterious or statistically complex, but it must be geared toward your specific needs. It should clearly spotlight good performance as well as bad, thereby rewarding "on target" personnel and highlighting needed improvements.

It is essential that your people be completely involved in applying any measurement/improvement techniques. The material in this chapter furnishes all the building blocks needed to quickly create a monitoring system that serves as an effective barometer of internal performance levels.

There are two systems:

- Manual System: clerical preparation of performance reports and trend analyses
- Automated System: computerized generation of performance reports, exception reports, graphic trend analyses, and planning models

You can choose to implement the manual now and the automated in the future, or go directly to the automated system.

EXPECTED PAYOFF/BENEFITS

The reports you create should identify problem areas, enabling you to take corrective action and improve performance. This will better satisfy customers, reduce operating costs, and improve corporate profitability.

These are the payoff/benefits you should advertise for your program:

1. reduce reject rates
2. decrease rework costs
3. enhance customer service by making products more competitive
4. give your line supervisors and higher management an accurate, current picture of a specific product's performance
5. identify present and potential problem areas so that you can take corrective action
6. operate a relatively low-cost program—that is, the benefits resulting from the installation will outweigh the cost of implementing and maintaining it

This approach is flexible and allows you to tailor the system to your specific needs. Concepts are translated into reality through a building-block approach, which takes you from some basic manual steps to a simple and cost-effective automated reporting mechanism.

INTRODUCTION TO THE MANUAL SYSTEM

The manual system has the following major benefits:

- pinpoints current performance and on/off target status
- detects short- and long-term trends
- helps plan future strategies
- provides simple, inexpensive reports

The approach features clerical preparation of performance reports and trend analysis. Use the steps on the following pages to install the system.

1. Select a Team and Target

Choose a team of up to five people. Combine talents to form a diverse group (pilot department line managers, staff members, operations analyst).

Carefully choose a pilot department where operating performance will be measured and analyzed. Place primary emphasis on quality, timeliness, cost, and productivity.

PRODUCTIVITY IMPROVEMENT AND COST CONTROL   137

2. Select Quality Assurance Checkpoints

Suppose you choose Department 998 as the pilot for your quality control system. You are concerned about the *scope* of the quality checks, which areas to test, what you would like to measure and how much measurement should be done.

Chart your workflow if your analysts have not done so already. A summary workflow is usually the best way to spotlight locations where problems or bottlenecks may occur. Exhibit 34 illustrates a typical department's workflow. Identify checkpoints as likely spots to measure performance and develop possible indicators.

3. Develop Performance Indicators

Using the department's workflow and quality assurance checkpoints, develop specific indicators to measure performance or volume.

In selecting its indicators, Department 998 management is concentrating on quality, timeliness, cost, and productivity. Other categories of performance—such as staffing, production volume, etc.—can be added.

As illustrated in Exhibit 34, this company identified typical indicators for the checkpoints.

An indicator is a quantifiable measure of performance in meeting a predetermined goal. Indicators provide useful and practical information that will assist in planning, monitoring, controlling, and improving your operations. Although indicators typically serve to identify problems, they also highlight satisfactory or exceptional performance.

Indicators are generally grouped together by type (quality, timeliness, productivity, and so forth).

They can also be grouped by:

- type and responsibility: reject rate by person, unit, section
- reporting level: department, area manager, or senior manager
- product, cost center, activity, etc.

Listed below are some typical performance indicators. Note that some of these can be external indicators based on customer feedback.

- rejects per 100,000 items produced (quality)

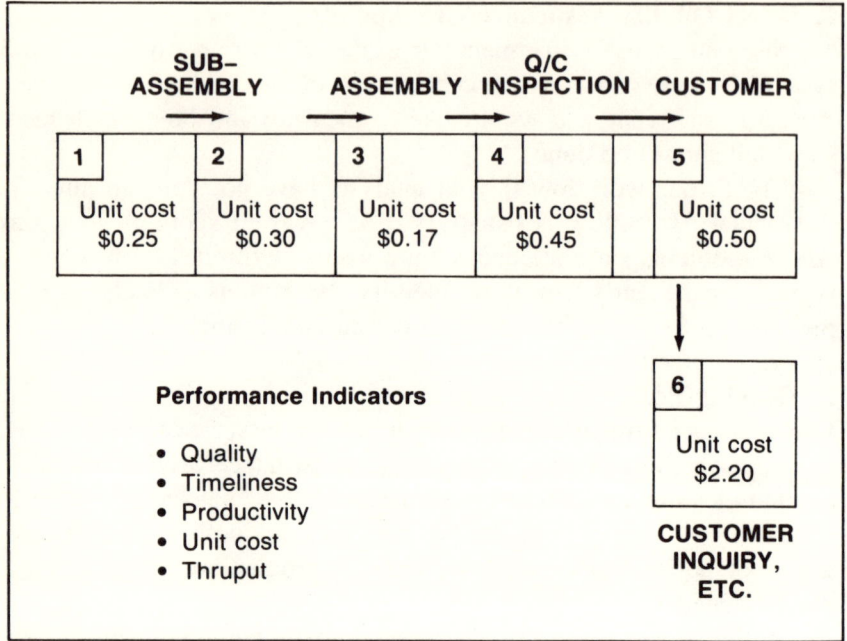

Exhibit 34.
An actual workflow performance chart

- percentage of products shipped on time (timeliness)
- operator items per hour (productivity)
- percentage of invoices mailed on time (timeliness)
- manufacturing expense (cost)
- customer inquiries handled in x minutes (timeliness)

4. Establish Volumes

Regardless of the type of indicator, you'll need two figures to compute performance. Experts refer to the two figures as Volume 1 and Volume 2. The first item is generally a *total* volume, such as the entire production volume for a day, week, or month. Volume 2 is most often exceptions or variances—number of rejects, late volume, and so forth.

Example by indicator types:

Performance Indicator	Volume 1	Volume 2
Q01 Quality %	Production Volume	# Rejects
T01 Timeliness %	Production Volume	Late Production
P01 Productivity (Items per hour)	Total Volume	Production Hours

Make all your calculations from the two volumes, as in the following examples:

- *Q01*
  Reject Rate = (Volume 2/Volume 1) × 100
  Quality % = 100 − Error Rate
  Calculation: (42/1367) × 100 = 3.07% (Reject Rate)
  Calculation: 100 − 3.07 = 96.93% (Quality %)
  The timeliness indicator (T01) is calculated the same way.
- *P01*
  Productivity: Items per hour = Volume 1/Volume 2
      1367/7 = 195 items per hour

5. Performance Report and Trend Analysis

Exhibit 35 is a basic Quality Control Performance Report. This example shows three indicator types—Q01: quality, T01: timeliness, P01: productivity. You can report others covering staffing, unit cost, production volume, and so on, in a similar manner.

The indicator is listed in Column 1. From the two volume figures (Columns 2 and 3) you calculate the performance (Column 4). Comparing performance to goal (Column 5) gives you an "on/off target" condition (Column 6).

You should use an on/off target **trend statement** (such as the comments you see in Column 6), or equivalent code number, to interpret and project performance. The trend statements are categorized as follows:

QUALITY CONTROL PERFORMANCE REPORT

Period Ending: _____ Area/Dept: _____ Prepared by: _____

(1) Indicator*	(2) Vol. 1	(3) Vol. 2	(4) Performance	(5) Goal	(6) On/Off Target
Q01	1367	42	96.93	96.00	On & Stable
T01	1367	34	97.51	98.00	Off, Improving
P01	1367	7	195	170	On, Reexamine goal

*Q = Quality %, T = Timeliness %, P = Productivity (Items Per Hour)
Remarks/Action:

Exhibit 35.
A sample QC performance chart

- Off target, improving
- Off target, stable
- Off target, reexamine goal (performance substantially better/worse than goal)
- Erratic—cannot determine trend at this time

You can also prepare a performance graph to help interpret trends.

6. Define Goals

With a good idea of the pilot department workflow, indicators, and volumes, you are ready to set your goals.

PRODUCTIVITY IMPROVEMENT AND COST CONTROL   **141**

Here are the ways to define goals:

- *management expertise,* your educated opinion
- *performance history,* over a reasonable period of time
- *negotiated goals,* referring to your departments or divisions that jointly set a goal for the quality, timeliness, average age of inquiries or other indicators
- *industry standards,* such as an acceptable number of rejects per 100,000 products produced

It is not true that all indicators must have a goal. Your departments may merely keep track of machine down-time percentage or a specific employee's errors.

Remember that a goal is a realistic and *quantifiable* statement of the level of performance you feel you can achieve. Given your manpower and other resources, do not set goals which are unrealistic. Certain indicator types, such as production volume forecasts, may not lend themselves to a stated goal or an on/off target situation. The status is listed as N/A (not applicable).

Note that both the computer and manual systems can help determine goals when you examine reports and accumulated history. Therefore, your goals may be increased, decreased, or changed at any time.

7. Volume Sampling
Decide what percentage of the total volume to measure. Keep in mind that the larger the percentage measured, the higher the confidence level and your cost. The chances of a truly representative sample drop with smaller size samples, as does the expense.

8. Calculate Performance and Status
Using the indicator volumes, calculate performance as per previous examples. Compare this result to your goal. For positive indicators (quality %, timeliness %, and so on), you are on target if performance is greater than or equal to goal. For negative indicators (reject rate, late production, etc.), on target is performance less than or equal to goal. The following table shows some examples.

Indicator	Goal %	Performance	Status
QUALITY % (Positive)	96.0	98.3	ON TARGET
LATE PRODUCTION % (Negative)	2.5	3.7	OFF TARGET
LATE PRODUCTION %	+6.0	+8.2	N/A

AUTOMATED PERFORMANCE MEASUREMENT SYSTEM

The automated system features computerized generation of performance reports, exception reporting, graphic trend analyses, and planning models. The following material is derived from an automated system which has been working for over five years. Even if you're not yet in a position to automate your efforts, it will give you some background information to consider.

In a typical operation, there can be tradeoffs. Quality may improve at the expense of timeliness because of extra time spent checking transactions. To decrease errors, added checkpoints might entail extra cost. On the other hand, emphasis on items per hour (productivity) could have a negative impact on quality rates. A **report option** should allow you to group related indicators for determining *overall* performance of a unit, section, cost center, activity, and so on.

Combining performance history and a graph can be very valuable in determining trends and projecting performance. An ideal automated quality control system has computerized graphs and narrative history on one page. It's easy to do with a computer, as you can see in Exhibit 36.

Note the combination of volume and quality performance on the same graph. The left-hand axis represents production volume; the right-hand axis is the related quality percentage. You should have the choice

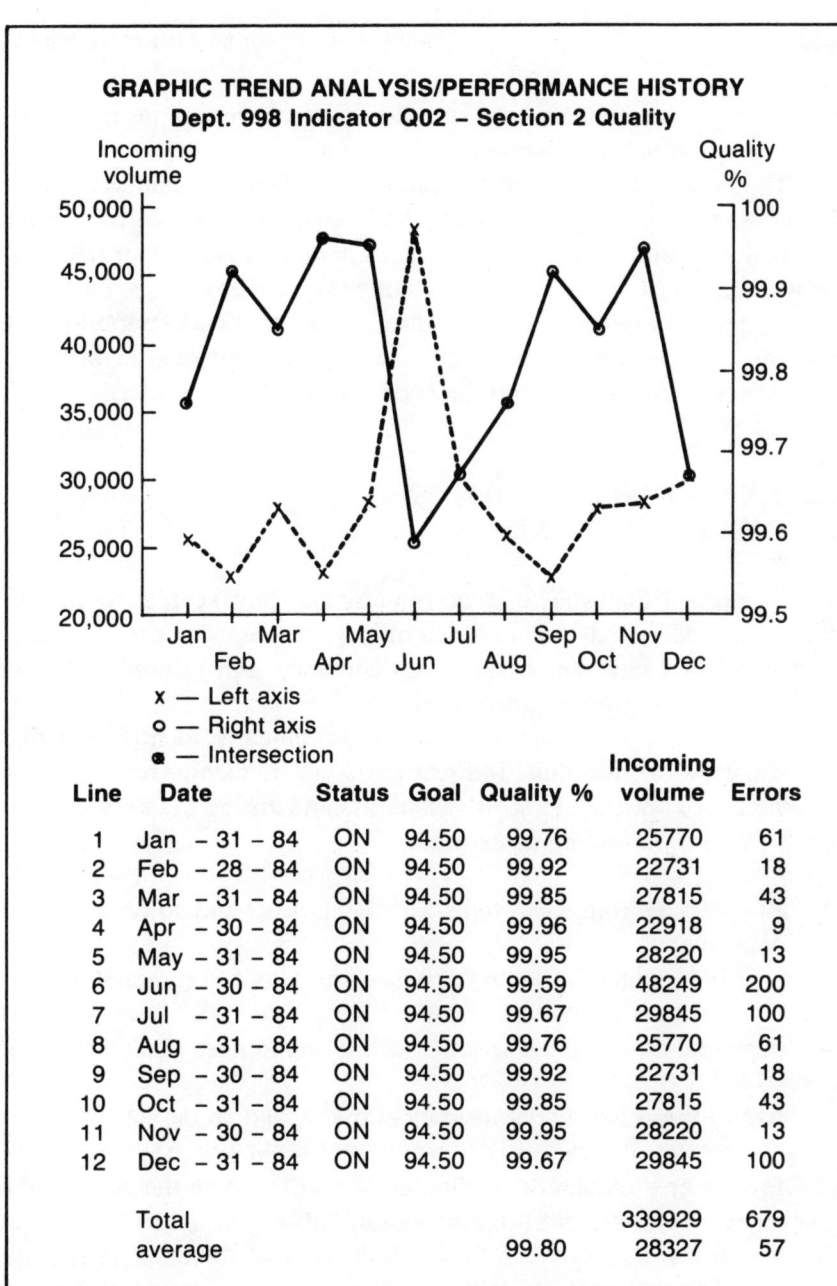

Exhibit 36.
Actual computer-generated trend analysis

of plotting performance versus volume, goal versus performance, current versus previous volume, and so on.

The data concerning the indicator are plotted automatically. Such items as date, goal, performance, and volumes need not be entered again. In addition, the computer stores and employs proper headings as well as adjusting the scale of horizontal/vertical axes.

To reduce reporting costs further, use **exception reporting.** The program should prompt you to choose indicators meeting certain specific criteria (department, product, on/off target status, etc.).

APPLYING COST ACCOUNTING TO SPECIFIC OPERATIONS

It is important that your cost accounting function keep accurate, detailed records so that you can determine unit costs for each phase of production and pinpoint shortages. In addition, such records will serve well in budgeting for future periods.

Direct costs are those that can be specifically identified with a particular production unit. Indirect costs are frequently referred to as overhead or controllable costs. Many manufacturing systems separate costs into the following categories:

1. energy, covering such items as heat, power, and so on
2. personnel
3. human resource variable expenses, such as fringe benefits, hospital/medical insurance, and the like
4. depreciation for fixed assets, such as buildings, equipment, and so on
5. fixed expenses such as insurance, taxes, and so on

From a cost reduction standpoint, it is crucial that the controllable expenses be isolated from the noncontrollable. These can be reduced by the various techniques referred to throughout the book, especially those in Action Checklist #11.

There is a clear difference between the terms "profit center" and "cost center." The profit center involves revenue and expenses and is expected to generate a profit. A cost center just incurs expenses and does not produce income.

Product costs are those directly connected with manufacturing the item, as opposed to general or administrative expenses, which are not able to be allocated to the product.

One of your big expenses may be data processing. It is worthwhile to mention the two major methods of charging for these services.

Direct Charge: In this the actual usage is charged to the users. In order to do this, you will need to set up some specific ways to measure the expenses for the data center for CPU time, printing, collating, support, personnel, and so on. In effect, a separate cost accounting system needs to be developed.

Allocation: Using this method, the cost is charged to the user department by a formula which is derived from looking at other budgeted items, or distributed on the basis of statistics developed by your computer people.

Even fixed costs, which traditionally have been left alone by many companies, can be attacked in a positive way. Think of the "step" effect. If you have certain fixed costs, which traditionally have been at one level, and because of added requirements you must bring in new equipment, you add to your fixed costs in increments or steps. By taking a serious look at the proposal, you may be able to use the principle of cost avoidance. This technique will reduce the necessity for the step effect of fixed costs.

ACTION CHECKLIST # 11

Productivity Improvement and Cost Control

ACTION FOCUS	N/A	STRONG	SATIS-FACTORY	NEEDS SOME IMPROVEMENT	WEAK: NEEDS MAJOR IMPROVEMENT	ACTION PLAN, RESPONSIBILITY
Create a productivity awareness culture at all levels						
Publish productivity goals in company media						
Establish a performance measurement and improvement system						
Set up a research/exchange network to exchange information						
Select quality assurance checkpoints and performance indicators						
Choose reliable volume figures including sampling						
Calculate productivity performance and determine trends						
Define goals and "status" (on or off target)						
Use graphics and exception reporting to save time						
Isolate controllable from noncontrollable costs						
Distinguish between profit center and cost center						

PRODUCTIVITY IMPROVEMENT AND COST CONTROL 147

	Employ direct charges or allocation for data processing services	Pinpoint standard costs for products and component parts	Assure that cost accounting records agree with other financial items	Maintain control over major expense and/or capital categories	Report frequently on actions concerning controllable expenses	Use cost avoidance techniques to prevent expenditures	Involve a steering committee on high cost projects	Have cost accounting participate in production contract preparation				

10

QUALITY CONTROL AS A COST REDUCTION METHOD

The *Wall Street Journal,* in its issue of April 10, 1985, called attention to one of the preeminent causes of poor quality. According to quality control expert Philip Crosby, any company (including yours) will get just what it asks for. If you request a 10 percent defect rate, you will get just that. Other experts claim that many firms think of quality control as a proliferation of inspectors in the assembly line or posters asking people to be more quality conscious.

According to the article, the most important factor in raising quality levels is *attitude,* from that of the chairman of the board to that held by production workers.

Mr. Crosby cited the example of the Tennant Company of Minneapolis, Minnesota. This corporation, which manufactures maintenance equipment, had a big problem with defects.

The first thing it did was to quantify the money spent in rework and service caused by rejects. The major change recommended and installed was a series of classes for the staff employees. Also, tremendous emphasis was placed on change of attitude. What that involved specifically was management convincing its people that everyone was very serious about quality.

Over a four-year span, manufacturing defects were reduced by 52 percent. The cost of quality (COQ) was cut in half from 1980 to 1984.

WHAT QUALITY CONTROL REALLY IS

The Wharton Management Report (a television series) claims that:

- A satisfied customer will tell *three* other individuals about your product and/or service.
- An unhappy customer will tell *fifteen* other people.
- 90 percent of customers will buy again if their complaints are quickly resolved.

One company uses a quality control device called "Daily Dose of Reality." Here's how it works. Wait until your customer has the product for six weeks. Call and ask, "How's it working?" You'll get a good clue to your *customer's perception* of your product's quality.

Many people think of quality control as a series of sampling techniques and product inspections that result in the calculation of defect rates which are then expressed as percentages. This common treatment has severely limited companies in utilizing the full potential of quality control as a vehicle for lowering costs and improving productivity.

Quality is an economic consideration. Simply put, it costs you money to build quality into a product. It is not unusual for a company to spend 15 to 40 percent of its total operating costs on quality-related activities.

This has been referred to by management specialists as the "phantom department." You should address quality in terms of its monetary contributions to the expense side of the ledger. If you translate defect rates into expense dollars or pounds or whatever, the impact can be seen more clearly. Having done this, you can then utilize quality control as a significant cost reduction technique as well as a vehicle for improving product quality. Specifically, this is referred to as the **cost of quality** approach.

However, before you apply specific cost of quality techniques, it is essential that you establish a firm foundation for quality control in your organization. Quality control policies apply to *all* areas of your business, not just the production shop.

ESTABLISHING A QUALITY POLICY

You can definitely get a competitive edge through improved quality. The major ingredients for this are management commitment and a positive companywide attitude.

Edward Deming, one of the foremost quality control experts in the world, claims that 94 percent of all defects can be attributed to management practices rather than directly to production workers. Many executives disagree with that number, but no one argues the validity of the concept that management has a prime responsibility for guaranteeing quality control.

A company should have a clearly articulated policy on quality. This written policy succinctly states the broad objectives of the company relative to quality issues. Base your policy on a solid sense of where your business is and where it would like to be in the quality arena. A broad statement such as "we are committed to the best" is of little value if your company is not prepared to back it up in terms of both employee motivation and economics.

Exhibit 37 gives you a sampling of items to be considered for your quality policy. Use it for planning your overall document. Make copies and elicit input from colleagues and managers.

ORGANIZING YOUR QUALITY CONTROL

If you have not already done so, consider designating a key individual as Quality Control Manager. This person would be held accountable for implementing quality policy and ought to report to a high-level executive.

Quality is not only a production shop concern. It permeates the entire organization in terms of impact on customer service, cost control, and productivity improvement.

Some of the functions and activities are listed in the following chart. You can assign the responsibilities to appropriate people in your organization.

QUALITY CONTROL POLICY FACTORS

1. **Market Factors**

    A. Do we want to be the best in the market? ___ Yes ___ No

    B. Will we use quality to gain a competitive edge? ___ Yes ___ No

    C. Should we simply maintain *current* quality levels? ___ Yes ___ No

    D. Should we stress ___ pricing ___ quality to our customers?

    E. What costs are we prepared to pay for excellence?
    _____

    F. If quality and service are stressed to customers, what is our liability in terms of warranties and/or claims?
    _____
    _____

2. **Internal Factors**

    A. Should our quality assurance effort be ___ focused ___ company-wide? If focused, what areas?
    _____
    _____

    B. What will be the impact in terms of extra cost on
    staffing? _____
    training? _____
    awareness? _____

    C. What incentives (if any) should we provide to employees for improving quality?
    _____
    _____

Exhibit 37.
Planning form for creating a quality control policy

Quality Control Responsibilities

Function	QC Related Activity	Responsibility
Quality Control Program	planning, implementation	
Sampling	sampling programs	
Production	product inspection	
	process control	
Design	engineering	
	testing	
	standards development	
Customer Service	field testing support	
	performance surveys	
	customer complaints	
Purchasing	vendor analysis	
Advertising	review correctness of copy	
Warehousing	procedures for proper storage/ retrieval of parts	
Parts Distribution	procedures for assuring that parts are distributed correctly	
Word Processing	reduce rework corrections	
Other	_____	
	_____	

ANALYZING SPECIFIC PROCESSING COSTS

Here are two important questions for you to ask:

1. How much does it cost to maintain the current level of quality for my customers?
2. What proportion of these costs can I reduce while still producing an acceptable level of quality?

The magnitude of quality-related costs, with their concomitant profit drain, has led to the need to isolate and measure these costs. This encourages the establishment of a cost of quality program. Such a program permits you to determine product cost of quality and cost of quality as a percentage of total operating expenses. An effective cost of quality program improves productivity by reducing quality costs while maintaining or improving quality levels. This concept has long been applied successfully in the manufacturing sector.

A successful COQ program will also turn into an excellent decision support tool. It helps you to determine which products have high quality costs and isolates specific problem areas. The impact is reduced costs and/or more effective pricing strategies. The historical approach to controlling quality is to place heavy emphasis on checking and "cleaning up" the product before the customer receives it. This is an extremely expensive proposition. Fortunately, there are other approaches that not only result in the same or better quality levels, but have significantly better bottom-line payback. By reallocating quality dollars, you can improve both the quality of your product and your return on assets.

The relative costs of original processing versus rework are illustrated in Exhibit 38. It starts with a scheduled run of 1,000 items, five steps and a projected production cost of $1,670.00 ($1.67 each).

Note the following:

1. 950 products were processed defect free (steps 1–5).
2. 50 items with defects were caught by Q/C inspectors. They are processed a second time from steps 1–4. *Rework* cost = $58.50. Distribution cost = $25.00.
3. Of 1,000 items produced, 50 "escaped" quality control inspection and were reported as defects by *customers*. The additional pass through steps 1–6 increased the cost by $193.50.
4. Total inquiry, rework cost (the "phantom department") = $252.00.
5. The original production cost was $1,670.00.
6. Increased percentage over goal = *15.1%*.

These added costs are avoidable through allocating quality expenses properly.

QUALITY CONTROL AS A COST REDUCTION METHOD

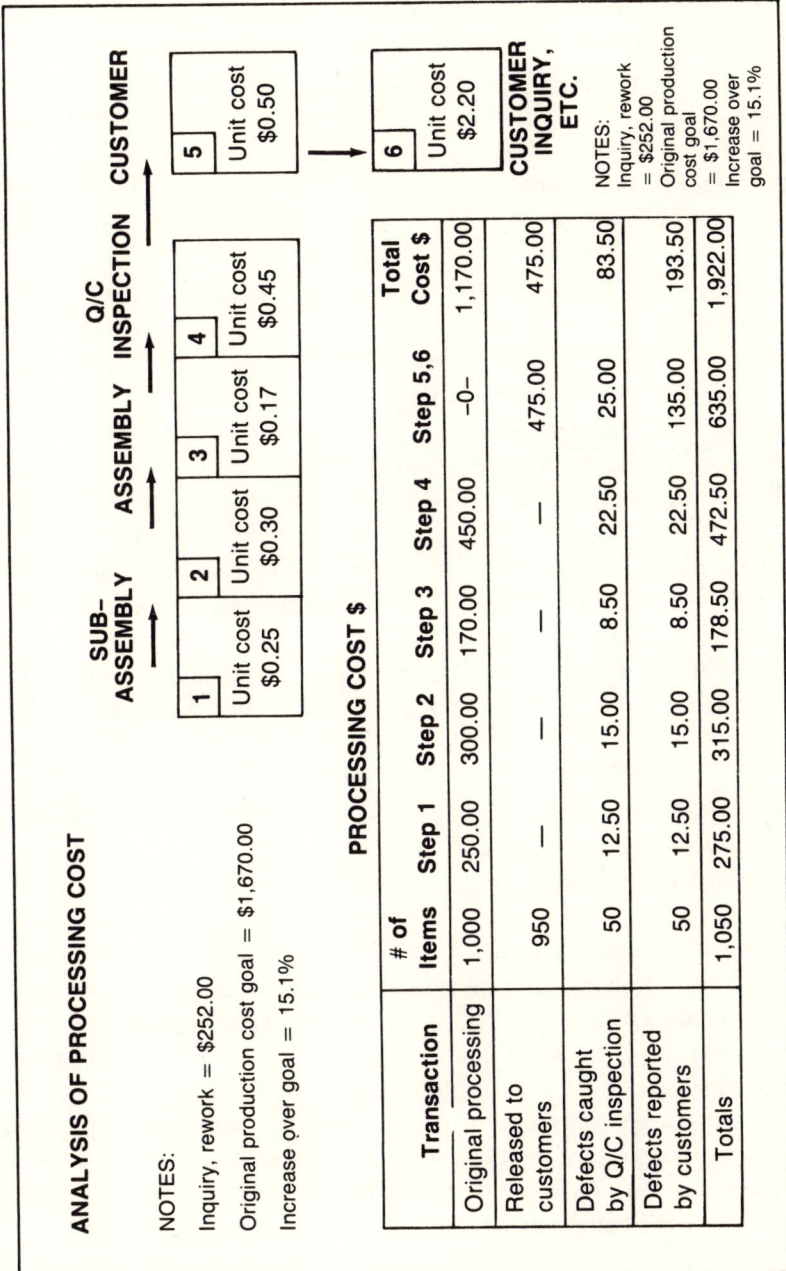

Exhibit 38.
An actual manufacturing cost analysis

QUALITY COST COMPONENTS

Once you've determined your "extra" costs, separate them into four categories:

Prevention costs are those involved in preventing defects. Expenses relating to product design, manufacturing specifications, job training, quality control planning, report generation and analysis are examples.

Appraisal costs have to do with the evaluation of quality levels. Is quality up to par? Is the item defective? Have we done the right job? Appraisal dollars pay for activities such as inspecting, checking, sorting good items from bad, and so on.

Internal failure costs are those incurred correcting defects discovered prior to delivery to the customer. Money spent on rework is a cost stemming from internal failures. So are extra expenses of handling scrap, delay costs, production stoppages, and the like.

External failure costs are those relating to defects discovered after delivery of this product. These expenses can be critical and costly because they involve customer complaints, inquiries, warranty claims. Most important, they represent potential loss of business from the affected customers *plus* those additional ones who become aware of your quality problems.

RELATIONSHIPS IN QUALITY COST COMPONENTS

The purpose of analyzing quality costs is to attempt to strike a balance between the value of quality and the cost to produce that value. Analysts study costs of quality to try to take advantage of two relationships that exist between quality expenditures and defect rates.

The first relationship links appraisal costs with internal and external failures. As more appraisal work is done, increasing appraisal costs, more defects are caught internally (increasing internal failures and rework costs). As more defects are caught internally (before delivery), fewer are caught externally (decreasing external failure costs).

Generally speaking, managers increase appraisal efforts to improve the quality of the output and lower the external failure rate. Often, reductions in external failure costs are negated by increases in appraisal and internal failure costs. Sometimes, both appraisal effectiveness *and* cost can be improved by switching from a checking procedure to a statistically valid sampling technique.

So, while individual costs may be affected, the total often remains nearly unchanged because the decreases in external failure costs are offset by the increases in appraisal and internal failure costs. Total prevention costs are unaffected.

The second relationship links prevention costs with internal and external failures. As prevention costs rise, both types of failure costs tend to fall. Moreover, in many cases appraisal costs may be reduced. The reasoning behind this relationship is that prevention efforts reduce defect rates and associated failure costs. Put simply, fewer defects mean less rework. On top of this, as prevention reduces defect rates, appraisal efforts can be scaled down because the level of quality has increased.

The point is that money spent on *prevention* buys much more than that spent on the other quality cost categories. To aid you in quantifying cost of quality and suggest how to better allocate these expenses, use Exhibit 39. Specifically, try to allocate more money on prevention than appraisal.

When you are ready to institute or improve your own program, use Exhibit 40 as a sample process document. Answer each segment step by step, assign responsibility, and show completion dates.

THE RELATIONSHIP BETWEEN COQ AND PRODUCTIVITY

An increase in prevention costs means fewer defects and higher quality. If fewer defects result in lower quality costs, it's also an improvement in productivity at the same time. By reallocating quality expenditures, you can improve both the quality of your product and your return on assets.

COST OF QUALITY COMPONENTS WORKSHEET

Component	Money Spent	%	Action/ Responsibility
1. Prevention			
Product Design Specs	_____	___	_____
Job Training	_____	___	_____
Quality Control Planning	_____	___	_____
Quality Analysis & Reporting	_____	___	_____
Subtotal *Prevention Costs*	_____	___	_____
2. Appraisal			
Inspecting	_____	___	_____
Checking	_____	___	_____
Sorting Good from Bad	_____	___	_____
Subtotal *Appraisal Costs*	_____	___	_____
3. Internal Failure			
Rework	_____	___	_____
Delay Costs	_____	___	_____
Production Stoppages	_____	___	_____
Scrap	_____	___	_____
Subtotal *Internal Failure Costs*	_____	___	_____
4. External Failures			
Handling Customer Inquiries	_____	___	_____
Customer Complaints	_____	___	_____
Warranty Claims	_____	___	_____
Adjustments	_____	___	_____
Subtotal *External Failure Costs*	_____	___	_____
TOTAL COST OF QUALITY	_____	___	_____

Exhibit 39.
Calculations for cost of quality components

COST OF QUALITY PROGRAM

	Responsibility	By Date
1. *Identify the quality problem.* Define job functions to be analyzed plus known quality problems.	_____	_____
2. *Develop and analyze the distribution of quality costs.* Pinpoint how much money is being spent on prevention, appraisal, internal failure, external failure.	_____	_____
3. *Determine the different defect types.* Calculate number of errors by type. Isolate those which are major contributors. Rank them by occurrence and accumulated percent to total. You may find that 20% of the types contribute 80% of the defects.	_____	_____
4. *Find out how the defects are generated.* Who is responsible and what are the reasons? This means meeting with managers, supervisors, inspectors and production workers.	_____	_____
5. *Propose solutions.* Use more prevention activities including product engineering, better specifications, quality control training, etc. Include timetable and quality goals.	_____	_____
6. *Implement changes and monitor progress.* Measure new quality and costs. Report to appropriate individuals.	_____	_____

Exhibit 40.
Planning process for cost of quality program

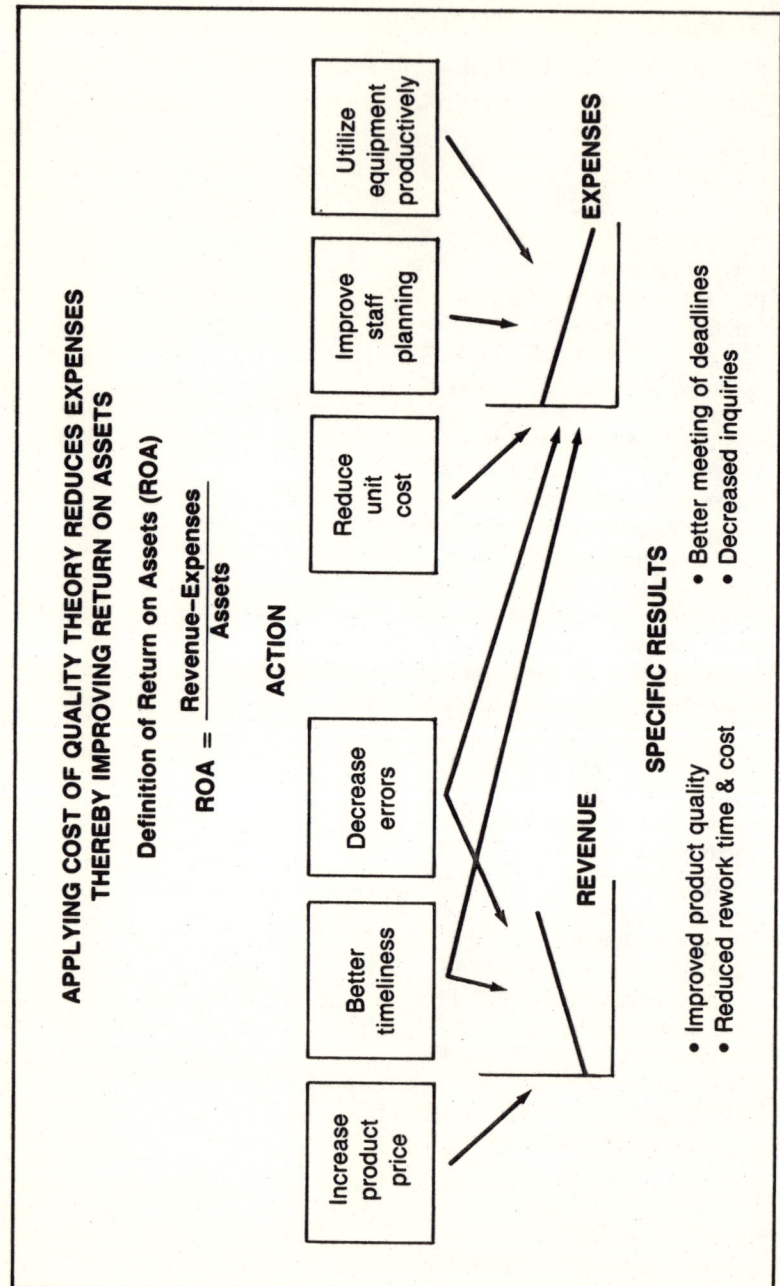

Exhibit 41.
An expert's graphic representation of COQ benefits

QUALITY CONTROL AS A COST REDUCTION METHOD 161

How all these different actions affect revenue and expenses is illustrated in Exhibit 41 which was created by a COQ analyst for his own firm.

When you are explaining and/or presenting cost of quality and productivity, you can use the chart shown in Exhibit 41. Many executives have photocopied illustrations like this and made transparencies or slides from them. The actions and results can be summarized as follows:

Action	Revenue		Expenses	
	Up	Down	Up	Down
Increase product price	X			
Better timeliness	X			X
Decrease errors	X			X
Reduce unit cost				X
Improve staff planning				X
Utilize equipment productively				X

EMPLOYING QUALITY CIRCLES PRODUCTIVELY

This technique, also known as Quality of Work Life or QWL, has a proven track record of improving quality while reducing costs. Its major philosophies are productivity through people; participation; and easy implementation. Here are the details:

Definition
The Quality Circle is small groups of volunteers who meet regularly to analyze problems and recommend solutions to management.

Philosophy
- People are experts in the work they do.
- Everyone has ideas and wants to contribute.

- People care about the success of the company.
- Everyone can help solve problems.

Steering Committee
- functions as quality circle board of directors
- sets objectives/policies/guidelines
- provides for system expansion
- acts as the support system

Circle Members
- composed of 6 to 12 individuals
- do similar work
- are volunteers
- meet regularly
- take special training

Facilitator
- reports to Steering Committee
- coordinates Circle activities
- provides training
- guides Circles through feedback
- maintains records
- guarantees communication to all levels of management
- supervises data collection
- promotes Circle growth
- monitors Circle progress

Circle Coordinator
- is a supervisor/staff member
- takes problem-solving training
- receives training in group dynamics
- is responsible for Circle activities

The Circle Requires Training In
- brainstorming
- data collection techniques
- pareto analysis (20/80 rule)

- presentation skills
- planning and scheduling tools
- cause and effect analysis

The Quality Circle Seven Step Approach
1. Identify a series of problems or opportunities for improvement.
2. Select the most important.
3. Analyze the current system.
4. Generate alternative solutions.
5. Evaluate pros and cons of the alternatives.
6. Select the most practical, cost effective solution.
7. Present findings, conclusions, and recommendations to management.

Potential Problems To Beware Of
- a tendency to look for "quick-fix" solutions rather than long-term adjustments
- members of the Circle (volunteers) may move to another department
- lack of valid data

On balance, Quality Circles are an excellent team approach to improving quality while reducing cost. Here are some interesting variations on Quality Circles.

The Milliken Company (fabrics) calls its group CATS (Corrective Action Teams). Once each quarter for three full days, the teams have a "Fabulous Bragging Session" for all members. Hundreds of teams each make a five-minute presentation of their success stories. The rules are: nothing negative and all savings small or large are reported. Management presents certificates to all presenters. By evaluation, the best presentations then are given to the company president.

The Ford Motor Company refers to its problem-solving groups as part of an "Employee Involvement Program." About 10 percent of the workers participate. Besides this, they present the "Q1 Award" to top quality suppliers. They also teach them how to improve quality control. The estimate from Ford is that these two actions alone have reduced the price of the company's Escort model by $400 per car.

THE ROLE OF STATISTICS
IN QUALITY CONTROL

Statistics provide the basis for gathering and interpreting the data obtained about the quality of a service or product. It is important that certain statistical aspects and terms are properly understood. If not, the conclusions drawn from improperly obtained or analyzed data can cause even more severe problems.

Two definitions are important—test (or inspection) and observation. When you inspect an item, you are comparing its characteristics against established standards which determine its fitness for use. Whether it satisfies the criteria or not is the result of the inspection. The result is known as an *observation*. In quality control, you can check a sample of items to determine the overall quality of a service or product.

Statistical sampling is used in many ways. It is an accurate and efficient method to determine whether a product is acceptable. Sampling is a decision-making tool that is particularly useful for you when:

- a lot is too large to inspect completely
- 100 percent inspecting is too extensive or time-consuming
- you simply want to employ the most cost effective measurement method for determining quality

One very important aspect for a valid sample is that every item has an equal chance of being chosen. If this condition is not met, the sample will be biased and not truly represent the total population. This equal chance of being chosen is covered by the term random.

A statistical tool called a **random number table** can be used for this purpose. These tables are generated by a computer and act as a guide in objective sampling. If you're interested in more extensive material on sampling, there are numerous books on the subject. Make sure you obtain one that relates directly to business, not to academics.

Briefly, suppose you wanted to select a sample of ten high-volume accounts from a population of five hundred such accounts. List the five hundred accounts establishing a "frame," a listing of all the units in the population. Since the population size is five hundred, refer to a random number table with a sequence of three random digits. You may decide to use the first two columns in the random number table. The first three-digit number is 132. Therefore account number 132 becomes the first account of your sample. The next number is 212, which means that the corresponding account is your second selection. The third number is 990 which is not within your frame so you disregard it. Continue this procedure until you have selected your ten accounts. You have saved the cost of looking at all five hundred accounts.

CONTROL LIMITS

Another good method of cost reduction connected with quality improvement is the establishment of upper control limits (UCL). What you can do is put a **trigger** in your reporting system that alerts you to a defect rate that exceeds a specific number.

Example: By examining past history and discussing a specific production item with pertinent members of the work force, you have decided that the UCL is at eighty-two errors per week. Direct your system to produce an exception report when the actual defect rate exceeds that. You will save money by avoiding the reporting of normal situations.

QUALITY CONTROL AT WORK

Here are some concrete examples of quality control's importance:

General Motors spent $24 million teaching quality control in just *one plant!*

At Ford Motor Company, quality has been the number one objective since 1979. Philip Caldwell, Chairman and CEO, stated in a 1985 interview that its quality level improved more than 50 percent in five years. He talked about recognizing that human resources are largely underutilized. Other points that he stressed were:

- use statistical quality control on high volume manufacturing
- don't waste time on quality control unless top management is committed

The Perdue Company grosses approximately $840 million yearly. To paraphrase President Frank Perdue, "It doesn't matter what your product or service. Your attitude should be an unlimited capability to improve quality." The company's share of market in selected areas is as high as 90 percent.

In a March 1985 discussion, author Tom Peters spoke with much eloquence about "a passion for excellence," not coincidentally the name of his recent best-selling book. He stressed that "markets don't buy; customers do and the need exists to treat the customer with courtesy." Among concrete examples of quality improvement, he mentioned the focus and attention at Hewlett-Packard, a large electronics manufacturer. One of their Q/C techniques is called MBWA. It stands for *M*anage *B*y *W*andering *A*round! It entails frequent on-site quality inspections by appropriate executives.

Action Checklist #12 is a good starting point for creating your own quality control program.

ACTION CHECKLIST # 12

Quality Control

ACTION FOCUS	N/A	STRONG	SATIS-FACTORY	NEEDS SOME IMPROVEMENT	WEAK: NEEDS MAJOR IMPROVEMENT	ACTION PLAN, RESPONSIBILITY
Call customers to find out how your products are working						
Designate a quality control manager and hold accountable						
Measure cost of quality by component						
Emphasize prevention rather than appraisal						
Calculate rework expenses over time to determine trend						
Employ Quality Circles productively						
Try a "bragging session" to highlight success stories						
Reward superior suppliers of quality materials						
Train resources in quality improvement						
Use statistical sampling for inspection						
Establish upper control limits and exception reports for rejects						

11

PRODUCT ENGINEERING AND PRODUCTION TECHNIQUES

The ideal production system places the right material in the right location at the right time, and schedules the right number of worker-hours and production time to meet a prescribed schedule. As time goes by, more and more manufacturers are using robots and computers to automate production for manufacturing.

Two major systems enhance production: Computerized Manufacturing Automation (CMA) and Manufacturing Resource Planning (MRP). MRP was discussed in the chapter on purchasing.

The Office of Technology Assessment of the Congress of the United States prepared a comprehensive study on each system. Its findings indicate extensive benefits in terms of coordinating plant operations, increased flexibility, better efficiency, more accurate/timely information. Users can also expect reduced inventory investment. That's what you should be looking for.

PA TECHNOLOGIES

The **programmable automation** (PA) technologies that you should know about are:

Computer Aided Design (CAD) is a sophisticated design tool to maximize a product's performance using the computerized representation of the product. Included functions are drafting and engineering.

Robotics: programmable devices used to move things along a prescribed path, loading/unloading, spray painting, welding machinery, assembly, and such.

Numerically Controlled Machine Tools (NC): machines instructed to do specific manufacturing functions, such as turning, drilling, milling, shaping, cutting, forming, shearing, and so on.

Flexible Manufacturing Systems (FMS): linking robots and NC to move and operate on materials.

Computer Integrated Manufacturing (CIM): a complete system which coordinates design, manufacturing, and information management.

Although all of the above technologies have great potential for manufacturing expense reduction, be aware of some pitfalls:

- complicated installation
- lack of standard programming languages and interfaces between PA devices
- relative difficulty for new people to use

For these reasons, many companies apply computerized manufacturing automation in phases. They start with pilot installations and measure the effect on productivity and quality.

COMPUTERIZED TECHNIQUES

On balance, future technology holds great promise for information flow improvement as well as reductions in operating costs and inventory investment. One state-of-the-art system existing today is "Machine Vision." The purpose is to spot defects through the use of laser beams. These intense lights are directed at hinges, holes, and gaps in assembled products. The system measures the degree of fit. One of the leading companies in this field is Perception, Inc., of Farmington Hills, Michigan.

Several other recent techniques are contributing to production increase and cost reduction. A number of large manufacturers are replacing large plants with new and smaller factories and turning to automation. They claim that increases in productivity are huge. This system is referred to as **scaled down** or **focused factories** using small teams of management and labor. One of the most dramatic improvements is the reaction to product changes and new technology. This avoids enormous investment in huge plants and other drags on production.

THE JIT TECHNIQUE

One of the most dramatic developments in recent years, in terms of improving productivity in a production environment, is the **Just In Time** system or JIT. This also has other names such as Zero Inventory, Stockless Production, or Kanban. The system, which was first developed in Japan, is now spreading quickly.

Some of the benefits are:

- inventory reduction in the area of 15 to 45 percent
- increased through-put time, between 20 and 50 percent
- improved labor productivity, between 50 and 80 percent

The goal of JIT is cost reduction through elimination of other than the minimum amount of people, materials, and equipment absolutely essential to production. Less inventory results in less capital tied up in a particular asset. In addition, carrying costs are reduced, as is the expense for an inventory control system. Fewer people are needed to control inventory and less space is used in the plant.

Another dramatic area of improvement is the better quality control which results from JIT. In terms of cost reduction, this will result in fewer hours spent on rework, less material waste, and fewer customer complaints.

MORE ON JIT

According to a recent survey by Arthur Andersen and Company, an international accounting firm, Just In Time has resulted in average reductions of the following:

- work in process inventory—90 percent
- manufacturing lead time—90 percent
- start up, scrap, and rework—80 percent
- set-up time—75 percent
- plant and warehouse space—50 percent
- direct and indirect labor—20 percent

The survey pointed out five areas to improve productivity:

1. Reduce set-up time.
2. Utilize space better by re-doing layout and creating smaller operating units with direct responsibility for getting production done.
3. Cut back on the number of suppliers and use those with high quality and reduced material costs.
4. Re-situate distribution centers closer to crucial customers, thereby increasing sales, pruning inventories, and reducing transportation costs. An important side effect is improved customer service.
5. Upgrade systems for controlling production processes including scheduling and measuring of performance and case studies of JIT manufacturing.

Various manufacturers have documented significant savings with Just In Time manufacturing. Here are several of them.

Whirlpool Corporation improved its inventory position by using a trucking company which unloads components directly through the Whirlpool plant door. The components are put directly onto the assembly line on an "as is" basis. Whirlpool tells the trucking company specifically what parts and sub-assemblies it requires, including the location and the specific time. The trucking company gathers the required materials from various suppliers, consolidates them, and delivers them promptly to Whirlpool's assembly plant.

The Caterpillar Tractor Company of Peoria, Illinois, is the world's largest manufacturer of equipment for earth moving, construction, and material handling. Moreover, it produces various kinds of engines. Caterpillar, working with GEISCO (General Electric Information Services Company), developed a worldwide around-the-clock information network. Under this system, Caterpillar and its suppliers exchange information through the GEISCO network. The estimate is that by the end of 1985 about 350 resources will be in this information network. The manufacturer claims reduced lead-time and decreased processing costs as opposed to the former system which made heavy use of paper.

The Coleco Company of Hartford, Connecticut, has had tremendous success with its Cabbage Patch children's dolls. In order to fully meet delivery deadlines, Coleco uses air freight (Emery) to deliver various components of the dolls from different suppliers on several continents. By using air freight, Coleco claims that the dolls can be packaged in two to three days. By using JIT manufacturing, Coleco has dramatically reduced production time while at the same time maintaining high quality.

The Master Lock Company in Milwaukee, Wisconsin, is one of the world's largest producers of combination padlocks. What complicates the inventory and production functions is that each one is unique in terms of its combination. Moreover, each lock has to have a specific label so that the user who is unable to open the padlock can get the combination directly from the manufacturer.

To address these two requirements, Master Lock employs an automated assembly system. This produces the product at high speed, tests each lock, engraves the serial number with a laser, then prints a label for the customer, listing all the instructions. The system is run by a computer that, in addition to controlling production, also drives a high speed printer to output the label data. Master Lock has achieved reductions in storage and production overruns as well as being more responsive to customer orders.

A sub-set of these new techniques is called "line-stop." Under this method, assembly lines are furnished with yellow and red lights. The yellow light is pressed when there is a problem and the red when the problem is bad enough to call for a stop in the production line.

This system prevents products with defects going through, and therefore lowers cost of quality.

To zero in on cost reduction in a production environment, carefully review Action Checklist #13.

The techniques mentioned here range in complexity from very simple to somewhat complex and in investment from a few dollars to many. However, they all have the same two objectives, to increase production and reduce costs.

PRODUCT ENGINEERING

The object of product engineering is to design up-to-date products that are sensitive to customer demand at a competitive price. The main operations consist of research and development (R&D).

Here are some concrete examples of cost reduction in the product engineering sector. Consider each in light of what similar efforts could do for you.

1. A large office equipment manufacturer carefully evaluated its product line. The *joint* effort between design and purchasing people resulted in:

    - 600 less parts for a specific product
    - motor size decreased by one-half for the same product

2. A medium-sized maker of electronic equipment achieved a return on R&D investment of 5:1 through spending money on standardization of parts.
3. A major electronics company decreased its inventory of parts from 1,350 to 150 items by eliminating parts with similar functions.
4. Some companies have reduced their costs by encouraging product engineers to attend trade shows. By doing this they gain valuable resource information quickly rather than through splintered, long-term efforts.
5. In other firms, teams of engineers and purchasing agents visit plants

PRODUCT ENGINEERING AND PRODUCTION TECHNIQUES 175

to determine key suppliers' capabilities in the areas of raw material production, quality control, distribution, financing, and so on.
6. Westinghouse Electric Corporation instituted a "Get 60" program whose objective was to decrease material costs by $60 million a year. The goal was surpassed by:

- putting new life into proven techniques
- upgrading technology to "state-of-the-art"
- increased emphasis on quality
- greater use of value analysis in product design

7. Union Trust Company of Stamford, Connecticut (a commercial bank), saved 5 percent of salaries and benefits through a formalized methods improvement program. This approach is applicable to manufacturing as well.
8. A soft drink bottler dramatically reduced its number of special packages and labels without affecting their attractive appearance from the customer's point of view. The result: lower expenses for product packaging.

Your cost reduction efforts for "better product/less money" operations can be substantially enhanced by using Action Checklist #14.

RE-MANUFACTURING

Manufacturers are putting together old and new parts to build products that are as good as, or better than, the originals at substantially reduced costs. Executives studying this technique estimate that 600 companies are now involved in this area.

An expert on re-manufacturing estimates that by using this method you can save 20 percent of the energy and 10 percent of the raw materials as opposed to building the product new.

As an example, American Telephone and Telegraph Company produces a re-manufactured phone for $30.00, which is $10.00 less than a comparable new model.

Pratt and Whitney utilizes re-manufacturing in its airline aircraft engine production. One of its jet engines is being re-manufactured at a cost of $900,000 as opposed to $1.6 million new. In addition, by adding new components, engine efficiency is boosted by about 6 percent.

THE PROBLEM OF MANUFACTURING COUNTERFEITING

According to recent estimates, approximately $20 billion in sales was lost because of counterfeiting of United States products. Aside from monetary losses, it has been reported that a number of fatal accidents have been caused by parts for automobile and aircraft which were not made by the original manufacturer.

To retard such a serious problem, American manufacturing companies will spend millions of dollars to attempt to authenticate products with such strategies as hidden magnetic or micro-chip tags, disappearing-reappearing inks, holographic images, digitized fingerprint of labels and other tricks that make their products hard to copy.

Here are some specific examples:

Light Signature Incorporated, working with clothier Levi Strauss, developed a special label and reader. They can tell whether the clothes are authentic by reading the label which has a unique fiber pattern. Levi Strauss claims it has ". . . virtually eliminated our counterfeiting problems in the U.S.'" The labels add about a penny to the price of each garment and a few more cents for the inspections of stores.

Allied Corporation, the producer of Fram Oil Filters, has a system which uses a magnetic tag and code number. This is then compared with the box code number using an inexpensive scanner. If there is any difference, the product is not genuine.

The most sophisticated method to determine counterfeits uses holograms, which are three-dimensional images. Although these currently are being used mostly with credit cards, they are being investigated for paper money and conventional manufacturing systems.

PRODUCT ENGINEERING AND PRODUCTION TECHNIQUES

ACTION CHECKLIST # 13

Production

ACTION FOCUS	N/A	STRONG	SATIS-FACTORY	NEEDS SOME IMPROVEMENT	WEAK: NEEDS MAJOR IMPROVEMENT	ACTION PLAN, RESPONSIBILITY
Improve accuracy of production forecasts						
Enhance delivery of small quantities of raw materials frequently						
Assure vendor compliance of wrapping in exact quantities						
Check conformity to raw material quantity specifications						
Encourage proximity of suppliers to plant						
Provide for quick, easy detection of defective products						
Be willing to make engineering changes when required						
Increase inventory control system's responsiveness to JIT						
Assure production equipment is operating at maximum capacity						
Verify that equipment is running at rated speed						
Provide breakdown analysis of machines to isolate "losers"						

178 HANDBOOK OF COST REDUCTION TECHNIQUES

	Do maintenance in advance of peak periods
	Have planned replacement program of automated manual equipment
	Intensify use of numerical control programs
	Use CAD/CAM
	Examine overall plant size versus "scaled down" installation
	Review tools, jigs, etc.
	Use standard parts for different types of equipment
	Employ air pressure, gravity feed and other natural aids
	Use automatic feed mechanisms rather than manual
	Check accuracy of gauges and other measuring instruments
	Use advanced power tools (drills, hammers, etc.)
	Review degree of cross-training and flexibility to meet changing situations
	Evaluate quality of oral instructions by supervisors
	Evaluate quality of reference manuals for job procedures

PRODUCT ENGINEERING AND PRODUCTION TECHNIQUES 179

Monitor operators' current productivity, overall trend, and quality											
Determine whether operators are meeting prescribed schedules											
Examine job setups: Operator versus setup specialist											
Analyze strength of safety inspections (better morale, cost avoidance)											
Encourage production employee cost reduction suggestions											
Use Quality Circles to address specific production problems											
Pinpoint exact production stations causing high number of rejects											
Determine precise reasons for parts breakdowns											
Insure that customer returns can be traced to their production source											
Use computer aided design (CAD) to maximize product performance											
Employ robots for moving materials along prescribed paths											
Consider numerically controlled (NC) machines for specific manufacturing functions											
Combine robots and NC machines to move and operate on materials											
Integrate design, manufacturing, information management (CIM)											

ACTION CHECKLIST # 14

Product Engineering

ACTION FOCUS	N/A	STRONG	SATIS-FACTORY	NEEDS SOME IMPROVEMENT	WEAK: NEEDS MAJOR IMPROVEMENT	ACTION PLAN, RESPONSIBILITY
Intensify long-range planning for new product development						
Improve short-term planning for product improvement						
Participate in setting quality standards						
Develop more accurate product unit costs						
Evaluate customer inquiries for clues to product failures						
Review appropriations for research and development						
Investigate budget versus actual variances for new product development						
Report on projects with schedule overruns						
Coordinate with cost accounting function on analysis of reports						
Review procedures on treating costs as expenses or capital expenditures						
Automate system for estimating product costs						
Increase degree of component standardization as opposed to special design						
Improve accuracy of production time forecasts						
Clarify parts identification method						

PRODUCT ENGINEERING AND PRODUCTION TECHNIQUES

Check staffing of product engineering and use of outside consultants										
Use microfilm for reducing records management space and costs										
Make parts lighter through use of different materials										
Examine production tolerances for possible reduction										
Alter design to reduce scrap materials										
Check product for temperature and/or pressure specifications										
Substitute less expensive metals or plastics										
Attend vendor trade shows to save research money										
Visit key resources' plants to check facilities, quality control, distribution, financing										
Revitalize proven techniques which are not being used										
Intensify value analysis in product design										
Reduce special packages and/or labels without affecting aesthetics										
Question whether new products will add volume or detract from existing items										
Determine timing of new product introduction to consumers										
Check out economies in packaging, handling, distribution										
Have representative consumers field test product										

12

COST REDUCTION MEASURES IN MAINTENANCE, MACHINES AND EQUIPMENT

Experts divide maintenance work into the following four categories:

1. *Emergency:* repair equipment right away.
2. *Routine:* repair when convenient.
3. *Safety:* repair equipment so as to resolve a hazard before production work continues.
4. *Contract Maintenance:* use of outside resources.

There are many ways to reduce your maintenance costs. First, total the number of hours spent on maintenance and then divide it up among the following categories.

1. Productive time and acceptable nonproductive time, such as travel, meal breaks, preparation.
2. Nonproductive time including:

   · idle time involving avoidable breaks
   · travel for transporting equipment and inventory
   · excess personal time involving such activities as eating,

drinking, and resting over and above that which is in labor management contracts
- early quitting and late starts
- waiting for people, equipment, inventory, etc.
- receiving instructions and assignments on the job
- receiving and disposing of tools

In many companies, these nonproductive activities amount to as much as two-thirds of the working day. Here's what the Emerson Corporation recommends to decrease nonproductive time:

- Check the way maintenance staff is assigned and the degree of supervision.
- Tighten up the work relationship of the Maintenance department with others in the plant.
- Improve the identification, measuring, and managing of the workload.
- Use planning, scheduling, and control techniques.
- Increase the accuracy and timeliness of maintenance information.
- Enlarge the role of Engineering personnel in planning and installation of manufacturing plants.

Further analysis of maintenance expenses suggests a quick series of basic questions:

1. Why is the work done?
2. How much does it cost?
3. Why is it being done now?
4. What methods are used to do it?

If your company maintenance is subject to peaks and valleys, it is probably difficult to keep the size of your staff down and yet provide for high volume. To address this, look into the advantages and disadvantages of **contract maintenance**.

By using an outside contractor, you can avoid:

- fringe benefits, some taxes

- unemployment, social security, certain government payments
- vacation pay, worker's compensation
- other customary fringe benefits
- replacement worries due to vacations and/or absence
- extra expense of parts and special tools

Reducing maintenance costs can be achieved by establishing subsidiary repair departments, rather than a central one. Pinpoint pockets of unusual repair requirements and place your subsidiary repair facilities there. This reduces the amount of travel and handling. One steel company reports a 30 percent increase in production while holding maintenance costs steady by utilizing such a strategy.

PREVENTIVE MAINTENANCE

One important cost reduction tool which also pays off in terms of smooth production is **preventive maintenance.** The benefits of this strategy are:

- performance of the major part of maintenance at regular rates rather than overtime
- important production equipment made available when needed (avoid downtime)
- reduction of maintenance expenses

Here's what several leading companies recommend:

Hartford Steam Boiler Inspection and Insurance Company: budget and control preventive maintenance expenses and avoid overtime whenever possible.

Waldorf Paper Products Company: keep preventive maintenance manageable in size; don't oversell. Also "emphasize the philosophy . . . ." In other words, increase workers' attention to expense reduction techniques.

Buick Division of General Motors: have supervisors list machines that shut down key parts of production. Have them identify unique equipment or those with high price tags. At the end of a shift, report on machine conditions.

Another manufacturer condenses its maintenance list and puts it at selected machines. Operators are reminded about startup procedures, downtime reporting, and so on.

New York City decreased repair time of its Sanitation Department vehicles by about 50 percent. It set standards for particular phases of maintenance and repair and insured that vehicles were lubricated and otherwise serviced equal to or better than manufacturers' prescribed recommendations.

Western Electric, in one of its plants, has several key maintenance people with repair kits on tricycles. Rush requests are handled quickly.

Dupont Corporation claims savings of 15 to 20 percent by holding line managers responsible for maintenance. They are helped by Engineering. The specific techniques entail establishing benchmark figures for comparison purposes, using activity analysis, and auditing results. As part of the audits, existing systems and procedures are evaluated. Instructions are standardized and documented.

The Tactical Air Command of the United States Air Force used motivation in maintenance. The Commanding General focused positive attention on his maintenance and support crews by making them take pride in their accomplishments. Pictures of the individuals with their equipment, special ribbons, awards, and parades were used. The result: average time for parts delivery was reduced by almost 90 percent.

MORE MAINTENANCE TIPS

If possible, teach production workers to do simple maintenance on equipment. Having spare parts available will also increase up time.

Have your Industrial Engineering staff establish standard times and costs for doing routine repairs on equipment. Measure actual versus standard costs and take appropriate action on major variances.

Try to avoid rush orders on maintenance. These will raise havoc with your schedules and most often cost extra money whether on regular or overtime basis. If your production plant is spread over a wide area, consider providing maintenance personnel with pocket paging or walkie-talkie devices.

Some production machinery can be fitted with attachments to alert you to the number of hours a machine has been running without maintenance. In this way, preventive maintenance can be done on the basis of time in use.

Here's a very simple method of alerting you to continually defective equipment. Place a form by the machines, and ask your operators to record each time there is a problem. This will also indicate whether a piece of equipment should be replaced for cost reasons.

You can lay the foundation for a sound maintenance program by tailoring Action Checklist #15 to your special requirements.

Here's another way to make your people more aware of reducing equipment expense. Next to selected pieces of equipment, place a sign that says "This machine costs $_____." It's a constant reminder to your operators to take good care of the machines.

ENERGY REDUCTION

One of your major costs is undoubtedly energy (heating, ventilation, and air-conditioning). Some specific case studies illustrate the great economies possible in energy savings.

1. One corporation reduced costs by $6 million a year through insulation of valves and pipe connections.
2. Raytheon, in one of its plants, reported a 16 percent reduction in electricity usage through dual usage of its air-conditioner as a heating unit.
3. Air Canada uses automatic timers to turn off lights at preselected times. Result: $50,000 savings per year.
4. A leading firm producing wood products gets about 80 percent of its power by burning waste by-products once *discarded*.
5. Armstrong Cork Company uses an "Energy Conservation Task Force." The members look for sources of heat loss and suggest changes.

6. According to statistics, you can reduce power consumption from 5 watts to 2 watts per square foot by using task lighting rather than ambient. Besides cost reduction, glare and reflections are decreased.

Here are a few other energy tips:

- Turn off vending machine lights.
- Employ a *variable* air volume system (savings from 15 to 20 percent).
- Use infrared scanning to locate heat loss sources.
- Look into local utility discounts for off-peak times; if the lower rates are available, consider shifting some work to the alternate time periods.

MORE CASES OF ENERGY CONSERVATION

The National Lighting Bureau in Washington, D.C. has collected a series of case histories demonstrating the savings to be derived by using high-pressure sodium lighting (HPS).

It claims that a California manufacturer achieved cost reductions of almost $80,000 per year by converting from incandescent lighting. Moreover, productivity improvement resulted in another $170,000 savings per year. The company also documented a further savings of $13,000 as a result of fewer accidents.

Another manufacturer using HPS in lieu of mercury vapor saved $35,000 in operation and maintenance costs and $20,000 from a reduction in rejects.

A third manufacturer claims a productivity increase of $173,000 annually, a 50 percent reduction in rejects or $60,000 per year, and a decrease in accidents. Moreover, savings of $24,000 a year were estimated for operation and maintenance.

The following case history shows how one company instituted a companywide energy project. Use Action Checklist #16 to help create your own.

One Company's TOM Project

R. J. Reynolds Industries is a conglomerate with many subsidiaries and divisions. It has a highly decentralized program that incorporates energy management into its daily business operations.

Both minor and major projects are publicized. Among the company's tuning, operations, and maintenance (TOM) projects are the following.

At a canning plant, a forklift operator was in charge of eliminating excessive lighting in a warehouse. He marked the location of lights on a floor plan and color-coded the circuits and switches that controlled each area's lights. The floor plan was posted beside the electrical control panel. This encouraged employees to locate and light only the area in which they would be working. The monthly electricity bill for the warehouse dropped by $1,000.

At a raw tobacco storage shed in West Germany, the ventilating system was run at night when electricity rates were cheaper.

Reballasting, relamping, and cleaning lighting fixtures in a cigarette production area cost $19,000 and saved $48,000 a year.

Construction of heat recovery systems at three gin and vodka plants cost $8,500 each and saved the company $6,000 a year.

These are routine improvements that cost little and have fast paybacks. But even major projects don't necessarily have long paybacks. The computerized energy management system installed at a tobacco facility cost $300,000 and is saving more than $100,000 a year in reduced electricity bills. Heat recovery devices at the same facility permit use of waste heat and vented steam to heat water for manufacturing processes. The total expenditure, more than $435,000; annual saving, about $175,000.

PURCHASING MACHINERY

There are pros and cons about keeping used equipment as opposed to buying new. You can:

- Inquire about the cost of reconditioning some of your present equipment.

- Sell obsolete equipment to scrap dealers and replace it altogether.

One of your initial moves should be to examine the advantages and disadvantages of machine purchase, leasing, and renting.

1. *Purchase Equipment.* The advantage is, you own it. In the long run, it is the least expensive way of acquiring machines. The most serious disadvantage is the chance of obsolescence.
2. *Leasing Equipment.* This involves a fixed term, such as three, four, or five years. At the end of this period, you generally have the option of giving it back to the vendor or purchasing it for the portion of the lease applied to the purchase price. In the long run, you end up paying more than a straight purchase.
3. *Rental.* The major advantage of this method is the smaller monthly cost. A second major advantage is that there is hardly any fear of obsolescence because under most rental agreements, you can cancel or change a rental for a good reason. The most compelling reason against rental is that you are paying forever.

When considering purchasing machinery, you should look at such varying factors as purchase price, operating costs, opportunity cost (the return on investment), and salvage value. To clarify opportunity cost, you could have invested your idle cash and realized a return of a certain percent.

The following chart illustrates how your decision might be made based upon two options.

Factor	*Machine 1*	*Machine 2*
Purchase Price	$325,000	$400,000
+ Operating Costs for 5 years	75,000	60,000
+ Opportunity Costs for 5 years @ 8% each	187,731	215,891
= Gross Cost	587,731	675,891
− Salvage Value	35,000	70,000
= Net Cost	$552,731	$605,891

Machine #1 is the better investment because it costs less.

TRAINING AND RELIABILITY

Here are other considerations for cost reduction on machines and equipment. Training operators is a crucial factor. Not only are you keeping your equipment costs down, but you're improving quality as well. The initial training on a new piece of equipment is perhaps the most important because it is more difficult to undo bad habits than to train people correctly from the start.

Safety training on dangerous equipment has two advantages. It can help reduce accidents (lost time, insurance claims) and decrease expenses. Many companies have safety training directors. If your company is too small to warrant this full time position, you can appoint volunteers to do this.

Availability and reliability of vendor service should be carefully considered before purchasing a piece of equipment. One of the best ways to determine this is to get a list of owners of comparable or identical machines. Be aware that vendors generally will give you a list of only *satisfied* owners. Contact some of your associates in other companies. That way you can get a fairly good idea of the important factors in vendor service.

No machine is expected to last forever. Therefore, dependability of spare parts is a major consideration. This involves not only the supply but the proximity of the parts warehouse to your own facility. Normally, a contract for equipment should contain a clause which spells out spare parts agreements.

It would be a good idea to closely examine your machines and equipment, and list those which are absolutely critical. These critical machines should be prioritized, with suitable backup available at short notice.

Depreciation most often is looked at from an accounting standpoint, in terms of schedules. You should also have a master plan for replacing inefficient machines. In the long run, it is better to scrap certain pieces of equipment and replace them with newer models than to maintain production with them.

MORE MACHINE COST REDUCTION IDEAS

You can apply a process known as value analysis to some features. Critically examine the purpose and the cost effectiveness of various pieces of equipment that you have. Occasionally, you may have machines which are there for showcase reasons. These do not generate substantial amounts of income, and should be dealt with in a bottom-line-oriented manner.

Equipment experts recommend the use of posters and other media to dramatize the need for equipment care. These should be posted in high traffic areas and/or near the specific equipment, so that employees are aware of your emphasis on taking care of the machines.

It is a good idea to conduct periodic work-flow analyses in order to determine whether there are wasted steps in the production process. Moreover, you can use these techniques to find out whether a straight line is being employed or if the products are zig-zagging through your plant.

Another dramatic way to increase productivity on your machines and equipment is through the use of proper operator's seating, efficient lighting, and ventilation. In this connection, it is a good idea to audit these environmental conditions periodically to determine if they are at their best.

In order to assist you in rating your machines and equipment from a cost reduction standpoint, check out Action Checklist #17.

ACTION CHECKLIST # 15

Maintenance

ACTION FOCUS	N/A	STRONG	SATIS-FACTORY	NEEDS SOME IMPROVEMENT	WEAK: NEEDS MAJOR IMPROVEMENT	ACTION PLAN, RESPONSIBILITY
Categorize productive versus nonproductive hours						
Check maintenance assignments and degree of supervision						
Improve workload identification, measurement, management						
Use planning, scheduling, and control techniques (e.g., PERT/CPM)						
Increase accuracy/timeliness of maintenance information						
Increase Engineering's role in plant planning, installation						
Investigate pros and cons of contract maintenance						
Perform major maintenance at regular intervals						
Teach production workers simple preventive maintenance						
Establish standard times and costs for routine repairs						
Take appropriate action on major cost variances						
Emphasize preventive maintenance philosophy at all levels						
List machines that shut down key parts of production						

Identify equipment with high price tags											
Report at shift end on machine conditions											
Condense maintenance list and post at selected machines											
Insure that vehicles are serviced at or better than prescribed intervals											
Use mobile repair kits (bicycles, etc.)											
Employ activity analysis and auditing											
Standardize and document maintenance instructions											
Provide pocket pagers or walkie-talkie devices to summon personnel quickly											
Fit machinery with attachments to record running time cumulatively											
Have operators record problems on special forms at the machinery											
Consider reconditioning used equipment											
Sell obsolete machines to scrap dealers											
Remind operators of machine cost, use a sign showing replacement value											
Have Engineering approve or originate design specs for buildings & equipment											
Request a formal work order to improve planning and chargebacks											
Examine "backlog report" for critical items to be expedited											
Perform periodic safety checks											

COST REDUCTION MEASURES IN MAINTENANCE, MACHINES AND EQUIPMENT

Use colored tags to mark equipment needing repair or service	Recharge batteries on vehicles such as materials handlers, etc.	Combine and/or consolidate vehicle delivery routes	Place computer equipment away from open windows (sunlight, dirt, temperature, humidity changes)	Keep computers away from electrical machinery to prevent interference	Cover printers, consoles, floppy disks, personal computers, etc.	Enforce no smoking rules in computer centers	Install anti-static mats; spray carpeting	Periodically clean read/write heads with special diskettes	Put printing elements (including daisy wheels) into cases	Clean print wheels, chains and platens periodically	Use nonabrasive solutions and lint free cloths on terminal screens and keyboards	Maintain floppy disks in envelopes and avoid writing on them	Keep staples, paper clips off disks to keep from demagnetizing

ACTION CHECKLIST # 16

Energy

ACTION FOCUS	N/A	STRONG	SATIS-FACTORY	NEEDS SOME IMPROVEMENT	WEAK: NEEDS MAJOR IMPROVEMENT	ACTION PLAN, RESPONSIBILITY
Stop leaks of heat and air conditioning						
Reduce temperature on thermostats during certain periods						
Insulate walls, floors, pipes, etc.						
Use solar heating where applicable						
Print employee reminders to put lights off						
Use automatic light dimmers and/or shutoff switches						
Employ timers to shut off equipment after prescribed time						
Appoint departmental "energy-watchers" to coordinate program						
Use alternate fuels including production by-products (waste)						
Audit energy bills and meters						
Examine equipment power requirements						

COST REDUCTION MEASURES IN MAINTENANCE, MACHINES AND EQUIPMENT

Upgrade wiring	Use heat exchangers, etc.	Track energy bills for unusual increases in costs	Use different temperature standards for winter versus summer	Keep doors and windows closed	Encourage employees to wear suitable clothing	Install air seals at loading dock entrances	Check energy efficiency ratings of electrical equipment	Convert lighting fixtures to more efficient types (mercury, sodium)	Remind employees to shut off vehicle engines when not in use	Obtain heating and air conditioning from a single unit	Recognize outstanding employees with appropriate awards	Upgrade furnaces for greater fuel efficiency	Seal up cracks around windows and doors, change to double insulated

198   HANDBOOK OF COST REDUCTION TECHNIQUES

Plug up leaks in steam lines	Clean and service boilers, fans and blowers	Use window coverings and insulating film to reduce energy consumption	Try spring loaded faucets to shut off water automatically	Reduce hot water temperature; avoid mixing with cold water	Consider premium awards for energy suggestions	Reduce exterior lighting to minimum safe levels	Use variable speed motors where applicable	Clean or replace air filters	Convert from ambient to task lighting	Turn off vending machine lights	Employ a variable air volume system	Use infra-red scanning to locate sources of heat loss	Take advantage of off-peak utility discounts; shift work accordingly

ACTION CHECKLIST # 17

Machines and Equipment

ACTION FOCUS	N/A	STRONG	SATIS-FACTORY	NEEDS SOME IMPROVEMENT	WEAK: NEEDS MAJOR IMPROVEMENT	ACTION PLAN, RESPONSIBILITY
Pinpoint pros and cons of equipment purchase vs. rental vs. leasing						
Train machine operators thoroughly; maintain progress reports						
Evaluate availability and reliability of vendor service						
Keep detailed records on dependability of spare parts						
Provide backup priority list for critical equipment						
Replace inefficient machines with newer ones						
Conduct safety training on hazardous equipment to reduce accidents						
Question equipment features for cost effectiveness						
Use posters and other media to dramatize need for equipment care						
Chart workflows to isolate wasted steps						
Chart workflows to see if straight line method is used						

13

EXPENSE REDUCTION THROUGH AN INTEGRATED MANUFACTURING INFORMATION SYSTEM

The major steps in traditional accounting systems are depicted in the first half of Exhibit 42.

1. Start with a source document to post the results in a journal.
2. Record journal entries in the ledger and then summarize.
3. Take a trial balance to reconcile debits and credits.
4. Produce the key financial documents, such as the income statement, balance sheet, and changes in financial position.

Traditionally, budgets may be a by-product of these systems. The one major flaw in this scheme is the lack of integration with the manufacturing process.

In order to address this, executives have attempted to put together manufacturing information systems that include the financial aspects. The bottom half of Exhibit 42 identifies the major organizational functions as Purchasing, Production, Marketing, and Financial. Within those major functions are numerous sub-functions, including:

- purchasing—inventory
- production—work in process and finished goods

TRADITIONAL ACCOUNTING SYSTEMS

Source Documents

Post Results in Journal

Record Journal Entries in Ledgers

Summarize

Trial Balance (Debits = Credits)

| Income Statement | Balance Sheet | Financial Position Changes |

BASIC MANUFACTURING INFORMATION SYSTEM

Purchasing
- Raw Materials
- Inventory

Production
- Work-In-Process
- Finished Goods

Financial
- Payroll
- Accounts Receivable
- Accounts Payable
- Cash Receipts and Disbursements

Marketing
- Sales

Statements
- Balance Sheet
- Profit and Loss
- Budgets

Exhibit 42.
Relationship between accounting and manufacturing information systems

```
┌─────────────────────────────────────────────────────────┐
│                  BASIC INFORMATION FLOW                 │
│                  (Sub-systems within function)          │
│  Expense                                                │
│                                                         │
│  • Procurement and vendor control ──────┐               │
│  • Receiving and inspection             │               │
│  • Accounts payable                     │               │
│                                         │               │
│  Production ──────────── Finance        │               │
│                                         │               │
│  • Inventory control      • Cash receipts and disbursements │
│  • Production control     • Property control            │
│  • Payroll and labor      • General ledger              │
│    distribution                                         │
│                                         │               │
│  Income                                 │               │
│                                                         │
│  • Marketing                                            │
│  • Shipping and transportation                          │
│  • Billing and collection                               │
└─────────────────────────────────────────────────────────┘
```

Exhibit 43.
A classic information flow relationship

- marketing—sales
- financial—accounts payable, payroll, and receipts or disbursements of cash

Exhibit 43 shows a classic, basic information flow in a manufacturing environment with twelve sub-systems in a typical manufacturing firm. This relationship holds the key for the practical analysis, design, and implementation of an overall integrated manufacturing information system as a basis for expense reduction.

EXPLAINING THE SYSTEM

The four cycles are expense, production, income, and finance. Each of these in turn has three sub-systems. Here are their objectives.

The Expense Function
Procurement and vendor control meet the raw material requirements of the production process while preventing excessive inventory accumulations; obtain quality material, on time, and at the lowest possible cost.

Receiving and inspection confirm the receipt of materials in a proper way according to company policy and procedures.

Accounts payable pays vendors in a timely manner, at the same time making sure that material was officially ordered, was actually received in proper condition, and is billed in accordance with the terms and conditions of the purchase order.

The Production Function
Inventory control maintains minimum stock levels, yet still insures that material flows smoothly through the system and that production line stoppages do not occur.

Production control produces a product, with concentration on quality, schedule, standards, budget, and performance; coordinates this function with Marketing, Engineering, Inventory. As a by-product of Production Control, makes cost distributions.

Payroll and distribution reimburses employees for their performance and maintains required records for government authorities. Interacts with other sub-systems to distribute labor costs by certain predetermined standards.

The Income Function
Marketing is the intermediary between production and consumption, so relates sales forecasts to the overall company business plan (Master Production Schedule) and production capacity in order to determine inventory levels, improve cash management, and so on. As another function, services accounts properly.

Shipping and transportation ensures that all merchandise sold is properly packaged and shipped in accordance with agreements. Coordinates with billing and collection because shipping/transportation documents serve as a basis for charging the customer. Accurate shipping documents provide audit trails for checking with carriers and for determining start dates for cash discounts.

Billing and collection sends an invoice for each shipment and follows up until the customer pays for the shipment.

The Finance Function

Cash receipts and disbursements. Cash is a current asset of the company and should be treated accordingly. Therefore, accounting controls should be very tight on the handling of cash. The two transaction types are receipts and disbursements. Receipts are generally referred to as accounts receivable. They involve recording and handling of incoming cash from customers. On the disbursement side, the accounts payable operation involves preparing checks and distributing disbursements to vendors, employees, and so on.

Property control. Fixed assets such as land, buildings, and equipment represent major investments in manufacturing companies. The focus areas are obsolescence, depreciation, and physical control. The objective of the property control system is to properly control and value fixed assets so that they directly reflect their true value on the company books.

General ledger prepares formal and informal statements reflecting the financial position at any point in time. The key documents are income statements, balance sheets, and budgets. Maintains audit trails so that a document or a transaction can be traced from its outset until its completion in the cycle.

AN MIS IN ACTION

Exhibit 44 shows a "live" integrated manufacturing system and how it works in practice. This particular one from Xerox Computer Services sets out three areas of manufacturing information systems: manufacturing, financial, and distribution. Similar to the previously outlined conceptual flow, each of these has its own sub-systems.

1. *Manufacturing:* procurement management, cost planning and control, material requirements planning (MRP), master production scheduling, repetitive manufacturing, random stores, production cycle, physical inventory, inventory management.

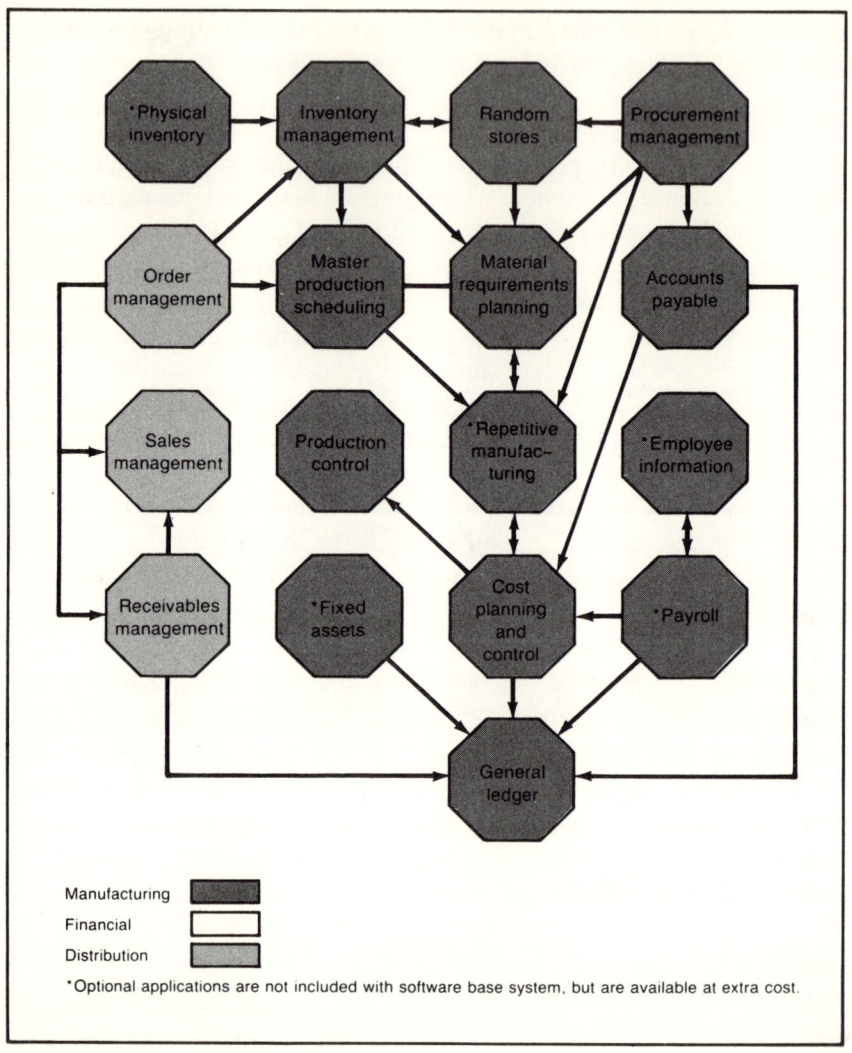

Exhibit 44.
An actual Manufacturing Information System

2. *Financial Systems:* payroll, employee information, accounts payable, general ledger, fixed assets.
3. *Distribution:* receivables management, sales management, order management.

The application software for this system was developed by Xerox Computer Services and is available in three ways:

1. Combination of its software with a current IBM computer.
2. A turnkey system where Xerox packages its entire software system on IBM hardware as a total system. One of the major advantages of this system is that it avoids the difficult task of identifying, evaluating, selecting, and installing separate components. These are data communications, database manager, report program generator, programming languages, systems security, and so on.
3. Remote job entry, utilizing an outside computer and software with terminals placed on your premises. With this alternative you avoid the responsibility associated with selecting, owning, and running hardware.

Whichever option you choose, you would employ a common database. In this way, every part of your company (manufacturing, marketing, distribution, engineering, procurement, finance, and planning) works with the same information. That information (such as last receipt of inventory, purchase order, or sales order) is instantaneously available to all users.

The Xerox sub-systems with narrative descriptions follow. These information modules will give you a good idea of what to look for in systems like this. Exhibit 45 at the end of this chapter illustrates a number of actual examples derived from this system.

Inventory Management
This application is designed to provide up-to-date, accurate information on stock availability in either a single or multi-stock environment. The records provide answers to many questions and keep a running balance of stock position. Critical to increasing profit is the ability to maximize inventory turns, while at the same time maintaining high customer service levels.

Physical Inventory
Inventory variance and value distribution reports are available. An

accurate and timely count of the inventory can be done in several ways, such as on a yearly basis, random counting, and so on. In addition, a request results in a generation of count tags of every part *or* selective parts in stock. Balances, ranking, and cycle counting also are available. Included in this module are order point and order quantity features.

Material Requirements Planning (MRP)
This sub-system provides timely information for users responsible for determining material requirements and designing product structures. It is possible to cost the current material plan including purchase orders and plant purchase orders, as well as to determine available quantities according to user-defined time periods. In addition, you can set multiple lead times for an analyst or buyer.

Master Production Schedule
This module provides valuable information for your people who are responsible for determining inventory investment, production rate, and delivery service. An additional feature is exception notification from the terminal screen. Importantly, you have the ability to reconcile forecasts to real demand. The master production schedule reconciles the resources of manufacturing to the requirements of marketing. The production planner has a "what if" modeling capability that enables you to see the effect of changes on the entire system instantly.

Cost Planning and Control
This provides the tools for operating a complete and comprehensive manufacturing and accounting system. Each order is classified and maintained as labor, material, other direct charges, or applied overhead. Standard and/or actual cost postings are supported. Report for audit trails and management planning and control of costs are available. Additional features are standard costs, variances, and relationships with payroll, inventory, etc.

Production Control
In a typical manufacturing plant, the production is either job shop or repetitive manufacturing. This module works primarily in a job shop

environment. Provided features are loading, scheduling, daily dispatch lists,"what if" simulations, or changes of crew size. Multiple scheduling techniques, such as forward, backward, mid-scheduling, are available.

There are basically three tasks that this application fulfills. They are:

1. *Capacity Planning:* Problems can be anticipated and headed off by various capacity-adjusting techniques such as working overtime, extra shifts, extra manpower, subcontracting, and alternative routing. This also provides the ability to group your orders by work center and allows planners to make adjustments for alleviating capacity problems.

2. *Capacity Control:* Tells you whether or not your capacity requirements plan is working. It measures what has taken place in your shop and spotlights how well the systems are meeting the production plan.

3. *Priority Control:* Provides an aid for shop floor personnel directing work center people to meet the overall production schedule.

Repetitive Manufacturing

This application is specifically designed for high-volume manufacturers to help minimize inventory levels and paperwork. Through the use of this application, you can achieve the results of Just-In-Time (JIT) inventory. You also substantially reduce inventories by keeping work in process to a minimum, thereby reducing or eliminating bottlenecks and providing parts to the production line only in the quantities needed and at the time desired.

Random Stores

This application allows you to store inventory (with the same part number) in multiple locations while maintaining separate costs and quantities for each item location. It's beneficial to companies which maintain lot-controlled inventories.

Procurement Management

Purchase orders automatically can use selected vendors with an allocation table of pre-established percentages. By doing this, you can be assured that any part is always obtained from the correct mix of vendors. Your purchasing agent can also create, adjust, or cancel requisitions/purchase orders on line. You can pinpoint receipts to their specific purchase orders.

Accounts Payable
This helps you improve your profitability through better liability management. The sub-system aids in improving cash flow while giving realistic time information and reducing clerical effort. Benefits include:

1. *Better Cash Management:* Maximizes the availability of cash, allowing you to profitably invest in other areas. Minimizes payments by automatically applying credit due from vendors and claiming all discounts where appropriate. In addition, defers cash payments until the last possible date, while still keeping good vendor relations.

2. *Reduces Clerical Effort:* The amount of paperwork is decreased because all information is entered into the system on line. As included in all applications, the user has menus and screens available and can modify them where appropriate. Included are "help" menus, which also can be changed.

General Ledger
A comprehensive financial system that provides your management with all the information necessary for audits, financial statements, ratios, and consolidations of multi-division information. It's an actual time system because any transaction being processed in any application area is *immediately* recorded in the general ledger and all affected applications, giving you up-to-the-minute profit statements and cash flow analysis. Other important features are audit trails and accurate journal entries and budgets.

Particularly useful with the general ledger, but true of all the applications, is the ability to down-load data from your mainframe database and use it on your personal computer for modeling and analysis or with applications such as electronic spreadsheets. Additionally, there are conversion tables for various foreign currencies.

Payroll

This application fulfills the fundamentals of recording hours worked and salaries paid. It stores correct tax tables. Clerical effort is reduced because the system provides on-line validation and balancing. Provision is made for an employee history file, as well as direct deposit and multiple paying methods. In terms of actual payroll, you can select from different cycles such as weekly, bi-weekly, semi-monthly, and monthly. A payroll register lists earnings and deductions for each employee.

The labor distribution feature allows the money and hours to be recorded for specific jobs, functions, projects, and cost centers for other activities. You select the break-out.

Fixed Assets

Three of the major features of this application are:

1. retaining information concerning the asset's original cost, depreciation, and location
2. wide variety of depreciation methods, such as straight line, double declining balance, and sum of the digits
3. forecasting, including the ability to effectively develop expense budgets and projections

Order Management

This module takes in all facets of the order entry/invoicing cycle. It includes sales orders and credit memos, credit checking, promised delivery day verification and back-order/backlog control. It is also integrated with inventory management, allowing you to verify the inventory status at the time of order entry.

The system maintains a cross-reference of superseded and replacement parts so that proper substitutes can be used. You can see the inventory for multiple locations and reallocate materials where necessary. In addition, there is multiple shipping date control, on-line credit checking, and the capability of Just-In-Time inventory procedures. There also are automatic back-order generators and automatic posting to the general ledger.

Sales Management

The purpose of this sub-system is to pinpoint profitability of products and product lines, customers, sales regions, territories, and sales representatives. It allows you to observe buying trends, conduct analysis of current activity and comparisons to past performance, and enables you to identify marketing trends. By retaining thirteen months of sales history, you can compare current year results of sales and bookings with those of comparable periods last year. By doing so, you can determine the profit of each product by customer, sales representative, and/or distributor, and so on. Another valuable feature enables you to convert all the rows of columns of figures into a graph, allowing you to examine trends and make forecasts more easily.

Receivables Management

Provides you with timely and accurate information on this current asset. Using a terminal, you can inquire about account balances, credit limits, and overdue accounts. Reports include detailed agings and statements. Additionally, the system produces a list of delinquent and/or inactive accounts, so as to improve cash receipts. You have a choice of balance forward or open item listing on accounts receivable.

You can run credit management reports for all or selected customers who have exceeded their credit limits or are delinquent. This helps credit managers make better decisions.

A FINAL NOTE

All the applications described here are supported by a series of end user tools known as Information Center Products. These tools allow you to specifically tailor the applications or their output to the unique needs of a user, department, or the company. All the enhancements are done through the use of "high level" English language based tools that require little, if any, understanding of data processing or programming.

The effect of an integrated manufacturing information system such as this one will be dramatic expense reduction. Action Checklist #18 will help you evaluate your present or proposed system.

PHYSICAL INVENTORY VARIANCE REPORT

AMERICAN MANUFACTURING COMPANY   PHYSICAL INVENTORY VARIANCE REPORT   6-30-XX   PAGE 2

TAG NO.	BIN	PART NUMBER	NSTK	DESCRIPTION	COUNT	ON HAND	VARIANCE	COST
101	SR2-1	1P1		NAME PLATE	11000.00	50.000		
110	SR2-1				123.00			
113	SR2-1				333.00			
				TOTAL	11456.00	50.00	11406.00–	52514.01–
102	CC2-1	1P2		MODIFIED COMM BOARD	22000.00	8000.00		
111	CC2-1				432.00			
				TOTAL	22432.00	8000.00	14432.00–	.00
103	TT3-1	15A1		SUB-ASSY CHASSIS	33000.00	155.00		
112	TT3-1				789.00			
114	TT3-1				555.00			
				TOTAL	34344.00	155.00	34189.00–	73625.00–
104	DF-41	15A2		ASSEMBLED CAGE	44000.00	9542.00	34458.00–	91600.00–
105	8A1-1	15A3		KEYPAD SUB-ASSY	256.00	634.00	378.00	28350.00
106	AA5-1	2P1		FRONT PANEL	666.00	300.00	366.00–	54900.00–
107		2P4		BRAIDED WIRE HARNESS	566.00	938.00	372.00	3373.36
108	MN4-1	25A1		SUB-ASSY TRANSFORMER	45687.00	100.00	45587.00–	.00
109	MN3-1	25AIN		SUB-ASSY TRANSFORMER.	333.00	60.00	273.00–	1820.00–

Supplemental tags assigned to the part (1P1).

Total quantity of all tag counts for the part.

This report indicates the variance between the physical count and the quantity on hand in the part record both in units and dollars.

Exhibit 45.
Actual sample from an MIS

VALUE DISTRIBUTION REPORT

AMERICAN MANUFACTURING COMPANY   VALUE DISTRIBUTION REPORT   RANK SELECTION A   6-30-XX   PAGE 1

DIV. PART NUMBER			YTD UNITS ISSUED	CUM UNITS ISSUED	CUM % ISS	ON HAND AT COST	CUM ON HAND AT COST	CUM % ON HAND	YTD UNITS AT SELL	CUM UNITS AT SELL	CUM % SELL
01 1P1	1	1 EA	658	658	25.23	570	570	1.36	12502	12502	3.14
01 2P1	2	1 EA	500	1158	44.40	275	845	2.01	4625	17127	4.30
01 1A1	3	1 EA	330	1488	57.06	297	1142	2.72	197984	215111	54.02
01 1SA1	4	1 EA	325	1813	69.52	166	1308	3.11	18119	233230	58.57
01 1SA2	5	1 EA	300	2113	81.02	0	1308	3.11	88500	321730	80.79
01 2SA1	6	1 EA	250	2363	90.61	156	1464	3.48	2998	324728	81.54
01 1A2	7	1 EA	245	2608	100.00	11357	12821	30.48	73498	398226	100.00
01 1P2	8	1 EA	0	2608	100.00	875	13696	32.56	0	398226	100.00

Year-to-date units activity

Units activity for this and all preceding parts relative to unit activity for all parts

Year-to-date unit activity with dollar extension

Indicates which one of the following ranking criteria was used:
A. Year-to-date units issued
B. Year-to-date units sold
C. Year-to-date units issued at normal selling price
D. Year-to-date units sold at normal selling price
E. Year-to-date units issued at client-selected cost
F. Year-to-date units sold at client-selected cost
G. Year-to-date units issued at margin (C–E)
H. Year-to-date units sold at margin (D–F)
I. Current quantity on hand at client-selected cost

This report calculates inventory activity by part and ranks each part using one of nine criteria. This report ranks parts by units issued year-to-date.

Exhibit 45.
Continued

MASTER PRODUCTION SCHEDULE

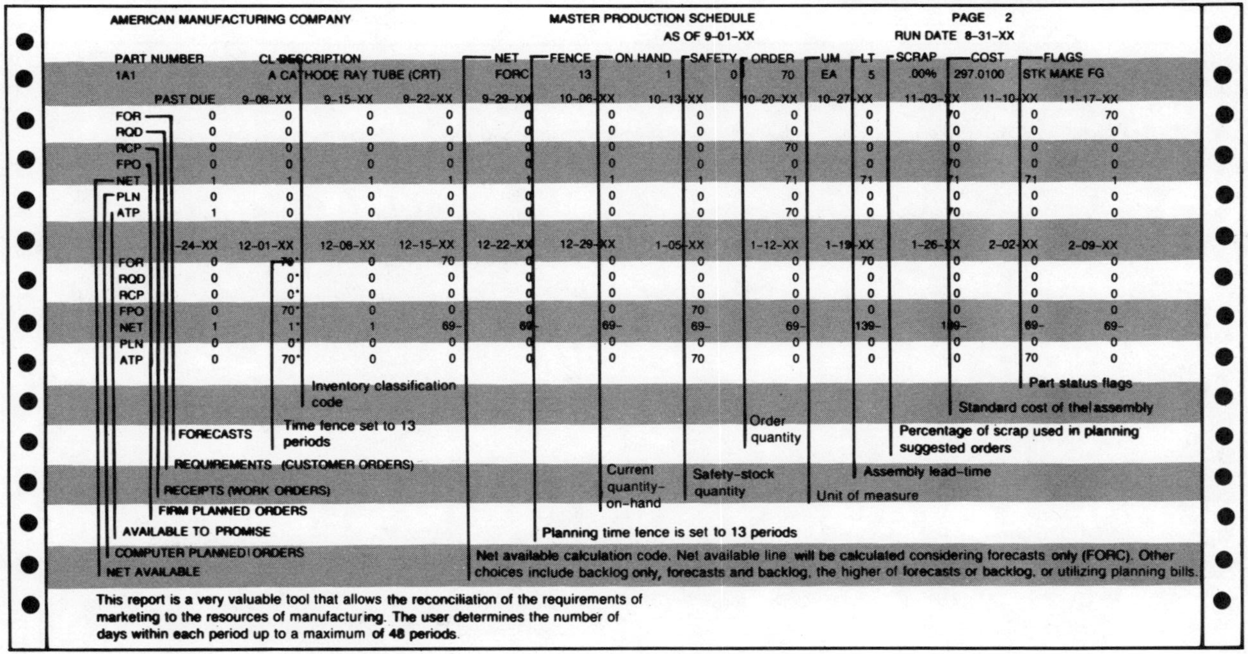

	PAST DUE	9-08-XX	9-15-XX	9-22-XX	9-29-XX	10-06-XX	10-13-XX	10-20-XX	10-27-XX	11-03-XX	11-10-XX	11-17-XX
FOR	0	0	0	0	0	0	0	0	0	70	0	70
RQD	0	0	0	0	0	0	0	0	0	0	0	0
RCP	0	0	0	0	0	0	0	70	0	0	0	0
FPO	0	0	0	0	0	0	0	0	0	70	0	0
NET	1	1	1	1	1	1	1	71	71	71	71	1
PLN	0	0	0	0	0	0	0	0	0	0	0	0
ATP	1	0	0	0	0	0	0	70	0	70	0	0

	-24-XX	12-01-XX	12-08-XX	12-15-XX	12-22-XX	12-29-XX	1-05-XX	1-12-XX	1-19-XX	1-26-XX	2-02-XX	2-09-XX
FOR	0	70*	0	70	0	0	0	0	70	0	0	0
RQD	0	0*	0	0	0	0	0	0	0	0	0	0
RCP	0	0*	0	0	0	0	0	0	0	0	0	0
FPO	0	70*	0	0	0	0	70	0	0	0	0	0
NET	1	1*	1	69-	69-	69-	69-	69-	139-	139-	69-	69-
PLN	0	0*	0	0	0	0	0	0	0	0	0	0
ATP	0	70*	0	0	0	0	70	0	0	0	70	0

This report is a very valuable tool that allows the reconciliation of the requirements of marketing to the resources of manufacturing. The user determines the number of days within each period up to a maximum of 48 periods.

Exhibit 45.
Continued

STANDARD COST BUILDUP REPORT

6-21-XX PAGE 1

ASSEMBLY PART NO. DESCRIPTION
1A1 CATHODE RAY TUBE (CRT)

STANDARD COST BUILD UP REPORT
UN   LAST UPDATE
EA   6-05-XX

COMPONENT PART NO	DESCRIPTION	AC	MB	QTY/ASSY U/M	MATERIAL	LABOR	OUTSIDE PROC.	BURDEN	TOTAL
1P1	NAME PLATE	C	B	1.0000 EA	11.0000	0.0000	0.0000	0.0000	11.0000
1SA1	SUB-ASSY CHASSIS	A	M	1.0000 EA	15.5000	9.4069	0.0000	7.8194	32.7263
1SA2	ASSEMBLED CAGE	A	M	1.0000 EA	158.9000	26.7718	0.0000	21.4513	207.1231
	SUB-TOTAL				185.4000	36.1787	0.0000	29.2707	250.8494

JOB STEP	FUNCTION CTR	MACH	DEPT	LABOR RATE	BURDEN RATE	SET/UP TIME	RUN TIME	LABOR	BURDEN	TOTAL
10	10	10	700	3.0000	25.00	0.3500	0.2550	1.8150	0.4538	2.2688
20	20	20	500	5.0000	110.00	0.5000	0.5000	5.0000	5.5000	10.5000
30	30	30	700	3.0000	25.00	0.7500	0.5000	3.7500	0.9375	4.6875
120	120	120	500	5.0000	110.00	0.1000	0.0750	0.8750	0.8625	1.8375
140	140	140	700	3.0000	25.00	0.0000	1.0000	3.0000	0.7500	3.7500
	SUB-TOTAL							14.4400	8.6038	23.0438

ASSEMBLY BUILDUP COSTS							370.8000	102.8406	25.0000	80.2227	578.8633
CURRENT COSTS ON FILE							173.3700	45.0100	19.0000	58.7300	297.0100
VARIANCE							197.4300	56.9306	6.0000	21.4927	281.8533

- Make or Buy part indicator
- Assembly or component indicator
- Labor routing for the assembly
- Standard departmental labor burden rate
- Component parts from the assembly's bill of material
- Standard departmental labor rate
- Unit of measure indicator

This report builds the cost of assemblies by accumulating the cost of component parts, based on the bills of material, and the production/assembly cost, based on the routing information associated with the assembly parts. Costs are calculated and displayed by the elements of material, labor, burden and outside processing. For each assembly the report compares the total build-up cost by element to the previous standard cost by element, and calculates and displays the variance between them. A report option allows the processing of all assemblies on file or the processing of only a single assembly.

The standard cost build-up reports is an invaluable capability for companies on a standard cost accounting system and also for companies which require product cost data for contract estimating, customer quotations, and pricing decisions.

Exhibit 45.
Continued

INPUT/OUTPUT CONTROL REPORT

AMERICAN MANUFACTURING COMPANY
PERIOD 12-14-XX TO 5-31-XX
PAGE 1
RUN DATE 5-31-XX

WORK CENTER		1 12-14-XX	2 12-21-XX	3 12-28-XX	4 1-04-XX	5 1-11-XX	6 1-18-XX	7 1-25-XX	8 2-01-XX	9 2-08-XX	10 2-15-XX	11 2-22-XX	12 3-01-XX	PERIOD TOTAL
10	ASSEMBLY													
	CAPACITY	0	350.0	350.0	350.0	350.0	350.0	350.0	350.0	350.0	350.0	350.0	350.0	8,050.0
INPUT:	PLAN	300.0	300.0	300.0	300.0	400.0	400.0	400.0	400.0	400.0	400.0	400.0	400.0	8,570.0
	ACTUAL	250.0	300.0	489.3	0	0	0	0	0	0	24.0	0	0	1,063.3
	CUM DEV	50.0	220.0-	409.3-	109.3-	290.7	690.7	1090.7	1490.7	1890.7	2266.7	2666.7	3066.7	7,506.7
OUTPUT:	PLAN	500.0	500.0	500.0	500.0	500.0	500.0	500.0	500.0	500.0	500.0	500.0	500.0	12,000.0
	ACTUAL	300.0	650.3	567.5	0	0	0	0	0	0	0	0	0	1,529.8
	CUM LEV	200.0	49.7	17.8-	482.2	982.2	1482.2	1982.2	2482.2	2982.2	3482.2	3982.2	4482.2	9,999.9
100	SLITTING OPERATION													
	CAPACITY	0	800.0	800.0	800.0	800.0	800.0	800.0	800.0	800.0	800.0	800.0	800.0	18,400.0
INPUT:	PLAN	600.0	800.0	600.0	600.0	600.0	600.0	600.0	600.0	600.0	600.0	600.0	600.0	14,800.0
	ACTUAL	1,002.3	500.5	750.3	0	0	0	0	0	.9	0	0	0	2,254.9
	CUM DEV	202.3-	97.2	53.1-	546.9	1146.9	1740.9	2346.9	2946.9	3546.9	4146.0	4746.0	5346.0	9,999.9
OUTPUT:	PLAN	1,000.0	1,000.0	1,000.0	1,000.0	1,000.0	1,000.0	1,000.0	1,000.0	1,000.0	1,000.0	1,000.0	1,000.0	24,000.0
	ACTUAL	1,234.6	289.4	1,489.5	0	0	0	0	0	0	0	0	0	3,013.5
	CUM DEV	234.6-	476.0	13.5-	986.5	1986.5	2986.5	3986.5	4986.5	5986.5	6986.5	7986.5	8986.5	9,999.9

This report compares the planned and actual input (in standard hours) to the planned and actual output for a work center. It highlights potential production line problems caused by excess or insufficient capacity.

Exhibit 45.
Continued

ACTION CHECKLIST # 18

Integrated Manufacturing Information Systems

ACTION FOCUS	N/A	STRONG	SATIS-FACTORY	NEEDS SOME IMPROVEMENT	WEAK: NEEDS MAJOR IMPROVEMENT	ACTION PLAN, RESPONSIBILITY
Meet raw material requirements of production process						
Prevent excess inventory accumulations						
Provide current, accurate stock status						
Highlight significant variances between book and physical inventories						
Indicate fast and slow sellers						
Produce preprinted count tags						
Allow flexibility in count cycles (annual, monthly, cyclical, etc.)						
Generate timely, accurate master production schedules						
Permit modeling ("what if") to simulate effects of changes						
Calculate bills of material value						
Compare planned versus actual labor hours in detail						
Schedule parts shipments on a planned rather than crisis basis						
Avoid extra shifts and overtime by adjusting capacity						
Check off receipts to appropriate purchase order						

Project cash flow through relationship to Purchasing sub-system	Provide for Just-In-Time applications to reduce inventories	Allow random stores feature to handle multiple locations	Automatically select vendors to keep acceptable mix of resources	Maximize cash discounts and vendor credits	Enter input on-line to reduce data entry costs	Post financial information directly to journals, ledgers	Prepare balance sheets, P&L, budgets as by-products of system	Generate all mandated and optional payroll forms, reports	Provide proper audit trails for internal and legal purposes	Allow downloading to personal computer for electronic spreadsheets, etc.	Produce depreciation schedules for fixed assets (land, building, equipment)	Integrate with comprehensive order-entry system	Evaluate sales performance by person, geographic area, customer, product	Age accounts receivables, print reports on inactive or delinquent customers

14

COST ESTIMATING AND CONTROL TO REDUCE EXPENDITURES

Your company's assets, liabilities, and net worth appear on its balance sheet. In order to estimate manufacturing cost, look at the other major financial statement on which such expenses are summarized—the income statement, also called the profit and loss statement or "P&L."

The three major components of cost of goods manufactured are labor, raw materials, and factory overhead.

These should be part of a standardized, systematic **chart of accounts** which lists account numbers and names. Many financial experts recommend a format like the following:

CHART OF ACCOUNTS

Balance Sheet Items		Income Statement Items	
Acct #	*Category*	*Acct #*	*Category*
100-199	Assets (current & fixed)	400-499	Income (revenue)
200-299	Liabilities (current, long-term)	500-599	Expenses
300-399	Equity (net worth)	600-699	Special, Tax Items

221

By making them uniform, all your concerned employees can find specific manufacturing expense items in your manual or computer system. This also allows for less costly preparation of financial statements. When you need detailed analysis, you can do this more easily by preparing comparative expense runs.

The format would look like the following:

COST OF GOODS MANUFACTURED ($)—COMPARISON

(Date)

Item	Last Year Current Month	This Year Current Month	% Change	Last Year Cum.	This Year Cum.	% Change
Direct Labor	25,160	27,843	+10.7	327,100	347,800	+6.3
Raw Materials	14,158	13,749	−2.9	182,470	180,625	−1.1
Plant Overhead	17,051	17,186	+0.8	224,300	225,500	+0.5
Total	56,369	58,778	+4.3	733,870	753,925	+2.7

Note the percent change of direct labor (both for the current month and cumulatively). This account should be checked further. Raw materials and plant overhead appear to be at or about the same as comparable previous periods.

Use systematic, agreed-upon production standards. Have clear-cut definitions of profit centers, cost centers, charts of accounts. Track your production forecasts by months and quarters. Compare them to actuals and refine future projections. Improve timeliness of cost reports by computerizing where appropriate. Match "dates sent out" with "action taken dates" to measure how timely the response is.

Request explanations of variances between budgeted and actual expenses. Research your competitors' costs to determine whether they are higher or lower for comparable/identical products.

Use the latest systems techniques for tracking expenses. Maintain a clear distinction between fixed and variable costs. Keep in mind that variable ones are more controllable.

You can take concrete cost reduction action by having your people study the following specific line items:

1. *Direct labor:* excess overtime, production delays, degree of operator training
2. *Raw materials:* purchasing department procurement expenses, inventory carrying costs, purchase order generation expenses
3. *Plant overhead:* fixed and variable occupancy costs, marketing expenses, administrative costs, travel and entertainment

Tip: One medium-sized manufacturer graphs the above elements for thirteen weeks to see what the quarterly trend is.

COST PER DIRECT LABOR HOUR

Generally, time cards are only used to record time in/time out. By definition, direct labor expenses are directly incurred when producing the product. If you want to categorize direct labor, you can employ a **job card.** This is the primary form for collecting times attributed to specific products, productive versus nonproductive time, and so forth. It can accompany the employee as he or she goes to different locations as well.

A good format is shown in the top half of Exhibit 46. Summarize the Lost Time Codes and Lost Time along with the causes in the Remarks section. Rank the causes by time lost and take corrective action. See the example in the bottom half of Exhibit 46.

ANALYZING AND CHARGING MANUFACTURING COSTS

Product costs are usually divided into: material, direct labor, and overhead. The last factor is categorized as follows:

Job Card For _JOHN DOE_ Date _Mar. 15, 1986_

Cost Center (Process Center)	Location	Start Time	Stop Time	Lost Time Code*	Lost Time	Part or Product Number	Quantity Produced	Remarks
127	Section 2	9:00	11:00	1	.30	706	200	Lack Raw Mat.
231	Section 2	12:00	2:30	5	1.00	1310	600	Machine Down
245	Section 2	2:45	5:00	2	.30	1220	250	Unfamiliar With Equip.

Supervisor's Signature _____

Lost Time Codes: 1 = Waiting for Material   3 = Inspection   5 = Maintenance
                 2 = Instruction   4 = Equipment Stoppage   6 = _____

Monthly Report: Cost Center 127

Reason	% of Lost Time	Action
Waiting for Material	20.6	Contact Vendors
Maintenance	13.4	Train Operators

Exhibit 46.
Creating a job card measurement

- indirect labor
    - ——production (supervision, material handling, clerical quality control, and process engineering)
    - ——purchasing and production control (material control, scheduling receiving, storing)
    - ——other (industrial engineering, cost accounting, human resources)
- maintenance and repairs
- occupancy
- noncapital equipment and tools
- supplies
- communications (telephone, etc.)
- heat, light, and power
- travel and entertainment
- depreciation on equipment
- dues tuition and membership
- transportation and material handling
- various administrative costs

You can actually use one of the following ways to charge manufacturing costs:

1. *Actual Cost:* the actual value.
2. *Standard Cost:* predetermined rates and allocation.

And you can record inventory valuation by:

1. *Absorption Costing:* charge to inventory the direct labor, direct material, all manufacturing overhead.
2. *Direct Costing:* charge to inventory the direct labor, direct material, *variable* manufacturing overhead.

In order for you to control these often substantial costs, the first step is to assure that your accounting records are current and accurate. Then you should:

- Isolate and reduce overtime by expense category.

- Have your supervisors note reasons for variances from budgeted amounts.

BREAKEVEN POINT

This is the point at which the monetary value of sales and fixed plus variable costs *coincide*. There is no profit or loss. Its importance lies in being able to reduce variable costs to achieve a profit. Of course, profits also could be achieved by increasing the selling price. The usual cost reduction techniques apply. So when you calculate the breakeven point, as shown in Exhibit 47, you reach the general conclusion that cost reduction opportunities apply to all variable costs.

CALCULATION OF PRODUCT BREAKEVEN POINT, PROFIT (OR LOSS)

Given:
- Unit Selling Price — $ 1.30
- Unit Variable Cost — $ 0.80
- Monthly Fixed Costs — $15,000.00

- Choice of monthly unit sales:
  - 25,000.00
  - 30,000.00
  - 35,000.00

Revenue = (Unit Selling Price) × (Unit Sales)
Variable Costs = (Unit Variable Cost) × (Unit Sales)

Factor ($)	UNIT SALES		
	25,000	30,000	35,000
Revenue	32,500	39,000	45,500
− Variable Costs	20,000	24,000	28,000
− Fixed Costs	15,000	15,000	15,000
= Profit (Loss)	(2,500)	0	2,500
Comments:	Loss	Breakeven	Profit

Exhibit 47.
A sample breakeven calculation

IMPACT OF PARTS SHORTAGES ON LABOR COSTS

A balanced production line operates at the lowest possible cost. In practical terms, the simple fact is that a shortage of parts impedes production, thereby causing a number of reactions:

- using overtime to produce the required parts
- rushing to make up for the lost process time, thereby generating more defective assemblies—this has a "ripple effect" in raising quality costs, customer complaints, and inquiry/rework expenses as well

Have your managers explain all overtime on a simple report like this:

OVERTIME REPORT

Date	Reason	Add'l. Hours	Labor Costs	Effect	Action
3/18	Parts Shortage	3	36.00	Defect Rate Up 2.7%	Called Purch. Dept. 3/20

Compiling these statistics and requiring action will give you a handle on the cost of parts shortages as well as mandating positive action steps to curtail them.

COST OF PROCESSING A SALES ORDER

The most practical way to measure this function is to prepare a summary flowchart. Use reliable estimates and/or standards. List the steps, time, unit cost and extend the total. It would look like this:

SALES ORDER FLOWCHART

Step	Time	Unit Cost
Salesperson Writes Order	15 minutes	3.15
Order Processing Clerk Checks	3 minutes	0.63
Data Entry Clerk Inputs Into System	2 minutes	0.42
Computer Produces Order	Separate Calculations	1.50
Total		5.70

The cost reduction/avoidance opportunities are present at all four steps. See Exhibit 48 for ten specific opportunities.

NETWORK ANALYSIS

By using network analysis (for example, PERT/CPM) for planning, scheduling, and controlling a project, your company can:

- make project planning more specific
- document the detailed steps
- key management in on problems before they occur
- improve communications between all levels of the organization by using the same material for each level
- graphically portray complex projects in a way nontechnical people can understand
- zero in on where resources may be wasted or needed
- fix responsibility for varying parts of the project

PROCESSING A SALES ORDER
POSSIBLE COST REDUCTION OPPORTUNITIES

	Yes	No	Action
(A) Salesperson Writes Order			
• Is form design conducive to clearly writing information?	___	___	___
• Could we use some preprinted fields (product identification, etc.)?	___	___	___
• Could the form be redesigned to be optically scanned?	___	___	___
• Is all the data needed?	___	___	___
(B) Order Processing			
• Is clerk completely trained in spotting errors?	___	___	___
• Could we sample orders rather than 100% verification?	___	___	___
• Should we check key accounts more thoroughly; small ones less?	___	___	___
(C) Data Entry			
• Does system alert terminal operator to obvious errors (account number can't be alphabetic, etc.)?	___	___	___
• Could salesperson enter order *directly* from the field, thereby bypassing steps A, B?	___	___	___
(D) Computer Produced Order			
• Can computer *automatically* generate related sales, exception reports (fast and slow sellers, net profit by item, etc.)?	___	___	___

Exhibit 48.
Specific avenues for potential sales order savings

Its emphasis on control rather than accounting-type historical reports gives you caution flags. This is better than being informed after the fact. An additional feature is the ability to use simulation. This involves revising time for a specific activity and measuring its impact on the entire project. PERT/CPM is most effectively employed when a) it is a new project, b) the project is a "one-shot" deal, c) schedules and expenditures are crucial.

PERT/CPM IN ACTION

One large manufacturer used a PERT/CPM network for a familiar job—mailing promotional letters. The three major steps were:

1. State the objective *precisely:* "Mail Advertising Letters to Customers."
2. Define all important events leading to the objective. Show which ones must be completed before a subsequent one takes place.
3. Prepare an arrow diagram—the heart of the critical path method. Each part of the project, called an operation, is shown by an arrow. The arrows need not be drawn to scale, only their *sequence* is important. The chart developed by the company showed dependent and independent events in a network. Here is a capsulized version without graphics.

The operation mail letter *cannot start until the operation* type letter *is completed. That means that neither of the two operations* write advertising copy *and* prepare artwork *can start until the preceding operation,* design advertising, *is complete. However, these two operations can be done at the same time.*

The operation stuff envelopes *cannot start until both operations* print circulars *and* print envelopes *are complete. It does not say that both these operations must be completed at the same time, merely that the following operation cannot begin until both are finished.*

The company created an arrow diagram to illustrate time estimates and find the critical path. Once the diagram was prepared, the next step was to estimate how long each operation would take. The important thing involved thinking about only one operation at a time. The people who know the job best should do the estimating.

To find out how long the whole job would take, the company added the times along each chain of arrows. The chain of activities with the longest total time of any in the diagram became the **critical path.**

If any of the critical operations took longer than estimated, the entire project would be delayed by the same amount. On the other hand, activities like *prepare mailing lists* or *address envelopes,* which were not on that path, could be delayed without affecting the project completion time. These activities had **float time.**

CALCULATING TIME ESTIMATES

Because of the difficulty in arriving at one mutually acceptable time estimate, experts sometimes recommend you use three times.

1. The "optimistic" estimate is the expected time if everything goes perfectly, with no delays for any reason.
2. The "pessimistic" is the interval to be expected if more than the usual problems occur.
3. The "most likely" time estimate generally lies between 1 and 2, but can be equal to either one. It represents what the estimator feels is the best approximation of the time required to complete the activity, taking into consideration normal delays.

You can calculate a time estimate (TE) using the following formula:

Formula: $TE = \dfrac{a + 4m + b}{6}$

Explanation:
a = Optimistic (10 days)

m = Most Likely (8 days)

b = Pessimistic (13 days)

Calculation:
$TE = \dfrac{10 + 32 + 13}{6}$

$TE = \dfrac{55}{6}$

$= 9\ days$

PERT/COST CALCULATIONS

A version of PERT/CPM concentrates on measuring **costs** of a project as well as time. The benefits of using PERT/COST include:

- more accurate time and cost estimates
- early identification of anticipated cost overruns and underruns
- quick highlighting of potential schedule advances or slippages
- accurate measurement of progress versus plan
- determination of the impact of proposed project changes through analysis by simulation

In addition, a PERT/COST system can be invaluable in budgeting personnel needs by skill and time period (for example, four mail stuffers required in May).

The system is extremely powerful when you can tie it directly to budgets, cash-flow projections, and so forth. This will show budgeted versus actual costs and projected expenditures for the project.

COST REDUCTION RATIOS

Management cost ratios (MCR) are a way to guage whether your managers' time is spent on their most important activity—management. Here's how one executive calculated his company's MCR.

Factor	Example
1. Manager's Salary	$ 30,000
*2. % Time Managing 60	* .6
3. = Management Cost	$ 18,000
4. Non-Management Cost (1–3)	$ 12,000
+5. Worker Costs (Salaries of people reporting to manager)	100,000
=6. Worker Cost	$112,000
7. "MCR" = Management Cost/Worker Cost (18,000/112,000)	= 0.16

A good ratio is 0.2 to 0.3. A low ratio (less than 0.2) indicates too wide a span of supervision, possibly resulting in production and quality problems. A high ratio (greater than 0.3) points to excessive levels of management, inordinate salaries, or similar problems.

Review Action Checklist #19 for cost estimating and control measures.

ACTION CHECKLIST # 19

Cost Estimating and Control

ACTION FOCUS	N/A	STRONG	SATIS-FACTORY	NEEDS SOME IMPROVEMENT	WEAK: NEEDS MAJOR IMPROVEMENT	ACTION PLAN, RESPONSIBILITY
Use scientific, agreed-upon production standards						
Make exact definitions of cost/process centers, chart of accounts						
Keep track of record of production forecasts						
Improve timeliness of cost reports						
Take action on budget, expense variances						
Research competitors' costs for comparable/identical products						
Use latest systems techniques for measuring expenses						
Distinguish between fixed and variable expenses						
Employ a job card for tracking lost time causes						
Use MRP to better schedule parts deliveries						
Have managers explain overtime and its effects						

Reduce cost of salespersons writing orders									
Decrease expenses of order processing									
Improve data entry operations									
Have computer generate orders, automatic sales reports, exception reports									
Let EDP routines produce fast and slow seller reports									
Computerize reports of net profit by item, etc.									
Employ PERT/CPM to plan schedule and control projects									
Add cost estimates to PERT/CPM									
Use breakeven analysis to determine profit points									

15

COST REDUCTION STRATEGIES IN MARKETING

You can accomplish expense reduction through a coordinated program of market research. Market research is a practice which attempts to describe the market you are trying to reach in a comprehensive and accurate way.

Here are the fundamental questions you should be asking to make this technique work for you.

1. What is the size of the market in units and money? What are the expected growth rate and the potential profits? What share of the market can we expect, and where are our potential customers?
2. Who exactly are our customers? Why should they buy our product, in terms of advantages and disadvantages? Will the product have repeat sales or is it a one-time deal?
3. What is the competitive price?
4. What does the customer perceive the purpose of the product to be?
5. How do we help sell this product, in terms of media such as television, magazines, newspapers, radio, and so forth? What selling points do we talk about to attract customers to the product?

6. How can we most effectively move the product from us as the manufacturer to the customer?

By clearly answering these questions, you will improve your marketing research effort, and concurrently save time and money.

COMPUTERIZED MARKETING RESEARCH

Here's how several companies, including BehaviorScan in Chicago, Illinois, are using television and computers to monitor purchases made by typical families, bringing a new dimension to this art and helping reduce costs.

The reported benefits of the system are twofold: Research takes one year instead of the traditional eighteen months. Cost of product testing for the average new product is reduced from over $3 million to less than $2 million.

Here is the way it works. Approximately 2,000 people with television sets receive specific advertisements instead of regularly scheduled commercials. This group is divided into two or three segments and each is shown a specific commercial.

When they go shopping, they use a special credit-type card which is handled by the cashier. The purchased items are scanned by an optical reader and the computer records the purchases and the consumer's name. This information is then summarized for the client.

A different version is being used by another marketing researcher with a tool called "people meters." The participants in the test punch in about every quarter or half hour the name of the person in the house who is watching television. In this way, the researcher knows the demographic profile of television watchers.

SEGMENTATION ANALYSIS

Another very different technique for cost reduction and market research improvement is called **segmentation analysis.** What this involves is looking at your market, or potential market, from three different viewpoints:

1. demographic (age, sex, religion, education)
2. geographic (county, region, state, country)
3. psychographic (whether the people are conservative or liberal, achievers, followers, and so on)

Companies such as General Motors and Proctor and Gamble have split their markets into manageable proportions, as well as saving considerable sums of money in marketing research.

You can get more information on this technique from various marketing directories and trade associations, or from almost any large public library or governmental agency.

Tip: In asking customers about your product, rather than requesting that they identify what they are looking for in terms of benefits, inquire as to the problems they have. In about 200 studies, the people came up with about 156 problems per product. The idea is to key in on those problems which can be turned around into better product development.

NEW PRODUCT DEVELOPMENT

Here's a twist which will improve your marketing of new products. Look at development from your competitor's standpoint. Ask the following crucial questions:

1. How would your competitor go about increasing its share of the market?
2. What new products would your competitor introduce?
3. What weak spots in your own product line would your competitor attempt to take advantage of?
4. How would your competitor attempt to put your company out of business altogether?

CHECKLIST FOR
NEW PRODUCT DEVELOPMENT

Positive answers to most of these key questions will give you a strong combination of successful design in marketing coupled with effective cost reduction.

1. Does your development strategy take into consideration long-term effects? As an example, are you conducting basic research into major new opportunities?
2. Are you allocating enough resources to the initial phases of new product development? By doing this, you will intensify the degree of major innovative steps, minimize failure, and maximize your personnel's creativity.
3. Are you targeting the right market to get answers that will help you design the right products for your customers?
4. Are your R&D and marketing people working as a team? This involves setting joint goals and establishing proper communication between the functions.
5. Are you fully utilizing your creative people?
6. Have you carefully defined your products' usage from a customer standpoint? By doing this, your advertising and other marketing efforts will be pinpointed toward your target groups.
7. Should you use pre-testing on selected groups of consumers?
8. Are you using the full range of information available to you from your test marketing models, interviews, and the like?
9. Have you installed a control system for monitoring the new products' introduction? Will your system identify actions which cause you to respond and improve your products' performances?
10. Have you identified added cost reduction and/or profit potential from products which are in the maturity stage of the product life cycle?
11. Do you have the best staff working on your products? Here is a chance to look at your individuals, your functions such as marketing, research and development, advertising, and the team effort, or lack of it, working on product development.
12. Are you using the most up-to-date techniques for improving the design and marketing of new products? What is your competition doing? What's being exhibited at trade shows?

Exhibit 49.
Questionnaire for new product development activities

See Exhibit 49 for specific areas you should probe in new product marketing and development.

BALANCING CUSTOMER SATISFACTION WITH COST REDUCTION

Here's how to handle the delicate balancing act between assuring customer satisfaction and achieving cost reduction. To achieve these two goals, you should:

1. Have a clear statement of policy for your customer relations department.
2. Assure that adequate information reports and records are available in terms of customer returns, quality control, product development, status, and so on.
3. Provide for a coordinated system of handling inquiries whether by mail, telephone, or electronically.
4. Insure that inquiries are handled promptly and courteously, according to a priority plan for each type.
5. Provide standard answers for routine inquiries; this assures consistency of handling customers and at the same time reduces the expense of such contact.
6. Make sure to differentiate between product complaints and product liability complaints.
7. Review your warranty and guarantee material for clarity and conformity to legal statutes.

Focusing on the customer adds value to your sales effort. Here's a specific example of how this works. A large distributor, McKesson Corporation, installed sophisticated customer systems which provide almost instantaneous inventory management reports. By doing this, it reduced its delivery time from four days to one day, and vastly improved customer service. Here are some specific ways to cut customer service costs without alienating your customers.

1. In addition to analyzing customer complaints, check your overall systems for length of the order cycle, delivery, billing accuracy.

2. If your sales people are writing orders in the field, place heavy emphasis on accuracy at that point and on delivering them immediately rather than holding them for long periods. Keep in mind that incorrect order information will have a multiplier effect, not only on your customers, but with extra expense in inquiries, transportation, and in your order replenishment systems.
3. Consider having some of your key customers write up their own orders. Train them in how to do this.
4. Encourage large order sizes.
5. Notify your customers in advance about shipments so that they will not be confused, thereby incurring extra transportation costs for you.

THE PERSONAL TOUCH

One of the most effective ways to improve customer service in line with overall cost reduction is for corporate executives to take a personal hand in keeping in touch. Joseph A. Baute, the chief executive officer of Markem Corporation, listens to specific customer complaints. He picks up the phone, telephones his company headquarters in New Hampshire, and rearranges deliveries when necessary.

At Syntex Corporation in California, president Richard G. Rogers eats breakfast with his employees each morning. He asks them questions, thereby keeping in touch with the status of customer service.

The chief executive of the Pennsylvania cutting tool maker Kennametal Incorporated, Quinton C. McKenna, frequently visits his manufacturing locations. Contrary to many executives' policies, these are announced in advance. McKenna, at random, invites several employees to lunch or dinner. In this way, he keeps in touch with the status of production equipment, customer relations, and so forth.

RETAIL CUSTOMERS

One of the most costly areas of selling to customers is the entire retailing effort. Recently, increasingly successful efforts have been made in computerized shopping, often known as electronic retailing. As an example, a relatively new company called Compusave Corporation has developed a combination of kiosks with computer terminals. The customer is taken through a menu which describes a series of products. The touch screen system is used so that there is practically no keyboarding involved. When the customer has zeroed in on the product line he or she is interested in, a video tape presentation instructs the prospective buyer on how to make a purchase, using the screen for the sale itself.

In one extremely competitive retail industry, the phonograph record business, manufacturers are reducing costs by restricting the number of unsold records which can be returned for credit. Moreover, there is an industrywide effort to prune down the number of items offered for sale.

GETTING DOWN TO BASICS

The purpose of the marketing function is to direct the flow of goods from the manufacturer to the customer. The activities are often referred to as the four "Ps" of marketing. They are:

1. *Products:* Develop the correct product for the selected market segment.
2. *Price:* Establish a fair price for the customers to satisfy them as well as to generate a profit for the organization.
3. *Place:* Make the product available to the customers through an efficient distribution network.
4. *Promotion:* Inform customers about the product through selling, advertising, and other means.

A recent survey determined that three factors were involved in losing about 90 percent of all customers. They are (in ranked sequence):

1. lack of interest on the part of the company's employees—68 percent

2. unsatisfied complaints—14 percent
3. better pricing from another manufacturer—9 percent

The other nine percent is accounted for by customers buying from friends or relatives, moving to another part of the country, or miscellaneous causes.

HOW TO USE THE 20/80 PRINCIPLE FOR PRUNING OUT LOSERS

You can use a long-established principle called the 20/80 rule for getting rid of items in your inventory which are generating little or no sales and are also costing you money. The 20/80 rule states that: 20 percent of your items generate 80 percent of your sales and/or profit. To use the rule, you simply generate a ranked report looking something like the following:

Item Number	Sales Percent	Cumulative Sales Percent
1	25	25
2	20	45
3	10	55
100	1.01	100.0

Typically, in this analysis items 1 through 20 would generate 80 percent of the sales. Items 21 through 100 would account for 20 percent of the sales. If you have a small number of items, you could do this manually, but a computer would be a must for a large number.

MORE MARKETING TIPS

Here's a tip which will improve your cash flow, speed up distribution, and reduce your paperwork. Instead of passing on transportation

COST REDUCTION STRATEGIES IN MARKETING

costs to your customers, increase your minimum order figure and inform them you will pay the freight if the minimum is met or exceeded.

Make more money on filling orders for repair parts. This procedure will do two things for you: reduce your costs and increase customer satisfaction. Put together a repair kit with an assortment of parts most frequently needed. Include it with the product.

Reduce sales calls costs through increased telephone usage.

1. If your sales people make business calls from their residences, ask them not to charge them to your phone number. By doing this, you will avoid the extra expense of an operator-assisted call. Have your people submit a statement to you for payment.
2. More selling by phone decreases the costs normally associated with a sales call. The key to this is that the sales calls must be planned and organized. Have your marketing staff develop a series of phrases that sales people can use. Moreover, supply a list of the main contacts so that your representative can get directly to the individual who is the decision-maker.
3. Frequently, a toll-free number is a tremendous customer service tool. However, you should bear in mind that a certain portion of calls may come in after your normal closing time. As a result, you will have to provide a 24-hour service.
4. Your analysis of the pros and cons of telephone usage should include the breakeven point for taking orders on low-priced items. As a guideline, one company established a $15 minimum for a phone order.

To look at the many cost reduction aspects of marketing, review Action Checklist #20.

ACTION CHECKLIST # 20

Marketing

ACTION FOCUS	N/A	STRONG	SATIS-FACTORY	NEEDS SOME IMPROVEMENT	WEAK: NEEDS MAJOR IMPROVEMENT	ACTION PLAN, RESPONSIBILITY
Ask customers about product problems						
Look at development from your competitors' viewpoints						
Tie your advertising budget to unit cost						
State your customer satisfaction policy clearly						
Assure that adequate information is available on returns, defects, etc.						
Provide for handling inquiries on a priority basis						
Insure that inquiries are treated promptly and courteously						
Standardize answers for routing inquiries (consistency)						
Differentiate between product and product liability complaints						
Review warranty/guarantee material for clarity, legal conformity						
Concentrate on reducing replenishment cycle and delivery time						
Conduct research into long-term opportunities						
Allocate enough resources to intensify innovation and minimize product failure						
Target the right markets						

COST REDUCTION STRATEGIES IN MARKETING

Improve goal setting and communications between R&D and marketing														
Better utilize your creative people														
Define product's usage from a customer's standpoint														
Use pre-testing on selected consumer groups														
Employ full range of test marketing models, interviews														
Install control system for monitoring new product introduction														
Identify events to alert you to improve product's performance														
Look for added cost reduction/profit potential from maturing items														
Check systems for length of order cycle, delivery, billing accuracy														
Emphasize accuracy on field-written sales orders														
Speed up transmission of field-written orders to main office														
Experiment with key customers preparing orders (train them)														
Encourage larger order sizes for full-load shipment														
Pre-notify customers of deliveries—avoid refusals														
Have corporate executives keep in touch with customers, employees														
Visit selected facilities; question employees at random														

248　　　　　　　　　　　　　　　　HANDBOOK OF COST REDUCTION TECHNIQUES

Consider computerized shopping (electronic retailing)												
Selectively restrict customer returns of unsold items for credit												
Substitute better training for some sales commissions												
Re-examine product design and mix												
Use up-to-date techniques for product improvement and marketing												
Size up your competitions' efforts												
Check exhibits at trade shows to see how up-to-date you are												
Determine market potential and size (units, money)												
Measure potential growth rate and profits												
Project share of market and possible customers												
Identify consumers' needs relative to the products												
Set competitive prices												
Use selected media (print, television, radio)												
Employ segmentation analysis to sell specific consumer groups												
Employ videotape for sales training												
Institute cost control on sales catalog												

COST REDUCTION STRATEGIES IN MARKETING

Review advertising budget	Conduct profitability analysis by customer	Conduct profitability analysis by product	Conduct profitability analysis by sales rep	Conduct profitability analysis by territory	Review sales promotion budget	Use outside printer versus in-house overtime printing; look at duplications	Maintain direct mail lists	Use lowest postage rates for sales material	Determine effectiveness of trade show participation	Review procedures for bidding on contracts	Analyze your product prices versus competitors	Compare your product quality to the competition	Do cost analysis of individual sales calls	Analyze routing of sales rep calls	Use economic order size relative to transportation expenses

	Prepare justification for repair facilities	Review commission percentage and payment method	Check processing of salespeople's paperwork	Increase degree of selling by telephone	Investigate effectiveness of toll-free calls	Control commission expense	Examine training costs	Prepare breakdown of distribution costs	Analyze trade discounts	Reduce cost of doing initial sales forecasts	Decrease cost of revising forecasts	Tighten marketing integration with inventory management	Calculate ratio of fixed to variable costs	Determine reasons for delivery refusals	Detail administrative costs

16

ORGANIZING SYSTEMS WITHIN YOUR PROGRAM

A system is a series of organized activities to achieve a specific business objective.

The purposes of systems techniques are to:

- reduce expenses, thereby increasing profit
- improve productivity
- provide accurate, timely information

Fast-breaking advances in management technology are rapidly rendering more and more of today's systems techniques obsolete. With the pressure of competition, lack of skilled personnel, and tight money playing their part, your company may be increasingly forced to adopt radical changes in organization and management in order to keep up in today's competitive business arena. To fulfill this vital role, today's systems must handle new responsibilities extending far beyond the traditional areas of systems and procedures in the past. Progress requires not only the mastery of technical tools, but continual preparation to meet greater challenges ahead.

COMPONENTS OF A SUCCESSFUL SYSTEM

What does the good system include?

1. the applicable policies (what management wants done)
2. the equipment
3. the forms
4. the personnel, including supervisors and managers
5. the office layout
6. the reports and records
7. the work flow
8. the procedures

The growth of systems techniques is the direct result of expense explosion and efforts directed toward its control.

Mastery of the techniques goes hand in hand with the personal qualities of your staff. Assess your people on the eleven attributes of a good systems analyst listed in Exhibit 50. Everyone involved in your approach to systems should have some degree of competence in each of those areas.

SYSTEMS TECHNIQUES FOR COST REDUCTION

An entire book could be written on systems techniques that contribute to reduced expenses and lowered costs. Some of the major ones are touched on briefly in this chapter to give you an idea of what to look for in creating a more extensive program.

Work Analysis and Work Simplification
The purposes of work analysis (also referred to as work measurement) are to:

- compare actual job performance against a predetermined standard, and show variations

THE ELEVEN QUALITIES OF AN EFFECTIVE SYSTEMS ANALYST

Quality	Has Skill	Needs Training
1. Able to work with people		
2. Can define and solve problems		
3. Communicates as a writer and speaker		
4. Understands data		
5. Knows systems techniques		
6. Can analyze an operation		
7. Able to design practical alternatives		
8. Skilled in selling a proposal		
9. Plans the implementation carefully and completely		
10. Has great timing—knows when to install; when to delay		
11. The systems achieve what was forecasted		

Exhibit 50.
Checklist of attributes for a good systems analyst

- plan and schedule work more effectively
- improve forecasting of manpower needs
- determine the least costly work method, including defining the cost

Work Simplification (a sub-category of work analysis) is the application of coordinated steps to arrive at a better operation. Here are five steps in applying work simplification.

STEP ONE   *Select an important job.* Choose either an operation which has many people doing the same thing, or a few people whose work represents a bottleneck in the operation.
STEP TWO   *Break the job down into components.*
STEP THREE   *Question every detail.*
STEP FOUR   *Develop an improvement proposal.* The key words here are eliminate, combine, simplify, change sequence, change location, revise equipment, reassign personnel.
STEP FIVE   *Install the improvement and monitor progress.*

Use Exhibit 51 to lay the foundation for a work simplification program of your own.

Records Management

The purpose is to provide three major functions: storage, retrieval, destruction. Properly file documents and reports so that information is available when needed. Part of records management involves efforts to reduce labor costs and filing space expenses through the use of micrographics and other tools.

Control the storage, protection, and disposal of records in accordance with governmental and other regulations. Part of this is a vital records program, including back-up if required. Vital records are those which would cause your company to go out of business or cost you substantial sums if they were lost or destroyed. In addition to paper, punch cards, tape reels, and disk files are also part of the vital records program.

Chapters 4, 5, and 6 give you substantial background on cost saving measures for paperwork and forms.

ORGANIZING SYSTEMS WITHIN YOUR PROGRAM 255

Work Simplification Worksheet: _____ **Operation** _____

(1) Step #	(2) Task Description (Components)	(3) Old Time	(4) Action Code*	(5) Responsibility	(6) New Time	(7) Time Saved (6)−(3)	(8) $ Saved

*Action Codes: 1 = Eliminate 2 = Combine 3 = Change Sequence 4 = Shift Location 5 = Revise Equipment 6 = Reschedule/Reassign Employees 7 = Other

Exhibit 51.
A worksheet to analyze work simplification

Equipment and Layout Improvement

Save time and reduce labor costs through elimination of unneeded steps and the use of modern equipment—a system of physical functions.

Typical time and cost reducing equipment used are postage meters, collators, and folding and/or inserting machines, rather than processing mail by hand. Using electronic calculators and computers improves calculating and producing reports.

In the area of layout improvement, shifting desks can reduce transport distance and/or the number of steps for processing a specific form or operating your mailroom. One company reduced its office expenses 40 percent by rearranging workflow. You can apply this principle by doing what they did. Trace the steps of a function and number them sequentially. See if the flow is smooth or continually crosses itself. Measure the distance before and after the improvement and calculate the time difference. On the shop floor or in the office, production work can be positively enhanced by equipment and layout improvement.

Ergonomics

Ergonomics deals with designing equipment to help in the work environment. The purposes of ergonomics are to reduce the physical and mental stress; hypertension; fatigue; eye, neck, and back strain which often may accompany long hours at production equipment, computer terminals, and other machinery.

Management Science or Operations Research

The application of scientific methods to operational problems provides management with a quantitative basis for making decisions. This replaces judgment by "the seat of your pants."

Some of the tools of management science are:

Sampling Theory: Make a quality control inspection of every tenth or twentieth item as opposed to every item. The benefits are tremendous savings in cost, while still getting a solid feel for what the total lot looks like.

Simulation: Construct a model to test proposed solutions. You can raise or lower inventory to see what the effect on customer service is, for example.

PERT/CPM: Use for planning, scheduling, and controlling projects. You can use PERT/CPM to reduce expenses in building or modernizing a plant or distribution center or office; marketing and/or shipping a product; installing a new or revised office system; or training employees.

Systems Study and Report

The purposes are to document the present operation and make a systems proposal to improve it. The systems report is the written proposal. The systems study has ten important steps, starting with defining the assignment and ending with a proposal. The study steps are illustrated in Exhibit 52 at the end of this chapter.

As an outline for a systems report, you can use the four-step approach:

1. *Summary:* state the purpose of the report; for example, "to improve the inventory control system."
2. *Background:* "for the past two years, our inventory investment has increased while the level of service declined."
3. *Findings:* "the present manual system is inadequate."
4. *Recommendations:* "that we consider automating . . . use the XYZ computer and ABC program."

A well organized systems study and concise report avoids extra costs as it solves problems and/or exploits improvement opportunities.

Teleconferencing and Videoconferencing

Think of the costs for employees attending out-of-town meetings. Salary, transportation, hotels, meals, tips, parking, long distance calls, and other items really add up. One major survey reported that 75 percent of the executives studied claimed an increase in personal productivity resulting from video- or teleconferencing. They also stated that there was a marked decrease in traveling expenses.

Electronic Mail

In this era of information dependence and geographic dispersion, electronic mail is truly the closest thing to "super mail." It allows you to send messages more directly and much faster than standard mail. It also avoids telephone tag and either eliminates or reduces paper.

Facsimile Transmission
You can "phone" documents from location to location in minutes. "FAX" is no more difficult than a telephone call, with the addition of a few steps, such as pressing a send button and receiving it on the other end.

Personal Computers
There are basically four major cost reduction functions that personal computers can perform for you:

1. *Electronic Spreadsheets* are a major tool for decision support. One of the most powerful features lets you answer "what-if" questions such as, "What would be the effect on my net profit if sales increased by 10 percent?" The reverse side of the coin is "goal seeking"—"What sales must I achieve to get a net profit of 4.7 percent?"

2. *Word Processing:* create letters, memos, and other documents—then easily add, delete, and change any text until it meets your specifications. Save the material and print it out error free.

3. *Database and File Management:* set up a list of accounts and addresses, personnel information, and other kinds of databases. Quickly display records; add, delete, change them, sort them, create new files, and so on. Save money by eliminating redundant information.

4. *Computer Graphics* lets you display current data, trends, forecasts in charts or text.

With the use of integrated software, many features, such as word processing, electronic spreadsheets, computer graphics, databases, and electronic mail may be displayed on a screen simultaneously. Individual "windows" can be adjusted in size and material moved from one module to another with utmost flexibility.

By doing this you avoid much redundancy and create custom-made reports easily. Another important feature with personal computers is the ability to do "down loading" and "up loading." Basically, your personal computer becomes a terminal allowing you to access data from a computer mainframe, manipulating it on your own computer. Conversely, you can communicate certain data from your equipment to the mainframe.

INFORMATION MANAGEMENT

The crucial complement to cost reduction is an **information management system.** Information is a resource. You can manage it on a timely and accurate basis and run your business properly, or manage it poorly and have your business grind to a halt. Four areas in information management can be crucial for you.

1. *Training* really takes in two aspects: training the information manager gives to himself and his staff; and training for your line managers to make them aware of the importance of information as a resource.

2. *Long-Range Systems Planning:* Planning for future systems development for computers and other equipment is important for two reasons. First, because of the age and condition of many company systems. Perhaps yours is one of them. Second, the vastly increased time, cost, and other requirements of modern projects, particularly those involving sophisticated real time, on line, and database systems.

3. *Systems Project Management:* The role of information manager is to make sure that the right projects for the company are being done by the right people with the right degree of user involvement and the right amount of effort, all meeting the right deadlines.

4. *Financial Control:* You must be sure that the overall information processing functions are properly planned and kept under good financial control. The basic principle is that information is a resource that can be budgeted and managed.

NETWORKS

An important aspect of systems techniques is **networks.** Traditionally, data processing people have looked at computers as their own bailiwick. A really significant achievement in the 1980s is the interconnection of all office technologies through networks. That means working with different kinds of machines, different languages and operating techniques. It entails putting them together, quite literally at your fingertips. With the introduction of networks, all the technologies which have been guarded closely must be merged into integrated networks. Four major advantages will accrue from this:

1. saving time, through the use of equipment on regular tasks
2. distributing work loads
3. becoming better informed by providing access to a tremendous amount of information now available
4. accelerating information through an organization, whether it's next door or around the world

EFFECTIVE BUSINESS COMMUNICATIONS SYSTEMS

The purpose, quite simply, is getting the right information to the right people, in the right format, at the right time, and at the right cost. The results range from carrying out simple orders to helping you make the right decisions. Here are some of the basic business communications you may encounter:

- policy: the statement of what management wants done
- procedure: the written, step-by-step instructions telling how a job is to be done
- directive: a general order issued by a central office
- memo: a short note written to help remember something or to informally communicate between individuals. Memos also serve as transmittal for reports.
- bulletin: a regular publication of an organization
- announcement: a formal notification
- manual: a place (such as a binder) in which to put permanent communications, such as policies, procedures, and organization charts

There are three important functions that well-designed manuals perform:

Instruction: The material teaches people about their jobs and trains them step-by-step. It helps in recruiting, selecting, and training new staff.

Reference: No one can remember everything about a company. The manual provides answers to routine questions without wasting people's time or giving incorrect information.

Review and Control: Documenting your operations sets standards and permits objective audits to determine if goals are satisfied. It also allows you to ask the question, "Is there a better way to do this?" Evaluating your employees' performance is made easier and less costly. Here is a 16-point checklist for preparing or improving your business communications.

1. *Define Assignment*

    · Is it a policy or procedure or both?
    · Does it cover one or several departments?

2. *Determine Objectives*

    · Zero in on what you're preparing.

3. *Collect and Organize Material*

    · Select all pertinent written material.
    · Interview people concerned.
    · Make sure the information is current and accurate.

4. *Establish Order of Steps*

    · The Communication can be presented in:
      —order of occurrence, first things first (most common)
      —order of descending importance (most important point treated first)
      —order of ascending importance (most important point last).

5. *Decide on Format*
    - charts
    - decision tables
    - narrative
    - playscript

6. *Write Material*
    - The key is to keep it short and simple and aim it directly at the user.
    - If it's a procedure, before your stamp of approval goes on it, read it as if you were the person doing the job.
    - Most of all, don't let the reader guess what you want him or her to do. Be specific!

7. *Choose types of illustrations, graphics*
    - forms
    - tables (two or more columns of written data)
    - charts (tables in pictorial form)
    - pictures (photos, drawings, diagrams, and maps)

8. *Provide Index, Table of Contents, and Glossary*

9. *Edit Material*
    - Present a letter-perfect document to the users.
    - Don't rely on them to pick up errors.

10. *Get User Approval*

11. *Issue Specifications*
    - type style, weight, and size—consult a printer for the right combination
    - size and construction of binder (allow room for later expansion when choosing ring size)
    - decide on copy arrangement

12. *Secure Management Approval*
    - Use audio-video techniques for an effective management presentation.
    - Determine the advantages and disadvantages, cost of material, bulkiness, degree of personal contact, ease of seeing in a room, and so on.

13. *Print, Collate, Bind, and Label*
    - Put together a package that the reader finds attractive and easy to read.
    - Make it simple to find the desired reference.
    - Allow for quick, inexpensive revisions and make it apparent what the latest version is.

14. *Distribute*
    - Set up an accurate distribution list on a need-to-know basis.
    - Follow up to ensure that the intended recipient has received it and has eliminated obsolete communications.

15. *Implement*
    - Observe (if you can) how the material is being used on the firing line.
    - Consider a questionnaire at a later date to determine if the user is still complying with the provisions.
    - Interview both the users and their superiors to get their reactions.

16. *Maintain and Control*
    - Keep the masters in a safe place (a back-up copy on microfilm might be a good investment).
    - Be sure that revisions get into the right hands and are inserted into the correct place in the policy or procedure.
    - Review the material periodically to make sure it is constantly up-to-date.

TEN STEPS IN A SYSTEMS STUDY

1. Define assignment
   - Product change, customer complaints
   - High cost of production
   - Bottlenecks
2. Establish objectives
   - Lower costs, increase profits by ___%
   - Improve information flow
3. Prepare project outline, schedule project phases
   - To whom will the project be beneficial
   - End result: new facility, better system
   - Start and complete dates
   - Location of study
   - Chronological steps and responsibilities
   - Address issues such as personnel, equipment, layout, organization, policies
4. Gather and analyze facts (document present system)
   - Interviews, questionnaires, charts (workflow, etc.)
   - Arrange and verify data
5. Schedule project phases
   - Use PERT/CPM, Gantt charts, etc.
   - Determine areas that can be worked on simultaneously
   - Assign responsibilities to appropriate personnel
6. Develop and cost justify new system
   - Consider alternate solutions (not just one)
   - Relate solutions to their effect on profit, customers, employees, schedules
   - Set up a parallel test (old and new system operating at the same time) so that results can be compared
   - Prepare cost/benefit analysis: present system, proposed system, benefits (tangible and intangible)
7. Sell the idea
   - Use written reports and/or oral presentations
8. Conduct live testing and implement
   - Try to maintain schedules
   - Keep everyone informed of progress
   - Avoid disruption of customer service
9. Monitor and evaluate
   - Are time schedules being maintained; are results satisfactory
10. Propose next steps
    - What came up to address next

Exhibit 52.
A systematic approach to a systems study

17

A POTPOURRI OF ACTUAL COST CUTTING TECHNIQUES

This final chapter contains a diverse menu of cost reduction ideas from a variety of operations/management perspectives. Many are based directly on actions and programs from successful companies in today's competitive marketplace.

Action Checklist #21 at the end of this chapter offers you a succinct review of many of the suggestions/tips/insights in these examples. You can make copies and pass them out to appropriate managers and staff to get your own cost reduction program into high gear.

BETTER BUSINESS PLANNING

Management tries to anticipate what will happen in the future. In the modern manufacturing environment, your business planning should match your company's objectives with its resources so that important activities can be accomplished.

The benefits of business planning are:

- a better framework for the business as it goes through various stages of its operation

- an improved way of communicating these factors to the people involved in converting plans into actuality

Long-range strategic planning generally concerns itself with periods of up to three to five years. Here are the recommended steps for basic business planning:

1. *Define the business ideas:* list in simple terms what your company is trying to accomplish.
2. *Establish goals and objectives:* define measurable accomplishments you want to achieve.
3. *Evaluate:* pinpoint whether the idea can work and if the goals and objectives are achievable.
4. *Project cash needs:* anticipate amounts of working capital for fixed assets and day-to-day operations.
5. *Identify sources and mix of funds:* decide amounts of debt (bonds) and equity (stock).
6. *Write a business development plan:* include the probability of success, cash flow requirements, and all the supporting operations to make it work.

Consider a technique called "sensitivity analysis." Using this approach, you can attempt to anticipate the effects on your business of various factors. Example:

- If my salaries go up by 10 percent, what will be the effect on cash flow two or three years from now?
- How will an increase of 20 percent in energy costs affect my net profit?
- What would a price increase of 6 percent a year for the next four years do to my share of market?

You can use a personal computer with electronic spreadsheet software to do such calculations. The important idea is to combine sound business planning with sensitivity analysis so that some future events can be anticipated and dealt with accordingly.

EFFECTIVE CORPORATE CASH MANAGEMENT

Cash management concerns itself with the planning, organization, and control of corporate funds so as to increase the return on this asset. Short range, it involves having enough cash on hand to operate your business on a daily basis.

Here are practical ways to improve your cash flow.

1. For accounts receivables, monitor major accounts closely and accelerate collections.
2. Establish a bank line with a local financial institution. Have a standby loan in case you need cash for emergency purposes.
3. Watch your inventories closely. If your pattern of sales is down, prune your stock accordingly. Conversely, if raw materials are in short supply be sure to have extra inventory to compensate.
4. Manage your accounts payable to take maximum advantage of discounts and other favorable terms.
5. To produce extra cash without incurring more debt, consider selling and leasing back fixed assets such as vehicles, equipment, and buildings.
6. Look into possible changes in your accounting methods for inventory evaluation.
7. Review your insurance policies to determine whether self-insurance is cheaper and more effective.

CASH MANAGEMENT SERVICES

Here are six major methods which can save you money and at the same time increase your availability of funds.

A *lock-box operation* starts with a centrally located post office box. Your customers mail checks to it. Pickups are made several times a day by the bank. It does all the processing, deposits the checks to your account and sends you the details. This reduces the amount of physical handling and waiting time for deposits and increases the availability of funds. It also eliminates the necessity for you to have a staff or supplement your present employees in the accounts receivable department.

Preauthorized checks are written by the bank on your account at specified intervals for recurring payments, such as insurance. The bank sends you the details and the checks go through normal processing. The benefits are predictability of cash payments, elimination of clerical operations, and reduced cost of collection.

Concentration banking takes funds from your various receiving locations and electronically deposits them into a central pool of cash. This pool can be administered and invested by your financial people. Transfers are most often made electronically.

Account reconciliation service, provided by a commercial bank, can provide a full range of services including checks issued, paid, outstanding, stopped, or voided. Included in this service are inquiry and tracking functions.

Zero balance accounts occur when you make arrangements with a financial institution to keep enough cash on hand for anticipated payments to vendors and employees. On a daily basis, your excess cash is "swept" into short-term interest-earning money market funds.

Electronic funds transfer allows you to instantaneously switch funds to any location around the world. This procedure should insure adequate cash on hand as well as cost reduction through on-line data entry and edit checking.

MANAGING HUMAN RESOURCES

One experienced executive with extensive involvement in the cost reduction aspects of human resources offered the following tips for actions in this area.

Trim overtime by adding shifts, staggering work time and hiring part-timers or agency people for peak periods.

Consider a service where a portion of your permanent employees are transfered to an outside company which will lease them back to you. In that way, you can save money on certain fringe benefits. These companies (independent contractors) take on many of the personnel headaches.

Check with your local unemployment office to make yourself aware of how lay-offs affect your unemployment taxes.

Review your current workmen's compensation policy and have it evaluated by several insurers to determine the lowest premium rates. As part of this, try to have your potential employees take preemployment physicals in order to catch disabilities which you might have to pay for later on. Take advantage of any free safety checks which your insurance companies provide.

Provide your job and exit interviewers with checklists so that they cover the required material in a timely manner.

Consider flex-time, establishing core hours when all employees must be present, and flexible time when employees choose their hours of arrival and departure. By doing this, you can decrease absenteeism rates because people have their own time to settle personal business, and at the same time increase their morale.

Reduce expenses by managing absenteeism. Here are some practical ways of doing this:

- Develop back-up people for hard to replace employees.
- Instill a team approach so that the other members can take over if one is out.
- Plan production schedules in order to avoid peaks and valleys.
- Have a "flying squad" of people who are well versed (cross-trained) in more than one of the important jobs.

Here is how General Motors has reduced its cost of personnel by attacking absenteeism head on.

> *According to GM, in 1981, 15 percent of its work force accounted for up to 90 percent of the absences. As a result of this, the following year the contracts stated that those employees who missed 20 percent or more time for such things as common colds would receive a six-month warning period and then if the absenteeism persisted, would lose an equivalent amount of bene-*

fits. According to General Motors, in one year the absentee rate of one of its divisions dropped from about 18 percent to about 13 percent. In total, GM estimates that this contract has saved it three-quarters of a billion dollars in three years.

Job enrichment is used by certain automobile manufacturers to improve products and employee involvement while reducing costs. At a General Motors plant in Pontiac, Michigan, workers from the production lines were asked to call new car owners to check on whether they were satisfied with the product. As a result of customer feedback, several product changes were made.

Ford Motor Company has a program called "A Day in the Life." This involves blue collar workers and white collar workers switching jobs for one day at a plant.

Health and medical plans can help reduce expenses. At a Honeywell (computers) plant in Florida, approximately 10,000 employees and their beneficiaries are participating in a plan called "Health Share." This features a flexible spending account—employees can join either a health maintenance organization (HMO) or a preferred provider organization (PPO). The purpose is to get employees and dependents out of the hospital as quickly as possible, thereby resulting in a decrease in premium costs.

The Aluminum Company of America has been able to decrease its medical costs by about 10 percent by asking people to return to work as quickly as they can, keeping safety in mind. They are given assignments which are less physically taxing than their usual ones until they feel they are ready to return to their customary jobs.

General Signal Corporation of Stamford, Connecticut, put together a health care cost containment task force whose purpose was to determine ways to control health care costs. As a result of this, employee contributions were changed and deductibles increased. Employee education was intensified so that people were aware of the provisions.

Here are some tips for a combination of safety improvement and cost reduction.

- Be sure that sprinklers are cleaned and maintained properly.

- Appoint a Plant Safety Committee. Have the members conduct safety workshops.
- Have your safety representatives check stairs to make sure they are not slippery.
- Keep floors dry and use as little wax as possible.
- Alert production workers about the potential dangers of bracelets, neckties, scarves, sleeves, and so forth around machinery. Put it in writing.
- Encourage people to have periodic eye examinations and to handle harmful fluids and liquids carefully.
- Post "No Smoking" signs prominently and keep combustible material a safe distance from curtains, drapes, and so on.
- Insure that several of your employees know elementary first-aid and that you have first-aid equipment handy. Make them aware of emergency numbers and the location of nearby medical facilities.

IMPROVED PLANT LAYOUT AND DESIGN

The objectives of improving your plant layout are better operations, reduced costs, more responsive customer service, and increased production output. Manufacturing layouts can be categorized as:

1. *Fixed Position Layout:* the material is held in one place while the personnel and equipment are brought to it. This is especially useful when the raw material is bulky or heavy and the production process is straightforward.
2. *Process Layout:* layout by function where production quantities are somewhat small.
3. *Product Layout:* large quantities and simple processes.

In order for you to save money on plant layout and design, there are several key questions you and your planner should ask.

- Is it one location or several?

- One building or several?
- One story or multiple?
- Is there a basement?
- What are the optimum ceiling heights, and the floor loading requirements?
- General types of construction needed?

Another consideration is the flow pattern which could be straight, in the shape of a "U" or an "L." Make provisions for heat, light, power, fuel. Provide for safe waste and pollutant disposal.

One simple, concrete way of reducing costs is through the use of conveyors. As a case in point, the Berton Company reported a productivity gain of over 10 percent by installing flow conveyors in one of its distribution centers. This replaced manual lifting of cartons as well as unproductive time walking back and forth to fill sales orders. The company also had a better sales performance due to more rapid order filling.

INTEGRATED INDUSTRIAL ENGINEERING

Industrial engineering is concerned with the design, improvement, and installation of integrated systems of men, material, and equipment. The industrial engineering department has many tools and techniques available to it, such as methods analysis, time and motion study, operations analysis, work measurement, and a range of control systems beginning with production through inventory and quality control.

Facilities planning is a branch of industrial engineering. Kelvin Cross of Wang Laboratories in Massachusetts suggests changing from assembly line methods to a "production module concept." With this concept, you specify areas of your plant as "work cells." In doing this, products are assembled from start to finish by small groups of employees called work teams.

By using work cells you can:

- change production schedules quickly in order to be responsive to demands for the product

- reduce inventory costs of work in process by minimizing the amount of materials on hand
- decrease throughput time (Cross claims that instead of waiting four or five weeks for an item to go through the production line, it can be made in just a few hours.)
- find defective products quickly—this is done by having quality control inspectors work directly with the operators
- increase pride by making people responsible for the product from start to finish

In addition to these benefits, Cross raises some question areas. For example:

1. What will be the impact on machine costs, inasmuch as each cell requires its own equipment? He answers that the savings in work-in-process will more than compensate for the extra machines.
2. More space is required but there is a reduction in piles of work waiting to be processed.
3. Products must be classified so that set up and change over time are minimized.
4. Your industrial engineering staff has to decide on the mix of equipment for each cell.

Cross claims that for Wang, the results have been a dramatic improvement in quality, a work-in-process reduction, and an output increase.

IMPROVED SECURITY

A leading publisher of security materials recommends you watch for the following signals which may alert you to possible employee theft:

- a mismatch between inventory records and physical counts
- missing or out-of-sequence documents
- unusual numbers of voided forms
- differences between bank deposit amounts, and receipts
- unusual amounts of wear on expensive tools or equipment

- paying vendor on proof of delivery rather than with normal receiving forms
- different serial numbers between originals and carbons of the same form
- alterations or erasures on forms printed on security paper
- documents not signed or countersigned
- inability to verify employment records of potential employees

Here are some signals of possible materials theft:

- materials missing from boxes or containers
- items found in trash
- empty cartons stored with full ones
- containers moved between closing and opening times
- frequent damage to expensive products
- authorization stamp held by people not normally charged with this responsibility

From a physical security standpoint, check these items:

- building, doors, entrances, windows, roofs
- perimeter fences, adjacent buildings, and other entrances
- internal, external, and emergency lighting
- control on locks for master keys and other vital keys (safes are included in this category)
- vehicle parking lots and access to loading docks
- building and perimeter alarms, including response by outside security forces
- training and alertness of security personnel
- access control for visitors and employees
- control of cash, including amount on premises, methods of depositing, handling, and separation of duties
- shipping and receiving areas, including surveillance of trucks, and so forth
- controls over inventory movement, counting, reconciliation with other records
- accounting controls over receivables and payables

- information controls to prevent piracy of trade secrets, marketing plans
- personnel background checks, orientation for new employees, exit interviews

Here are some simple things that you can do to safeguard your computer data:

1. Change the password frequently so that people who leave the company or get the password from others will be foiled attempting to get into your system.
2. Add to your password other fields such as project I.D. Include a telephone number which can be verified.
3. Limit the number of attempts to log onto your system. This prevents people from *randomly* using all kinds of numbers to tap into the computer. A good rule of thumb is three unsuccessful log-ons knocks the person out of the system.
4. Maintain a record of user activity and look at this log periodically to spot an unusual number of attempts to get into your system.
5. Be tough on violators so that the word gets around.

EFFICIENT MATERIALS HANDLING

A specialist in this important function offers some areas for you to investigate.

- Reduce idle machine time.
- Decrease production bottlenecks.
- Avoid rehandling of materials.
- Prune inventories.
- Utilize space better.
- Concentrate on excessive maintenance costs.
- Assure that high priced production employees are working on manufacturing products, rather than on handling material.
- Minimize damaged material and breakage.

- Avoid demurrage due to shortcomings in transportation.
- Inspect scales to make sure they are weighing correctly.

Select a way of checking incoming material. You have two choices: a *direct check,* in which materials are verified against a packing slip or invoice with quantities; and a *blind check,* in which an inspection is made without any counts to refer to. A direct check has a reference for your employees which may be beneficial, whereas a blind check tends to be slower but more accurate. Alert your receiving operation to look for the following conditions: damaged, incomplete, short, or overshipment, wrong materials according to the purchase order. Have a standard claim form for loss and/or damage. Prepare a tracer if a shipment is short according to the bill of lading.

There are some general guidelines which will help you store materials properly in warehouses as well as reduce costs. The first is proper planning and space layout, by kinds of materials. Protect high value items. Separate commodities which are flammable.

Place large bulky containers and very heavy items on special racks or pallets meant for this purpose. Store fast-moving items close to their final use point. Lay out aisles for easy access to raw materials. Make them sufficiently wide so that two pieces of equipment, fully loaded, can pass each other in opposite directions. In order to fully utilize most of your space, use forklift trucks. Special attachments are available to handle particular kinds of loads. Get general operating/safety manuals and verbal instructions from the forklift truck manufacturer.

The Quaker Oats Company made some major improvements in distribution costs. The first step was to appoint a distribution improvement committee, selected from field and headquarters people as well as professionals from the distribution department. The group made visits to the plants and encouraged projects which reduced costs. Specific assignments were made in each area touching on warehousing and materials handling. Objectives were set and a responsible individual assigned for each phase. A system called transportation management information tracks the cost savings and produces suitable reports for management.

Westinghouse has a novel way of reducing damage to outgoing

shipments. It places floor tile cement on the corners of large appliance containers. The boxes stick to each other. This prevents intransit damage caused by cartons swaying and falling off each other. When they are received, they come apart easily with no damage to the packaging.

Here are some other suggestions for reducing costs of deliveries:

- Use common carriers (such as intercity bus companies) who are specialists in handling small parcels.
- Consider changing from daily to every other day deliveries whenever possible.
- Ask some of your customers who request rush orders if they will send *their* trucks for them.
- Instead of employing *your* trucks for deliveries to post offices, or parcel services, ask them how much they would charge to come to your premises and get the packages.

VEHICLE ECONOMY

One of the most important ways you can reduce costs is to cut down on energy consumption. Among other companies doing it, the Xerox Corporation passed along better driving tips to its thousands of technicians who work on copiers.

The company estimates that just a 5 percent reduction in gasoline would save 600,000 gallons a year. Xerox gave each of its drivers a book called "How To Get More Miles Per Gallon." It covers such items as starts, timing traffic lights, avoiding excessive idling, and proper tire pressure. You can get a list of these measures from any local automobile or fleet management association.

OFFICE IMPROVEMENT

Using temporary office workers is a smart way to smooth out workload peaks and valleys. Here are ways to help you improve the quality of your work while you keep your costs down.

Assign one responsible person on your staff to manage the temporaries during their presence on your premises. Make sure your manager checks the work frequently during the day for quality and timeliness. Keep in mind that if you are not satisfied you have the right to replace the temporary with another one who is better.

Make sure the temporary agency has proper worker's compensation insurance (if required) and that it assumes any risks while its employees are performing duties for you.

Office copiers can be both a blessing and a problem. Know the peak times during the day that the copier is used. Are there lines, and what is the extent of the walking time? Waiting and inordinate walking add costs. Look into whether your people are collating by hand. An on-line collator and stapler attached to your copier probably would do a better job, less expensively.

Additionally, here are some features to look for in copiers:

- the ability to use plain paper rather than special stock
- dry toner instead of wet
- reduction and enlargement capabilities
- automatic document feeders, and large-capacity paper trays
- changing the density of the copy to compensate for poor originals
- duplex printing—ability to copy on both sides
- use three hole, predrilled paper, thereby eliminating the necessity to manually punch three holes (this is a common capability of most copiers)

Dictating is a concrete way of saving time and money. Because many reports, memos, and other correspondence should be conversational in tone, they offer people the ability to talk in natural terms. However, there is a built-in resistance to dictating on the part of some individuals. Here's how you can help overcome some of this resistance. Have your people organize their notes by just putting highlights on a piece of paper or on index cards. This will reduce the amount of time later on in dictating.

Another tip is to ask the typist to type the correspondence or report in *final* form. Psychologically, this makes them aware that you don't expect to have any errors.

Telephone costs can be a major outlay in many companies. There are two primary ways to control these costs:

1. Restrict the use of telephones to authorized phone calls.
2. Have people make calls in the most cost-efficient manner.

Many companies make the mistake of having every telephone have unlimited capabilities for outside calls. Ask your telephone company if it can install a line-restricting device. Place unrestricted telephones strategically so that only those people who need to make long-distance calls have access to these instruments.

Here are some additional points you can use to better control telephone costs:

1. Specifically list the options you must have such as local versus long-distance.
2. Make sure your employees know the best off-peak times for making authorized long-distance calls.
3. Encourage people to dial long-distance calls direct instead of using operator service.
4. Remind your employees of your policy on nonbusiness phone calls.
5. Make provisions to audit telephone bills (by exchange) to pick up possible abuses.

Many large organizations have the telephone company supply an equipment inventory listing from time to time. This will show you if you are paying for instruments that are disconnected, no longer on your premises or even listed in error. If an error is found, claim a refund back to the date the error was made. Issue written orders to the telephone company for all actions such as installing, changing, and disconnecting telephone instruments.

Many companies use telephones exclusively. People in job functions such as marketing, sales, reservations, customer service, and electronic data processing find that the use of lightweight telephone headsets leads to improved productivity because they free people's hands to make notes, look for documentation, and so forth.

In a recent study, a survey company estimated that productivity is increased by 43 percent, incoming calls are handled 72 percent quicker and in about 48 percent less time than previously.

Men and women who work in noisy places are reporting better results. These kinds of employees include financial services people, customer service agents, computer operators, and those who work near computer printers.

There is a trade-off when you use telephones because there is a lack of written documentation to support conversations. Look into Telex. Simply by using a teleprinter and dialing direct, you can communicate in writing to almost any place in the world. Since the keyboard is like that of a standard typewriter, the conversion to a Telex is quite easy.

SHORT INTERVAL SCHEDULING

There is an office improvement technique called **Short Interval Scheduling** (SIS) which proponents claim can result in payroll savings of between 30 and 40 percent. These savings are realized because of increased office production, reduced payroll costs, and elimination of bottlenecks.

The concept of SIS is that it provides control of routine operations by encouraging regular checks on employee performance at brief intervals. It also focuses attention on office production and scheduling activities for managers, while at the same time enabling supervisors to be constantly looking to improve operating methods.

Here's a brief outline of the recommended steps:

1. Develop work standards (units of measure). Typical of these are pieces per hour for invoices, labels, work orders, and so on.
2. Calculate the reasonable expectancy, that is, the quantity of work that can be produced by an average employee under normal working conditions in a specific period of time.
3. Study a typical time period and compute the average workload.
4. Have the supervisor break the workload down into daily, then hourly, batches and assign the work to the employees accordingly.

5. Have the supervisor maintain a "schedule control" in order to monitor the progress against the schedule.
6. Every two hours, have the supervisor check each employee and enter the actual quantity versus the plan. Calculate the variance.

MEASURING WORK PROCESSES

Here is a way that you can utilize the power of a personal computer to measure and improve productivity. There is a product called "Process Flow Analysis" (PFA), developed and marketed by Control Data Business Advisors. The process uses a personal computer to produce flow charts and reports for present or proposed systems. By analyzing the functions, activities, and tasks you can pinpoint areas for improvement. Control Data claims it has saved about $13 million for various companies. In addition, the benefits include one-third better order-turnaround time, and an increase in interest income.

Here are the types of reports available:

1. a flow chart of the entire process
2. flow charts of the activities and tasks
3. highlights of the different types of steps such as manual, input, decisions, etc.
4. a simple cross-referencing system that ties processes to policies and forms
5. progress reports for monitoring

Provision is made to record cycle times, unit costs, and milestones for project management. One of the major benefits of process flow analysis is a dramatic reduction in paperwork; another is faster generation of required reports for documenting such processes.

PAY FOR KNOWLEDGE

General Motors Corporation has achieved cost savings resulting from a concept called "Pay For Knowledge." Before this concept was implemented, the workers at one of the automotive plants only performed duties according to their written job descriptions. Then they would spend their idle time waiting for more work to be assigned.

Under this more flexible system, assembly-line workers are grouped into teams and individual job classifications rather than the multiple categories which previously existed. Now, each production worker can do several tasks. Moreover, they can rotate jobs to relieve boredom and improve efficiency.

General Motors claims that the cost of certain parts declined by 6 percent because of this system and that the number of supervisors required was also reduced. General Motors also points with pride to a dramatic improvement in car quality, and to the fact that other automobile divisions have requested that their parts be made in this particular plant.

SUCCESSFUL ELECTRONIC DATA PROCESSING (EDP)

Experts claim that the greatest benefits to be derived from EDP are in the high volume, repetitive applications such as payroll, accounts payable, invoicing, accounts receivable, general ledger, and financial statements. However, you will probably find in your own company other functions or applications which should be considered, or are already implemented, where other savings can be derived. Among these are inventory, order entry, marketing, decision support, and so on.

A noted computer consultant recommends that you separate data processing into development and maintenance. Development expenses go for feasibility, design, and installation. After that, all else is maintenance, which can run anywhere from 25 to 50 percent of your total budget.

To decrease supply costs:

1. Substitute stock paper for custom forms. By printing on prelined paper rather than pre-printed forms, you can save as much as 75 percent of cost.
2. Consider printing eight vertical lines to the inch rather than six.

3. For reports that do not go outside your company (and particularly for testing programs), flip the paper over on the other side thereby saving 50 percent of that expenditure.

You can protect yourself from human threats in three major categories:

1. *Personnel Controls*

    - Have background investigations on all individuals who work with the computer systems.
    - Change your access codes for entry whenever one of your employees in a facility leaves your employment.
    - Have the employees surrender their identification badges when they leave the company.

2. *Access Controls*

    - Install some form of electronic access device to the facility.
    - Have a receptionist or other trusted employee escort visitors in and out of your computer center.
    - Keep a signature list of vendor personnel such as repair/support people who must have access to your computer facilities.

3. *Procedural Controls*

    - Monitor operations from time to time to insure that your written procedures are being followed.
    - Prevent employees from operating the computer system alone. Have proper checks and balances.
    - Have your documentation in a safe area.
    - Control access to your data bases, files, and records by using passwords, project IDs, and so on.
    - If required for particularly sensitive data, try encryption or other special coding.

One of the most widely neglected and yet important ways of protecting your computer system and keeping costs down is the use of clearly defined audit trails. This allows you to trace a specific transaction all the way through from source document to input, processing, and output. In order to do this the transaction must have a unique number which is called a key, such as an account number, payroll number, and so on.

Another accepted way of protecting a system is to have a clear separation of duties between the people who have access to the computer as opposed to the people who design and program systems. Finally, have a corporate policy on information security which includes the measures to be taken in case there is a breach of security.

HOW TO CHOOSE A COMPUTER SYSTEMS CONSULTANT

Consultants can perform vital functions for you. First guideline: Don't use a consultant for something of a permanent nature. They are meant to work on nonrecurring projects when their special knowledge will be of help to you.

You can make a consultant's job more effective and less costly if you do several things.

1. Gather up all the representative reports, memos, correspondence, analyses of the job the consultant is going to take on. Be sure that the samples are representative of the whole.
2. Get specific answers to such questions as: Who are the information users? When do they need the information? How do they get it now? What is the frequency? What changes would they like to see in the future?
3. Make sure that any consultant you hire has the experience and references. Check current users, to find out how long the consultant spent with them, and if the fees were stated correctly.

Insist on clearly spelling out what your rights are on any programs. If the consultant develops software for your use, for example, is it for you exclusively or can he or she use it for someone else?

REDUCING COSTS OF AIR TRAVEL

The American Express Company estimates that about 40 percent of companies have no written travel policy and that many of those that do, have policies that are either obsolete or unenforced. Moreover, inadequate accounting for travel and poor documentation add to the problems.

Many companies are addressing these cost reduction opportunities by consolidation of travel agents, special arrangements with airlines, and purchasing blocks of discount tickets. Grumman Aerospace Corporation even has guidelines for travel expenses. It gives special prizes to the employee who produces the greatest savings on travel.

SAVING MONEY IN YOUR MAILROOM

This is an often neglected facility which can make a substantial contribution to cost reduction.

Carefully consider the layout of your mailroom and try to redesign it, if necessary, so that it is more functional for both incoming and outgoing material. In order to keep your staffing in line with demand, keep volume statistics by day, week, month, and types of mail. Identify the peaks, valleys, and priority, and then revise your staffing accordingly.

Many post offices offer discounts on presorted mail in volume. Check with your local postmaster for this possibility.

Here are some other tips to save you mailroom expense:

1. Make sure your scales are absolutely accurate. Many employees looking at a borderline piece of mail will go to the next highest cost category.
2. Redeem unused meter stamps with your postmaster for as much as 90 percent of their original value.
3. Subscribe to your post office for manuals and bulletins in order to keep you up-to-date on rates and other cost cutting methods.

4. Stress to your employees the importance of handling packages correctly to prevent damage.
5. Don't use first class mail for non-critical items like books and manuals.
6. Use your calendar to mail payments to vendors or employees so that the mail arrives on a Friday. By doing this, you can improve cash flow by drawing interest on the unused funds over the weekend.
7. Check into the possibility of selling some of your own mailing lists to companies that purchase them (direct mail outfits).
8. Have a written contingency plan in case of strikes, disasters, and unusual weather. Make arrangements with auxiliary carriers to handle incoming and outgoing mail.
9. If you have large volume, investigate the practicality of an accumulating printer (attached to the postage meter machine) which captures mail costs by department. The printer summarizes and allocates the expense.

Here is a concrete example of how an insurance company reduced its mailing costs. Union Insurance Group of Bloomington, Illinois, claims to have saved nearly $8,000 by using an *expanding mailer*. Under the previous system items were shipped in corrugated boxes at a cost of 83 cents each. They were often bulked up with paper or styrofoam and lacked a return address. Besides the cost of materials, there was the expense of labels, tape, and labor. The expanding mailers have as an additional feature a pre-printed return address and a stock number for reordering.

RECYCLING PAPER

J. Rodney Edwards of the American Paper Institute advocates recycling paper in order to save costs and produce extra income. In general, the kind of paper refined is clean and recyclable. Examples of this are index cards, computer punch cards, computer printout paper, letterheads, and business forms.

Here is a step-by-step approach recommended by Edwards:

1. Contact a local waste-paper dealer; ask about specific grades and prices.
2. Enlist the help of all of your employees to separate recyclable paper from other items. You might even ask them to give a portion of this income to a local charity or set it aside for a company social function.
3. Separate the paper at its source, in the office itself. Designate specific containers for recyclable paper.
4. Establish a collection system for getting the paper to the dealer.
5. Be sure your employees do not contaminate the recyclable paper with such things as beverages or food.
6. In addition, have them avoid placing into the recyclable container such items as carbons, newspapers, magazines, and cups.
7. Keep your people informed of progress so that they maintain enthusiasm for this particular program.

MANUFACTURING PRODUCTIVITY CENTER

Determine whether there are any comprehensive information research centers which you can utilize in your area, like the Manufacturing Productivity Center (affiliated with the Illinois Institute of Technology) which is located at 10 West 35th Street, Chicago, Illinois 60616.

These are some of the services which can help you hold down research costs:

- The Manufacturing Productivity Center (MPC) conducts studies for individual companies in such widely diversified areas as: metalworking, robotics, quality management, the use of computers, and modeling. In addition, studies are done in productivity improvement, computer aided manufacturing, and automation.
- On a cooperative basis, there are "multi-client programs" wherein a group of organizations share the cost and the results.
- MPC conducts conferences and seminars on a wide range of subjects concerning productivity, quality, production management, and CAD/CAM, among others.

ACTION CHECKLIST # 21
Tips/Suggestions/Insights

ACTION FOCUS	N/A	STRONG	SATIS-FACTORY	NEEDS SOME IMPROVEMENT	WEAK: NEEDS MAJOR IMPROVEMENT	ACTION PLAN, RESPONSIBILITY
Define business ideas, accomplishments						
Establish goals and objectives						
Evaluate for practicality						
Project cash needs for fixed assets and operations						
Identify sources and mix of funds						
Write a business development plan						
Check sales breakeven points						
Use sensitivity analysis to anticipate effects on the business						
Keep a minimum amount of cash in noninterest accounts						
Monitor major accounts receivable accounts						
Accelerate collections						

A POTPOURRI OF ACTUAL COST CUTTING TECHNIQUES

Have a standby loan for emergency cash	Prune inventories when sales decline	Maximize accounts payable discounts	Consider selling/leaseback of fixed assets	Revise inventory evaluation method	Use lock box service to handle accounts receivable	Employ pre-authorized checks for recurring payments	Centralize cash pool through concentration banking	Reconcile checks with account services	Arrange for zero balance accounts and invest extra cash	Switch funds electronically	Hire part-timers, agency people for peak periods	Transfer and lease back employees from independent contractors	Check effect of layoffs on unemployment taxes

HANDBOOK OF COST REDUCTION TECHNIQUES

Review Worker's Compensation policy to determine lowest rate											
Have potential employees take physicals											
Take advantage of free inspections by insurance companies											
Draw up specific job descriptions for recruiting and training											
Provide written checklists to interviewers (hiring and exit)											
Consider flextime											
Switch appropriate people from hourly to salary status											
Revise employment applications to reflect shift assignments											
Manage absenteeism by developing backup people											
Instill a team approach for flexibility											
Plan production schedules to avoid peaks and valleys											
Have production workers call customers for product reactions											
Switch blue and white collar jobs for one day											
Participate in flexible health care plans											

A POTPOURRI OF ACTUAL COST CUTTING TECHNIQUES

Lock in high interest rates for pension contributions	Appoint a plant safety committee with broad responsibilities	Use checklists provided by safety councils	Give first-aid training and equipment	Pinpoint location requirements such as dimensions, construction	Decide flow pattern: straight, "U" or "L"	Use conveyors to replace manual lifting and distribution	Provide for waste and pollutant disposal	Employ methods analysis, time and motion study, operations analysis	Use work measurement, control systems	Try production modules and work cells for group assembly	Pinpoint your risk category for broker or underwriter	Consider self-insurance	Form insurance cooperatives with other companies in your industry

Rewrite product liability insurance to be on a per claim basis	Evaluate your products from a customer misuse standpoint	Check accounting records for possible employee theft	Look for alterations, missing forms	Investigate amount differences between corresponding documents	Alert security personnel to signals of materials theft	Perform a security audit of buildings, perimeters, parking lots, etc.	Tighten access controls to critical installations	Observe receiving and shipping areas	Verify information controls on trade secrets, marketing plans	Review fire and emergency plans periodically	Change computer systems passwords frequently	Add project ID and telephone verification to computer security	Maintain and check logs of user activities

A POTPOURRI OF ACTUAL COST CUTTING TECHNIQUES 293

Provide backup for databases, files, and records										
Store duplicate tapes, cards in separate, secure location										
Look into comprehensive computer risk insurance										
Reduce idle machine time and production bottlenecks										
Keep high-priced production workers on making products										
Inspect scales for proper weighing										
Explore less expensive (slower) shipment methods (rail, water)										
Decide on direct or blind check of incoming materials										
Alert receiving people to damaged/incomplete/wrong shipment procedures										
Use special racks on pallets for bulky/heavy items										
Clear aisles for easy access and special equipment										
Employ forklift trucks for better space utilization										
Have shipping department properly prepare all documents										
Weigh outgoing shipments carefully										

294　　HANDBOOK OF COST REDUCTION TECHNIQUES

Audit freight bills periodically for proper categories												
Appoint a distribution improvement committee to encourage cost reduction												
Equip trucks with citizen band radios for road condition information												
Try common carriers for delivering small parcels												
Use other people's trucks for pick-ups at your premises												
Rent vehicles for peak periods												
Improve office manager's ability to plan, lead, instruct, communicate												
Upgrade manager's knowledge of office systems and procedures												
Increase their experience with budgets and accounting records												
Place word-processing operators close to users												
Assure that equipment is compatible												
Produce camera-ready copy with word processors												
Typeset with computerized equipment												
Reduce square footage and lost files through microfilm												

A POTPOURRI OF ACTUAL COST CUTTING TECHNIQUES 295

Decrease information retrieval time with microfilm	Determine all costs including waiting and walking	Use plain paper rather than special stock	Have dry toner instead of wet	Provide for reduction and enlargement	Consider automatic document feeders, large-capacity paper trays	Produce overhead transparencies directly on acetate	Equip machine with 2 paper trays (letter, legal)	Employ predrilled 3-hole paper	Organize dictation notes in outline form	Type correspondence on reports in final form	Triple space important documents for easier correction	Restrict placement of long-distance capable phones	Install line-restricting devices to prevent unauthorized calls

Inform employees about best off-peak calling times	Dial long-distance direct rather than with operator service	Enforce policies on nonbusiness calls	Audit bills by exchange to isolate abuses	Check equipment inventory lists periodically	Recover money for instruments billed in error	Issue written orders for installation, changes, and disconnects	Develop work standards (units of measure)	Calculate reasonable expectancy	Compute average workload	Assign hourly and daily batches	Maintain schedule control and monitor progress	Eliminate redundant or inefficient policies, procedures	Look for lack of key reports at all company levels

A POTPOURRI OF ACTUAL COST CUTTING TECHNIQUES 297

Quantify acceptable number of errors in clerical systems	Consider EDP for high volume, repetitive applications	Recommend computer for decision support	Maintain control with your own in-house system	Increase expertise, flexibility through service bureaus	Reduce expenses by time-sharing	Quantify extra costs for labor, supplies, energy	Separate EDP charges into development and maintenance	Substitute stock, prelined paper for custom forms	Flip printed reports over and use other side	Check pros and cons of used and leased computers	Let information systems services provide specialized reports	Investigate practicality of fault tolerant systems	Install computer systems in fireproof facilities

Enforce no-smoking rules	Keep backup copies of master and transaction files	Use noncombustible curtains and rugs	Assure quick communication with outside fire/security agencies	Place computer rooms above street level	Ground computer equipment against lightning	Conduct background investigations of computer personnel	Change entry access codes	Install electronic access devices	Escort visitors in, around, and out of your computer center	Keep a signature list of outside repair/support people	Monitor actual operations versus written procedures	Prevent employees from operating the computer system alone	Place documentation in a safe area

A POTPOURRI OF ACTUAL COST CUTTING TECHNIQUES 299

Control access to databases, files, and records by passwords, etc.	Use batch totals, control totals	Try encryption for particularly sensitive data	Establish clear audit trails for each transaction	Separate duties of people with computer access from those who develop systems	Publish a policy on corporate information security	Use consultants on nonrecurring projects requiring special knowledge	Look for functional knowledge (marketing, human resources)	Check for analytical and presentation skills	Gather representative samples of reports, memos, analyses	Delineate specific information requirements	Verify references and fees	Beware of consultants who move offices frequently	Determine your rights on jointly developed programs

HANDBOOK OF COST REDUCTION TECHNIQUES

Lay out the mailroom for incoming and outgoing items												
Identify volume fluctuations and staff accordingly												
Print current address lists to avoid misrouting												
Presort volume mail for postal discounts												
Adjust mailroom scales for maximum accuracy												
Redeem unused meter stamps with your postmaster												
Use automatic tape dispensers												
Subscribe to post office publications on rates, etc.												
Maintain meter-mail machines to prevent illegible stamps												
Open letters automatically rather than manually												
Stress proper package handling to prevent damage												
Substitute lower mail classes for noncritical items												
Mail payments on Friday to draw weekend interest												
Sell selected mailing lists to direct mail outfits												

A POTPOURRI OF ACTUAL COST CUTTING TECHNIQUES

Ship with expanding mailers using preprinted return addresses	Contact waste-paper dealers about grades and prices	Separate recyclable paper from other types	Designate specific containers	Establish a collection system	Keep beverages, food out of the special paper	Avoid carbons, newspapers, magazines, paper cups			

INDEX

Absenteeism, 269–270
Absorption costing, 225
Account reconciliation service, 268
Accounting systems, traditional, 201, 202
Appraisal costs, 156–158
Automated performance measurement system, 135, 142–144
Awards for suggestions, 28, 29, 38–40

Ballot boxes, in forms design, 72, 84–85
Baute, Joseph A., 242
Breakeven point, 226
Business communications systems, 260–263
Business planning, 265–266

Caldwell, Philip, 165
Capacity requirements plan, 112
Cash management, 267–268
Chart of accounts, 221
Closed loop system, 111
Computer aided design (CAD), 170
Computer graphics, 102, 258–259
Computer integrated manufacturing (CIM), 170
Computerized Manufacturing Automation (CMA), 169
Computerized techniques, 170–171

Concentration banking, 268
Construction standards, 16, 25
Consultants, 284
Contract maintenance, 183, 184–185
Copiers, 278
Cost accounting, 144–145
Cost/benefit analysis, 102–105
Cost estimating and control, 221–235
Cost of quality approach. *See* Quality control
Cost reduction committee, 9
Cost reduction coordinator, 4–5
Cost reduction specialist, 5–6
Counterfeiting, 176
Crosby, Philip, 149
Cross, Kelvin, 272–273
Customer satisfaction, 241–242

Database and file management, 258
Deming, Edward, 151
Depreciation, 191
Dictating, 278
Direct costing, 225
Direct labor costs, 222, 223
Dispatch list, 112
Document inventory, 93–96
Document value analysis, 98, 100–101

302

INDEX

Drucker, Peter, 133

Economic Order Quantity (EOQ), 122–124
Edwards, J. Rodney, 286
Electronic coding, 126–127
Electronic data processing, 282–284
Electronic funds transfer, 268
Electronic mail, 102, 257–258
Energy reduction, 187–189, 196–198
Equipment. *See* Machines and equipment
Ergonomics, 256
Exception reporting, 144
External failure costs, 156–158

Facilities planning, 272–273
Facsimile transmission, 258
Flexible manufacturing systems (FMS), 170
Flex-time, 269
Forecasting, 111
Forms analysis, 57–58, 59
Forms designs, 68–86
Forms management, 41–68
Forms specifications, 64–68
Free forms analysis, 102

Goals, definition of, 140–141

Health and medical plans, 270
Human resource management, 268–271

Industrial engineering, 272–273
Information management, 259
Integrated manufacturing information systems, 201–220
Internal failure costs, 156–158
Inventory controls, 16–18, 121–131

Job card, 223, 224
Job enrichment, 270
Job rotation, 282
Just In Time (JIT) system, 171–174

Layout and design, 256, 271–272
Leasing equipment, 190
Line-stop, 173–174
Lock-box operation, 267–268

Machines and equipment, 189–191, 199, 256

Mailroom expenses, 285–286
Maintenance, 183–187, 193–195
Management cost ratios (MCR), 232–233
Management science, 256–257
Manual system of performance measurement, 135, 136–142
Manufacturing costs, 221–223, 225
Manufacturing Productivity Center (MPC), 287
Manufacturing resources planning (MRP), 107–120, 169
Market research, 237–238
Marketing, 237–250
Materials handling, 12, 14–16, 23, 275–277
McKenna, Quinton C., 242
Micrographics, 99, 102

Network analysis, 228, 230–231
Networks, 259–260
New product development, 239–241
Newsletter, 9
Numerically controlled machine tools (NC), 170

Office improvement, 277–280
Operations analysis, 8
Operations research, 256–257
Optimized Production Technology (OPT), 114
Overhead, 223, 225
Overtime, 268

Packaging, 12, 14–15, 21
Paperwork analysis and reduction program, 87–106
Parts shortages, labor costs and, 227
"Pay for Knowledge," 281–282
Perdue, Frank, 166
Performance indicators, 137–139
Performance measurement and improvement techniques, 134–145
Personal computers, 258–259
PERT/COST, 232
PERT/CPM, 228, 230–231, 257
Peters, Tom, 166
Pilferage, 7–8
Plant order handling, 18–20
Preauthorized checks, 268
Prevention costs, 156–158
Preventive maintenance, 185–186

Print consolidation, 99
Process Flow Analysis (PFA), 281
Product engineering, 174–175
Product simplification and standardization, 12, 13–14, 21
Production/business plan, 108–109
Production control, 18–20
Production scheduling, 16
Production techniques, 169–181
Productivity, quality control and, 157–161
Productivity improvement, 133–147
Programmable automation (PA) technologies, 169–170
Promotion, 9

Quality Circles, 161–163
Quality control, 149–167
Quality control performance report, 139–140

Random number table, 164–165
Records management, 254
Recycling paper, 286–287
Re-manufacturing, 175–176
Renting equipment, 190
Retail customers, 242–243
Robotics, 170
Rogers, Richard G., 242

Safety improvement, 270–271
Sales forecasting, 16, 17
Sales order processing, 227–229
Sales planning and distribution, 19–20, 26
Sampling theory, 256
Scaled down (focused) factories, 171

Security, 273–275, 283–284
Segmentation analysis, 238–239
Sensitivity analysis, 266
Short Interval Scheduling (SIS), 280–281
Simulation, 256
Snapout forms, 74–75
Statistical sampling, 164–165
Suggestion systems, 27–40
Systems study and report, 257
Systems techniques, 251–264

Teleconferencing, 257
Telephone costs, 279–280
Telephone sales, 245
Telex, 280
Temporary office workers, 277–278
Theft, 273–274
Time estimates, calculation of, 231
Transportation, 16, 25
Travel expenses, 285
Trend statements, 139–140

Vehicle economy, 277
Videoconferencing, 257

Warehousing, 12, 14–16, 23
Waste prevention, 7–8
Word processing, 102, 258
Work analysis, 252, 254
Work process measurement, 281
Work simplification, 254, 255

Zero balance accounts, 268